NORTHUMBERLAND COUNTY LIBRARY

Please return this book on or before the last date stamped below unless an extension of the loan period is granted.

Application for renewal may be made by letter or telephone.

Fines at the approved rate will be charged when a book is overdue.

Eat My Globe

SIMON MAJUMDAR

JOHN MURRAY

First published in Great Britain in 2009 by John Murray (Publishers)
An Hachette Livre UK company

I

© Simon Majumdar 2009

The right of Simon Majumdar to be identified as the Author of the Work has been asserted by
him in accordance with the Copyright, Designs and Patents Act 1988.

A CIP catalogue record for this title is available from the British Library

ISBN 978-1-84854-017-0

Typeset in 12.25/15 Monotype Bembo by Servis Filmsetting Ltd, Stockport, Cheshire

Printed and bound by Clays Ltd, St Ives plc

John Murray policy is to use papers that are natural, renewable and recyclable products and
made from wood grown in sustainable forests. The logging and manufacturing processes are
expected to conform to the environmental regulations of the country of origin.

John Murray (Publishers)
338 Euston Road
London NW1 3BH

www.johnmurray.co.uk

To my father, Pratip Majumdar, for his constancy and to my mother, Gwen Majumdar, for, well, just about everything. Her yoghurt chicken is the one dish I crave more than any other and know I shall never eat again.

Contents

Acknowledgements

If I were to thank everyone who was of help before, during and after my journey, this section would be longer than the book itself, so I hope that those mentioned in these pages will accept that as my sincere appreciation of all they did to make *Eat My Globe* such a special experience. It would not have happened without them.

In the UK I would like to thank my agent, Euan Thorneycroft, and all at A.M. Heath for helping to turn an idea from a proposal into a book, the whole team at John Murray, including Eleanor Birne, James Spackman, Helen Hawksfield, Bernard Dive, Polly Ho-Yen and Nikki Barrow, for their enthusiasm and, most of all, their correct insistence that I overcome my obsession with the world's toilets. Any factual errors in these pages are mine, not theirs.

In the USA I would like to offer much appreciation to my publishers, the Free Press, and particularly to Leslie Meredith and Donna Loffredo, whose pictures should both appear in the dictionary under the word 'professional'.

Many people have provided support along the way, and I would like to offer particular thanks to Anthony Bourdain for a supportive quote and Jay Rayner for offering the sage advice that only someone with his level of success can give. Sybil Villanueva was the first person I trusted to read the manuscript, and all her suggestions were spot on. Sarah Giles and Kirsty Jones all kept my spirits high with regular e-mails, and Paul Smith brought me back down to earth and reminded me again of the fine phrase 'mardy old git'. I plan to use it regularly from now on.

Finally and, if the others will forgive me, most important of all, my thanks go to the Clan Majumdar: to Baba, Robin and Jeremy, to Auriel and Matt, and to Evan Arthur and Biba Florence, who are already proving that the apples have not fallen very far from the tree.

Introduction

Imagine you are sitting in a small bar in Andalucía. In front of you, an unsmiling man in a an ill-fitting white jacket is wielding a long, sharp knife and taking small, thin slices from an Ibérico ham which he has locked into a weathered-looking stand upon which the legs of many pigs have given their all.

As he slices, he places each piece of the deeply flavoured meat on a large plate in concentric circles, like the petals of a flower. Like yours, his attention is on the ham, only on the ham. It is as though nothing else on this earth matters, and it doesn't. This is, after all, one of the greatest foods on the face of the planet. Forget truffles and caviar. If you want proof of the existence of God that does not involve Natalie Portman doing something unsavoury for your pleasure, this is it. After what seems like an eternity, he has finished his cutting, and he places a few oily almonds in the centre of the plate and slides it towards you.

Next to the plate he places a small glass, a *copita*, which he then fills, close to the brim, with a buttery-coloured Manzanilla sherry whose saltiness will be the perfect foil for the richness of the ham and its creamy fat, flavoured with the acorns on which the pigs have fed before giving up their lives for our pleasure. Your mouth salivates at the prospect. You reach towards the plate, your fingers aiming for the choicest morsel.

Suddenly your hand is brushed aside, and you are brought back to reality by the words 'Oi, lardy, me first', as another hand, that of an older sibling, claims 'dibs' on the prime piece.

Welcome to my world. A world where food is everything, but the right order of the family hierarchy comes first.

I was probably five years old, or maybe even a little younger, when I first learned the natural order of things. There was nothing unusual in the fact that when my parents went out for the evening, they put the oldest of their children, my brother Robin, in charge. There was not even anything particularly out of the ordinary in the fact that he took the opportunity to spend the evening torturing us. That's what older brothers do.

What made this particular evening different was that this time Robin decided to declare himself a god, the Lord High Ruler of our home in Rotherham, South Yorkshire, and he bestowed on himself, the title of 'The Great Salami'. My older sister, Auriel, myself and my younger brother, Jeremy, were forced to crawl along the floor on our bellies paying obeisance to him with the words 'Oh, Salami'. You see, even then it was all about food.

To say that our family was obsessed with what we ate would be like saying that J.K. Rowling is comfortably off. Food was not just fuel to feed the plump bodies of the Majumdar clan. It was the very essence of who we were and indeed are, and that passion has remained the focus of our every waking moment and every conversation. At breakfast we would sit and discuss what was for lunch, at lunch what was for supper, and at supper what we had eaten for lunch and breakfast. There would be comparisons with previous breakfasts, lunches and suppers, and fond and wistful remembrances of breakfasts, lunches and suppers past. It was not uncommon for any one of us to be slumped on a sofa and suddenly cry out unprompted, 'those sausages were nice', and the rest would nod in enthusiastic agreement, even if said sausage had formed part of a meal over a week ago. We would all understand.

In my student days it was just the same. For reasons I have never quite understood, I chose to study theology and headed down to London – the alternative being Lampeter St David's, in the middle of Wales, where research told me that the sun only came out for thirty minutes every other June and pubs were open only on Mondays. These were heady days, when governments paid students to go to college and, unlike the poor mites of today, who will go to their graves still paying for their education, I got a grant – a nice, fat cheque for £600 – at the beginning of each term. It was supposed to last ten weeks and cover all sorts of important things such as rent and textbooks but instead it lasted about ten days as I spent it with wild abandon in the Indian restaurants and steakhouses of south London and the Turkish okabassi and Cypriot pastry shops of Green Lanes.

The Great Salami (hereafter to be called TGS, as I am lazy) had also moved south and was making pots of cash. He was happy to share the love and would take me out for meals. Not just any meals, but meals at places I had read about in food guides, meals at the restaurants dragging London kicking and screaming from the moribund food scene that had engulfed it since post-war rationing to being among the best places to eat on earth. TGS is a man of extraordinary generosity, even though that generosity obviously comes at the cost of our never trying to usurp his primary position in the Majumdar hierarchy.

On my twenty-first birthday my parents gave me £100 to spend on a meal, which I duly did. A very fine meal it was too, at an old-school trattoria called Gino's at the bottom of the Charing Cross Road. In the early 1980s £100 brought you a great deal, and I had no trouble finding companions to help me spend five hours blowing the lot. I can still recall what I ate: tortellini in a mushroom cream sauce, poussin flamed in cognac and served with rosemary and soft, melting chestnuts, followed by a frothy zabaglione made at the table by a waiter with a loud waistcoat and a liberal hand with the marsala wine. It was all washed down with any number of bottles of Valpolicella and my first tastes of a complimentary rough grappa, the burn of which I can, if I close my eyes, still remember.

You may think it odd that I can recall what I ate at a meal twenty-three years ago. In fact, I can recall just about every meal

I have ever eaten. It is a Majumdar family trait: we signpost our lives by what we have eaten and when. If I were to ask any one of my family about a significant event in our lives, they would look at me blankly until reminded of what we had to eat on that occasion and then it would all become clear. There would then follow a lengthy discussion about the dish in question and possibly even a heated debate about whether it was any good or not.

Heated debates about food are common in my life. There is nothing I hate more than bad food and, hard though it is to believe, I have been known to be ever so slightly opinionated about it. I try not to be judgemental but fail miserably, and a wife and any number of girlfriends have fallen by the wayside as they tried and failed to keep up with my fixation, trailing round after me as I take the long route home so I can go from restaurant to restaurant to see if there is something new on the menu or sitting opposite me as I dissect a meal that they have lovingly prepared. 'That was great, sweetheart. Couldn't you find the good lentils?'

I can recall a nascent relationship that came to a screeching halt when I was being treated to a meal at a very grand place on my birthday. I tried to be generous, knowing that my girlfriend had put a great deal of effort into choosing the location and securing the booking, but there is nothing I hate more than a lousy meal. I grimaced my way through the first course, sent the fish course back with a complaint about it being overcooked and sent the next course back with a complaint about it being undercooked. By now she was close to tears, although I was too engrossed in what was going wrong with the food to notice. I think it was my description of the sauce as 'jejune', a word that I had recently gleaned from a Woody Allen film and was using at every opportunity, that finally sent her hurtling to the bathroom in floods, only to emerge about thirty minutes later, ask for the bill and leave – never to be seen again. Such occasions are not uncommon in my life.

If anything, I am even more passionate and obsessive about

food now than I was when I was younger. Certainly I can afford to eat out more than I could when I was a student, but that is only part of it. My obsession has been fuelled by any number of cookery books, membership of websites and internet forums where people discuss the best food and restaurants and the advent of television channels in the UK and USA dedicated entirely to food, even if they just make me throw something at the screen as the chef smothers a great ingredient in an unnecessary sauce.

Quite simply, I adore food, and I also love people who are as passionate about growing, preparing and talking about food as I am about eating it. I love the glamour and glitz of the Michelin-starred restaurants and, if I were to bump into Gary Rhodes, I would probably faint like a bobbysoxer at a Fabian concert. I love the skill, craft and technique the great chefs show in transform-ing the mundane into the utterly fabulous and delicious. I love being presented with the wine list and the pop of the cork when that first bottle of many arrives. I love the little cups of foaming soup that the chef sends out as a little welcome and the *petits fours* that arrive to accompany the tinkle of tea being poured in fine china at the end of the meal and all points in between.

It's not just the smart places, however. If I had to choose my last meal, it would be a plate of fish and chips – from up north, of course – the crunch of bubbly, crisp batter breaking under the slightest tooth pressure to reveal glistening white fish, which has been allowed to steam inside its protective coating to a perfect flake. Alongside it, a mound of 'proper' chips, crunchy on the outside and soft and yielding in the middle. All washed down with a mug of builder's tea. Perfection.

A close second would come meat. I like meat a great deal. A journalist once described me as 'The Great Majumdar, a man for whom many animals have died'. It's true. If it once had eyes and a face and a mom and a pop, I want to eat it. A perfectly prepared steak, with a charred crust and rare and bloody in the middle, is one of the true tests of any chef's art. Many try, and most fail. Those who succeed are as worthy of note as any great artist.

If you eat meat, it is disingenuous not to eat all the animal from where your choice cuts may have come. So I like my offal, my entrails, my hoofs, noses and lips, my nether regions and innards, so often thrown away in these days of pre-packaged foods but often the source of the best flavours. Gnawing on the roasted head of a suckling pig at London's legendary St John restaurant and slurping up a bowl of tripe soup in Chinatown are regular treats, and yes, before you ask, I have eaten testicles. Jolly good they were too.

Food is the first thing I think of in the morning while I ponder a bowl of slow-cooked porridge with a spoonful of peanut butter and a chopped-up black banana, sipping on that glorious first cuppa, and it is the last thing I think of at night, as I sit down with a bowl of macadamia nuts and a tumbler of peaty whisky.

Food, I have realized, is not just what I eat: it is what I am and what I do. That realization and the realization that I am not alone in my obsession are what led to the book you have in your hands. It is what led to the whole notion of *Eat My Globe*, my desire to 'Go everywhere, eat everything'. It is what made me walk away from my old life of self-indulgent hedonism to head off around the world in search of the weird, the wonderful and the downright tasty. It is what took me from a comfort zone where my idea of hardship was finding only Chardonnay in a hotel mini-bar, on a trip that saw me endure nearly one hundred flights, the same number of different beds and the unspeakable horror of Chinese toilets.

Best of all, it was a realization that brought me into contact with hundreds of people all over the world who shared my passion for incredible things to eat and who opened up their lives and their hearts to let me share a meal with them or be part of the process that brings these treasures to our tables.

I hope that reading this book will not only give you some vicarious pleasure from reading about the people, the places and, of course, the food but will also rekindle your desire to go to places far and wide because 'they do great noodles' or to spend time preparing a meal for someone special, even if they can be, like me, an over-critical dolt. Most of all, however, I hope it just makes you really, really hungry and want to put the book down (after buying it and taking it home first, of course) and go and eat something incredible.

That is, of course, if an older brother does not steal it off you first.

Simon Majumdar
London, 2009

I

I Hate My Job

That's not quite true. In fact, until late 2006 I loved my job. I worked in book publishing and got to travel to far-flung places where I could usually score a decent meal on my expense account. I led a life that some other people would consider charmed or at least enviable.

A few years earlier The Great Salami and I had bought a flat together on the edge of London's fashionable Hoxton. The burgeoning bar and food scene fed our craving for decent cocktails and offered a pleasing variety of restaurants. Between us, we ate out about seven times a week. Neither of us was every going to be mistaken for cool at any point, so our perambulations around the achingly trendy neighbourhood often drew contemptuous stares from the young folk as we headed off for dinner or a drink. TGS suggested we have T-shirts made that said, on the front 'We May Not Be Hip Enough To Drink Here, But We Are Rich Enough To Live Here' and on the back, in larger letters, 'Fuck Off Back To Clapham'.

But that was a small price to pay for being able to walk to work to my office in Islington every morning. I could not wait to get there, switch on my computer and see what e-mails had flooded in from customers around the globe.

Of course, I had to have my breakfast first. Porridge. Porridge gets a bad press from so many people, who think back to the misshapen lumps of oaty mush they were forced to eat as a child. But for me there is no other way to start the day. If I don't have a great deal of time, then a microwave will suffice, but if I am on a more leisurely schedule, I will take the opportunity to slow-cook my coarse-ground oatmeal on the hob in a combination of milk and water until it is rich and creamy. I'll stir in a spoonful of crunchy, organic peanut butter before topping it off with a banana or a pile of berries, which will burst in the residual heat to release their juices. If I am feeling particularly indulgent, I will treat myself to a large dollop of Greek yoghurt, which will be slowly amalgamated into the dish as I eat it.

I was living a life that could hardly be described as uncomfortable, with a smart flat, a highly paid job and well within my tolerance levels of never living more than fifteen minutes from the nearest source of Madagascan vanilla extract. So what made me come in one day, sit at my desk and write forty-two e-mails to friends all of which read, simply 'I hate my job'?

With hindsight, it was a combination of things. Certainly the job had changed. It had gone from being an exciting and challenging opportunity to grow a business into a dreary procession of spreadsheets and arguments over budgets with colleagues. But it ran much deeper than that.

Two years earlier I had turned forty, and that milestone hit me in the face like a slap with a wet haddock – an un-dyed, lightly smoked one, of course, not one of those yellow monstrosities they sell on supermarket fish counters but a haddock never the less. At a quiet supper a few days after the event a friend said to me, 'Congratulations, you are now officially middle-aged'. As the words came out of her mouth, I could practically feel my prostate swelling inside me and see the remaining years of my life filled with night-time visits to the bathroom, with only a pathetic little dribble to show for it. There are many signs that you are hurtling towards the middle years. You become entirely invisible to attractive young women, that's a given. Worst of all, you lose all ability to move urinal cakes around the bowl. Men may deny it, but we all do it. Once I could have them moving around at a pleasingly brisk pace. Now a few begrudging millimetres and that's it, as they refuse to budge any more, taunting me with their fluorescent unmovingness. Bastards. It became increasingly obvious. I had more sand in the bottom of my egg-timer than the top. A sobering thought.

That same year my mother died. It happened quickly from that most pernicious of diseases, leukaemia, and I was not there to see it – a fact that did, and still does, haunt me. Most people you meet will tell you that they love their mother and that she is an incredible person. My mother truly was an incredible person, the biggest influence on my life and certainly the inspiration for my obsession with food.

Gwen Majumdar was one of three nursing sisters from south Wales and first met my father in the mid-1950s, when he came from India to complete his surgical exams at the Royal Gwent Hospital in Newport, a training centre for many doctors from around the former empire. Despite the moral restrictions of the day, many liaisons took place between the exotic young men with dark skin from the former colonies and the hot-tempered young Welsh women with fiery red hair.

My father, Pratip (known as Pat), asked my mother out, under the pretence of wanting to take pictures with a new camera in the local park. It is a ruse I used myself a few times in my teen-age years, with considerably less success, probably because I didn't own a camera. Despite the fact she was, at first, going to send her identical twin sister, Ann, she eventually went along and yours truly, along with three other siblings, was the result. To her credit she never once looked at us in times of profound disappointment and said, 'If only I had sent Ann.'

Theirs was a fairly chaste courtship. These were more inno-cent times, and my father – Baba, as he is known to his children – used to tell us to his great glee and my mother's great embar-rassment that on their wedding night, spent at a small hotel in the Lake District, he requested a hot water bottle from the management.

Despite the inauspicious beginning, the marriage lasted for over forty years, and my mum went from being Gwen John to

Gwen Majumdar, a wonderful combination of names that I have had to explain to people over and over again. It was not uncommon for the Indian doctors and the Welsh nurses to marry, and I suspect that the children of Myfanwy Bannerji and Blodwyn Patel have equally interesting stories.

Soon after they were married and not long after TGS was born, my parents moved to India, where this young woman, who had never strayed too far from the valleys, found herself in a high-caste Brahmin family in Calcutta, with servants and drivers to wait upon her but with precious little to fill her time. Fortunately households such as these also had cooks, and my mother spent her days peering in the kitchen and watching the various wives of the family work with the cooks to supply the constant supply of food required by the Bengali men, possibly the most demanding creatures on earth.

She returned to the UK with my father in the early 1960s with an ability to cook Bengali food that she used to good effect feeding her brood. I grew up on the thin but deeply delicious dahl made with red lentils, stews of bony fish flavoured with mustard oil and, best of all, a simple chicken dish with yoghurt and a few spices that is one of the great tastes of my life and to which I dedicate this book. Add to this the baking prowess inherited from my Welsh grandmother, and the smells emanating from our kitchen were a unique combination.

My mother's death shook me to the core, and I miss her every day, not only for her intense loyalty to her family but also for her fiery temper, which was often hilarious and aimed at the most quixotic of targets. TV presenters were a particular favourite, and she developed an unexplained loathing of Sue Lawley, whom she denounced as 'all fur coat and no knickers'. Local dignitaries too got short shrift. For a time she was a local magistrate and had soon acquired the well-earned nickname of 'The Hanging Judge' for her conservative views, which would have meant the return of flogging for dropping litter. Other magistrates were seen as too soft or lenient, which obviously meant they were 'communists' – ironic really, since my father's family had been leading members of the Communist Party of India, a fact that seemed to faze my mother not at all.

Most hated of all was my father's secretary, for whom she dreamed up exquisite punishments for whatever imagined transgression crossed her mind. Usually this meant buying expensive but appalling Christmas presents, and I can still recall the delight in her voice as she announced in a Welsh accent, which she never quite lost, that she had bought the victim a large bottle of 'Elizabeth Taylor's Passion. It's really disgusting.' My mother was not, it has to be said, someone you would ever wish to cross.

Most of all, however, I miss her for her food, for the stupendous smells of cooking and groaning tables that used to greet me on my return from school and, in later years, fleeting visits to Rotherham from London. She had no concept of the word 'ample', and both the larder and the fridge were constantly filled to bursting with the fruits of her labours. Pies and Welsh cakes, chutneys and pickled onions, curries and stews. It is little surprise that the fondest memories of friends who were lucky enough to visit are of the sheer volume of food she put in front of them and the clucks of disapproval if they turned down fourth helpings and bemusement if they did not want to try all the eight flavours of ice cream in the large family freezer.

I was forty and feeling it, in a job that I loathed and dealing with the loss of a parent, perhaps the hardest thing that any of us will have to face. Any one of these could make a person unhappy with their lot. Added together, they began to make me feel as though I was rapidly heading towards the sort of breakdown that could see me featuring in a newspaper story that ended 'and then he turned the gun on himself'.

The night of my negative e-mail-fest I returned home and flopped down on my deep, comfortable sofa with a large glass of a favourite Spanish red wine in my hand and stared out of the window at the glittering lights of London's financial district. The scent of onions frying, drifting up through a vent from the flat below, woke me from my torpor, and I realized that I had been sitting there in the dark for nearly two hours, and I had not eaten a thing since lunchtime. I got up determined to lose myself for a while in cooking – one of the few things that, at this point, I knew would stop me feeling quite so miserable.

Checking on what was in the cupboard, I saw a bag of red lentils and decided on a stand-by of Bengali dahl made with mustard powder, ginger and turmeric, cooked slowly with quartered lemons to give a gentle citrus flavour. For our family this dish is like chicken soup. I call it LSD, 'Life-Saving Dahl', the sort of dish you turn to when you need emotional as well as physical nourishment.

After toasting the lentils until they released a pleasing nuttiness, I added the dry spices and water, followed by the lemons. It began to bubble gently, and I turned my attention back to my wine. It was at this point that I noticed, among my cookery books, an old notebook that I had bought when – don't you dare laugh – I had decided to follow a course by that rather scary, perma-grinned, American self-help guru Anthony Robbins.

I can't recall the name of the course; it was probably something like 'Awaken the Unleashed Giant inside Your Inner Child for Abundant Success'. I don't even recall whether I ever listened to all the twenty-four CDs that came with the course before I got bored with the whole thing. I did, however, follow one piece of advice. I wrote down a set of goals to achieve once I had turned forty. As I absent-mindedly stirred the lentils, which were by now giving off a familiar whiff of lemon and spices, I began to read.

'1. Fix Teeth.' I am British and of a generation when teeth were considered things of function rather than of aesthetic worth. Consequently, by the time I hit my fifth decade, I had choppers that were healthy but looked like an abandoned cemetery. No one else seemed to notice or care, but it bothered me a great deal. Six months after my milestone birthday I found myself sitting in a dentist's chair being fitted with a brace. I can't pretend that I enjoyed the next two years, wandering around with a metal mouth like a teenage girl, but at least now the offending appliances are off I have teeth that are determinedly straight and pearly white. I am officially gorgeous.

'2. Have a Suit Made to Measure.' The made-to-measure suit must be every man's dream and ultimate clothing indulgence. It was worth the time and money: a striking suit of grey herringbone that garners admiring looks and comments every time I can find an occasion to wear it. The process, however, was not as much fun as I expected, particularly as the man taking my measurements made no attempt to spare my feelings. At the first fitting I offered up helpfully, having read about such things, 'I dress to the left.' The tailor looked at where my obviously less than John Holmes-like appendage was situated and sniffed, 'I don't think it is really going to make a difference, do you, sir?' Moving around to get a glimpse of my behind, he added, 'Sir has got quite a wide seat, hasn't sir?' as he pulled the tape across my rear end. I suppose, as a way of telling you that you have an arse like an old sofa, it is one of the nicest, but it did rather take the gleam off the whole occasion.

'3. Run a Marathon.' As an early riser, in the morning I can often be seen pounding the streets, wherever I happen to be, or lifting weights in the gym with all the prerequisite grunts. At the beginning of 2006 I decided that I should try and put all of this to good use and aim for the ultimate challenge. Timing meant that the next opportunity was the New York Marathon in November 2006, and the following months saw me running 40 miles a week until the big day.

The race itself was the single hardest thing I have ever done, particularly when my hip gave a loud 'pop' at the 23-mile mark and I had to limp the rest of the way through Central Park while well-meaning Americans shouted encouragement through mouthfuls of bagels and muffins. There is no chance in hell that I will ever repeat the exercise, but I did it and I have a medal to prove it.

I had listed a few other things on my goals list, most of which were either too stupid or implausible to worry about. It is, for example, unlikely that I am going to live on an island with Sophie Marceau and/or the woman from the Olay anti-wrinkle cream ad. Nor am I ever likely to own my home-town football team, Rotherham United, and take them to European glory. However, at the bottom of the page, in large, capital letters were four words: 'Go Everywhere, Eat Everything'.

I can't recall exactly what I was thinking when I wrote them down, but as I stood in the small, galley kitchen of my flat the seed was definitely planted. I chopped a large bunch of spinach and scattered it into the pot to wilt among the lentils, and then spooned my dahl into a large bowl into which I had placed a couple of hard-boiled eggs. The perfect comfort food. As I sat back onto the sofa and placed my supper on the coffee table in front of me, I turned the TV, tuned inevitably to a cookery programme, to 'mute' so I could still look at the pictures, and began to write in the same notebook what 'Go Everywhere, Eat Everything' could possibly entail. The more I wrote, the more excited I became.

A friend in the USA had been inviting me to the American Royal Barbecue competition in Kansas City for years. I adored sushi, yet I had never been to Japan. I knew nothing about Mexican food. I had always planned to go to Buenos Aires, arguably the home of the world's best beef. What would Beijing roast duck taste like in Beijing, or pad thai in Bangkok? What about Africa and, of course, my father's homeland, India?

By the time I had finished my second bowl of dahl – one is never enough – I had written down over forty things. At the bottom of the list I had written the words that you see on the front of this book, 'Eat My Globe'. I might not have gone anywhere yet except my living-room, but the journey had definitely begun.

The next morning in the gym, as I pottered along in my usual stately fashion on the treadmill, my mind kept turning to my list. People told me that Melbourne was a great eating city. What about mouldy shark in Iceland? Was it as disgusting as people say? Perhaps I could learn how to mix cocktails or persuade myself that wines from California were not all like melted sweets? What about whisky or gin? I loved them but did not know how they were made. What about my favourite things in the UK: pork pies, black pudding, cheese? It was no longer just mild curiosity; as I ran I began to think it was a real possibility. One hour and ten kilometres of sweat later, the decision was made.

I showered, dressed in a hurry and headed off on the short walk to work. For the previous few months, as I approached the office, I had begun to develop a sinking feeling in the pit of my stomach. In more recent weeks it had become closer to a panic attack, as I forced myself towards a day that I knew would be filled with arguments and tortuous meetings that achieved nothing. Today was different. I felt exhilarated. Not just from the great run, which had flown by with thoughts of food, but because I had reached the point of no return and there was no stopping me. A colossal weight had been lifted from my chest, and I was surprisingly well behaved, spending the morning smiling beatifically through a board meeting that would normally have contributed a great deal to my future ulcer.

Meeting over, I returned to my desk, switched on my computer and began to write a short, standard letter of resignation. I printed it out, signed it and placed it in a crisp white envelope, which I handed over to the owner of the company, my friend Zaro, who uttered words I was to hear more than once on the trip: 'Can I carry your bags?'

That afternoon I wrote forty-two e-mails to the same people who had received the previous rather depressing missive. This one simply read, 'I did it'. I am not sure quite what I expected, but, apart from a few return e-mails from people saying 'Ooh, that's brave', the world seemed to be fairly well attached to its normal axis. Inevitably, word began to get around to colleagues and clients that I was leaving, and I began to receive e-mails asking me what exactly it was I was going to do.

It was a good question. What the hell did 'Go Everywhere, Eat Everything' actually mean? I had done the easy bit, handing in my notice, and I had indulged in a few fanciful thoughts about jetting off. Now I had to do the hard bit of figuring out where to go, who to meet and how to pay for it all.

Money was an issue, of course. However, for the previous five years I had been putting by a decent sum away every month and had always promised myself that, when I reached a my set goal, I was going to do something different, even if I had no idea what that might be. I was fortunate enough to have no mortgage, and I was pretty sure I could get by for a year on the road even if, at the end of it, I would be penniless, jobless and could see myself standing on a street corner with a sign reading 'Will drop trou' for foie gras'.

For the 'who?' I turned inevitably to the internet. A few years earlier I had discovered food discussion sites. Sad though it may seem, it changed my life. Until that point, with the exception of my family, I felt like I was the only person in the world for whom food was the first thing one thought about in the morning and the last thing one thought about before heading up to bed.

The people with whom I worked were not like me. They wanted to have water-cooler conversations about music, a TV programme from the night before, a film or even politics. I joined in, but inside I wanted to talk about what to serve with hake (floury potatoes, in case you were wondering), the latest restaurant openings and what I had cooked the night before, why it was good or how it could have been better.

Then one night TGS sent me a link to a website called 'Chowhound'. I couldn't believe it. It was like discovering Narnia at the back of my refrigerator. There was a wonderland filled with people like me, where I could ask 'Where can I find a decent salami in east London?' or could write a thousand words about a new restaurant without people thinking I was stark raving bonkers. I felt at home immediately and soon began to post lengthy accounts of my dining experiences. One website soon begat another until I was, at one point, a member of four at the same time. I was easily one of the most active contributors, clocking up over 10,000 posts on one site alone as I became embroiled in lengthy arguments about such important matters as 'best Sichuan hotpot in London' and 'Lobsters tastier big or small?'

I am happy to admit now that I spent far too much time on these sites. I would look at them as I ate breakfast and lunch and often sneak peeks during the day, when I should have been doing something altogether more productive. But this was my world and these were my people, and I felt happy there and with them.

By 2006, however, I had weaned myself off them, primarily because I had started a blog with TGS called Dos Hermanos, on to which I was now posting the same extensive reports of every meal home or away. When it came to *Eat My Globe*, however, the food websites were a godsend.

Over the years I spent poring over these sites I met many people – at first virtually and then, as my travels allowed, in person. In the UK I began to organize regular get-togethers where those as afflicted as me could sit around large plates of food and have arguments in person. Business trips to New York saw me sitting with people I had never physically met before but knew everything about (often far too much about) and having astonishing meals in Manhattan, Queens or Brooklyn at restaurants or the houses of people willing to feed like-minded souls.

Now, as I prepared to head off into the world, I decided to call in every offer that had ever been made of a bed for the night or a home-cooked meal. I made a reappearance on one or two of the sites and posted about my planned trip. Almost immediately I started to receive e-mails with offers. Did I want someone to guide me around Mexico? Had I ever experienced a 'proper' Thanksgiving meal? Did I fancy a day on the barbecue trail in Texas? Would I like someone to put me up for a week in Melbourne? The response was astonishing but one that I later found throughout my trip to be nearly always repeated. Like nothing else I have ever encountered, food and the desire to share it bring out generosity in people wherever they are in the world.

The suggestions did not just come from over the Web, however. Friends from my 'real' life were soon chipping in. A Finnish friend dangled the possibility of a hunting trip in the Nordic countryside with an eighty-year-old man who only knew two words of English, of which one was 'vodka' and the other wasn't. Another suggested that I head up to spend a week in Scotland at a whisky distillery. So it went on. It would be a case not of what to do to fill my year but of what I was going to have to leave out for lack of time.

'When?' was pretty clear too. I had agreed that I would leave work at the beginning of March 2007. That gave me a little over two and a half months to plan. I spent most evenings in the next weeks flopped on the sofa with my laptop open and a large mug of tea to keep me fortified while I fired off e-mails to everyone and anyone I could think of. Slowly things began to take shape, and by the end of the year and with a few key dates in place I had my itinerary pretty much set in stone:

March and April: The UK and Ireland
May: Australia
June: UK
July: Japan
August: Hong Kong and China
September: Mongolia, Russia and Finland
October: The USA
November: Mexico, Argentina, Brazil and back to the USA
    for Thanksgiving
December: Home for Christmas and a little bit of a nap
January: Germany and Iceland
February: Thailand, Vietnam, Singapore, Malaysia
March: The Philippines and India

April: South Africa, Mozambique, Senegal and Morocco
May: Turkey, Italy, Spain

It was an intimidating list, but two things made me determined
to carry on.

The first was that, now I had told everyone what I was about to
do, I would look like a prize tool if I gave up at the first hurdle.
The second was that, as TGS put it none too kindly, 'an old git'
like me would never get this opportunity again. Circumstances,
finances and emotions had collided in a once-in-a-lifetime way,
which truly meant it was now or never.

My plans were well under way but were the cause of many
sleepless nights. I was not used to being out of work, and I developed a dread fear that I would turn into one of those people who
spend all day in their dressing gown, slumped on the sofa watching *Jerry Springer* while eating broken biscuits or baked beans out
of a can. Actually, I like baked beans out of a can, particularly if
they have those little sausages and burgers made out of reclaimed
meat in them, but that is another story.

I made a conscious decision to treat what I was doing as work.
I was not out of a job or on holiday. I was organizing a 'project':
the fact that I was doing it at home and was never more than five
seconds from a Chocolate Hobnob was just an added bonus. I
kept to my normal schedule. I got up at 5.30 every morning and
went to work. It is just as well that I did. I had no idea what was
involved in organizing a trip like this. Flights, accommodation,
visas, currency – it was more than a 9–5 job.

With the help of the internet I put together the schedule for
the first leg of my journey, and before you could say 'although
the bag will not inflate, oxygen will be flowing through the
mask', I had handed over the best part of £2,000 for my first set of
flights, to Australia and around Asia. There was now, officially,
no turning back.

2

Eating Britain (and Ireland)

Before I headed off around the world looking for great things to eat, I wanted to go in search of some of the astonishing food we have to offer closer to home. Britain and Ireland's relationship with their food is one of the most confused in the world. With the possible exception of the Americans, the British are probably furthest removed from the source of production of their food of any people on earth. You could point towards the huge sales of celebrity cookbooks and to the extraordinary popularity of cookery shows on TV as proof of a renaissance in the UK's interest in food. However, the truth is that the majority of people in the UK are perfectly happy to eat crap as long as it is cheap crap, served in huge portions, with little thought about why it is so cheap. It certainly isn't altruism. It is down to sourcing of the cheapest industrial ingredients and delivering them to customers through a process in which no skill or care is needed, carried out by lowly paid staff. In the ration-blighted post-war years the view was promulgated that cheap was good, and the majority of people in this country will still put up with food that borders on the inedible as long as the portions are filling and the dent in their wallet small.

This does not mean, of course, that good food has to be expensive. A plate of fabulous fish and chips from my home town of Rotherham costs well under £5 and can be as delicious, in context, as any three-star meal I have ever eaten. You can buy cuts of meat such as brisket or lamb breast from any decent butcher for less than it costs to feed a cat for a day. Slow-cook the brisket with winter vegetables or roll and stuff the lamb breast and you will have something delicious, nourishing and affordable.

It is hard not to view as schizophrenic a country where mediocre chefs can become megastars, selling millions of books and DVDs, but where you can still find the words 'Thai Vegetarian Schnitzel' scribbled on the blackboard menu of a pub.

It certainly is not down to a lack of ingredients. Britain and Ireland have some of the best raw materials in the world, but precious little of it ever finds its way onto our dinner plates. Despite the farming problems of recent years, we have fantastic beef, pork and lamb and spectacular seafood from Scotland or Cornwall; and don't get me started on the wonders of English asparagus. We have hundreds of varieties of apples and pears, artisanal bakers and more cheese-makers than France. Yet it is still a rarity to see these appearing on menus with any regularity, and much of what we produce is whisked off to more appreciative audiences in Europe.

In part, of course, cost is involved. Producing good food is not cheap. It is less intensive than standard methods of farming or fishing and requires time and patience. Consequently the end-result is going to cost more, which requires a long, hard education process for suppliers, retailers and consumers alike.

It is also down to a lack of confidence. Like an abused child, Britain has lost confidence and any sense of worth in what it produces and how to cook it. Nearly a century being the butt of the world's jokes means that we British have lost all pride in some of the fantastic things we produce – foods that, if they were made in any other country, would be national treasures. Foods that, when made with ingredients of the highest quality, are as good as anything you will taste anywhere in the world. I thought about this a lot as I was planning my trip and drew up a short list of things I adored but which have a bad reputation in the UK, primarily because most people's exposure to them has been, badly made, mass-produced examples. I decided go in search of just three things. My list read: black pudding, pork pies, cheese.

My first call was to Debbie Pierce, the co-owner of the Bury Black Pudding Company, who agreed to let me go up north and spend half a day watching the making of their splendid blood sausages. A three-hour drive from London and I found myself in the 'raw' room of their facility, resplendent in a blue overall, some over-sized blue Wellington boots and a hairnet covering nothing but my smoothly shaved scalp. This was what it was about: meeting people who were as obsessed with food as I was. All summed up in one huge mixing bowl of blood, barley, spices and back fat in a beef intestine. Fantastic.

There are few foods that divide people quite as much as a black pudding. Some people, me included, love it and become fanatical about it in all its forms. Others, usually those who have never tasted it, declare that they hate it. When asked why, they usually squeal, 'You know it's made of blood, don't you?'

The first time I ate black pudding would have been at a Majumdar family breakfast. Our breakfasts, I am guessing, were very different from yours, primarily because everything on our plates was yellow. Baba prepared breakfast and cooked everything in the same pan in which Indian food had been prepared. The jaundiced yellow of residual turmeric imbued everything that crossed its less than non-stick surface. So our breakfast comprised yellow fried eggs, yellow fried bread and yellow bacon. I knew no different and, thinking this perfectly natural, once made quite a show of myself at my friend's house when his mum produced a tea containing a perfectly cooked but glistening white egg. I announced in loud screams to my fellow diners that it was obviously 'poison' and was sent the 100 yards back to my house in tears of disgrace. Even then I was a critic.

At the yellow family breakfast the only thing that had a chance to power through the turmeric shackles was the black pudding – thin round slices of it cooked in the fat of the yellow bacon – and it was lovely. This was good black pudding, from the local butcher, none of the mass-produced rubbish that littered the supermarkets then and now. I loved the crunch when I first bit into a black slice. I loved the slight spiciness, and I loved finding a blob of hot fat. Special days, even if I am looking at them through glasses tinted with a very yellow hue of turmeric.

Most of my schoolfriends thought I was, in the vernacular of the day, 'a bit of a spacko' for liking black pudding, but then they thought I was ' a bit of a spacko' for many reasons, including, but not limited to, the fact that I was a fat Indian kid who brought poppadums to school. I was never one to follow the crowd, however, and my love of the by-products of pork production continued and, as I got older and travelled more, I realized that not only was I not the only one who liked the stuff but that just about every country had its own version. The French had boudin, which was soft and silky smooth to the tongue. Well, it would be, wouldn't it? The Spanish had morcilla, which was appropriately spicy, laced with paprika and plumped out with rice. It was a party in your mouth, and everybody was invited. The Germans, true to form, were not interested in any frills and came up with the simple but delicious blutwurst. All of them fine attempts and, heaven knows, I tried enough of them. But none could compare to our own black pudding.

By the time my food obsession was able to flow unchecked in the early 1990s the pudding had undergone a bit of rehabilitation and was no longer considered just the gross using-up of abattoir leftovers. A new wave of chefs inspired by British ingredients had decided it was hip. I chose it every time I saw it on a restaurant menu, and I used it at home when I cooked for myself and others, taking great delight in preparing meals that guests declared fabulous, only for me to explain to them what one of the main ingredients was. Conversion by stealth.

So that we don't labour the point, let's just agree, I am a fan of the black pudding, and no, I am not a spacko. I don't care what anyone says.

If you are going in search of the best black pudding, then there is only once place to go: Bury, Lancashire. A small town rapidly becoming subsumed into a suburb of Manchester, Bury is known for two things. One is that it was the birthplace of Robert Peel, founder of the police force. (Nope, I didn't know this either, but they are inordinately proud of this fact in Bury, and there is a large statue in his honour in the town square.) The other is black pudding.

What Graceland is to Elvis, Bury is to black pudding – its spiritual home since the early part of the twentieth century, when the town had over a dozen pork butchers and as many pig farms and they needed some way of using up all that blood. Every morning would be spent catching the blood, mixing it with local barley and blends of herbs, which changed from shop to shop. By opening time the puddings had been stuffed into skins and boiled and were lining the shop windows. By lunchtime they would be gone, the locals knowing a good thing when they see one.

In my slightly childish imaginings I had hoped a black pudding factory would have a conveyor belt from the outside, where smiling, innocent little porkers would be loaded, 'oinking' happily before entering a dark, satanic building with at least three chimneys puffing out acrid, black smoke. Inside would be a nightmare version of a Heath Robinson machine involving crushers, mincers, grinders, slicers and an extra crusher, just in case the first one did not crush enough. There would be a few vain squeals from the porcine victims before they were dispatched, and out of the other side would plop nicely packaged little puddings ready for the eating. As a pleasing afterthought there might be a side-door through which you could perhaps see a pie or two.

Instead, what I got was a tidy, bright, purpose-built unit on a small industrial estate. Hardly the charnel house I had been anticipating, and I have to admit to a slight disappointment. But I pressed on and was soon sitting in the neat boardroom of the Bury Black Pudding Co. with a cup of tea in one hand and my notepad in the other. I was introduced to Richard Morris – the son of James Morris, a legend in the black pudding world – who gave me a history lesson, before Debbie gave me the tour.

The raw ingredients room and cooked ingredients room

are strictly separated and required a change from blue to red uniforms as I moved from storerooms of fat and dried blood to ones that housed the finished product, hanging from lines like miniature clown's trousers out to dry. Very interesting, but all I wanted to do was to taste the puddings. Debbie picked one particularly plump specimen off the rails and cut it in half. She made me another cup of tea and took me back to the boardroom, leaving me alone to sample the freshly made beauty. It was everything I expected and more. The casing melted away to reveal a dense, dark inside with the herbs and flavourings, particularly white pepper, giving a result that had length, almost like a fine wine. 'Château Pudding, sir? It's the 2007. An exceptional year for blood.'

After the initial flavour came the mouth-feel, the creaminess of the fat with the slight bite of barley followed by the final touch of the herbs and spices. Make no mistake, this is a very special thing indeed; if you have not tried one, you are missing out. As I went to leave, Debbie filled a bag with samples of black pudding, which, true to form, once TGS got involved, lasted about an hour after I arrived back home.

Pork pies are another thing that people either love or hate. I will give you one guess in which camp my size 10s are firmly planted. The main drawback is the few simple ingredients: ground pork, jelly made from the pig's trotters and a pastry casing made predominantly from fat. OK, even I will admit it doesn't sound great when you put it that way.

Another problem is one of image. If you ask most people to describe the average pork pie eater, they will no doubt conjure up a picture of a bearded man with a large belly. In one hand he will have a pint of real ale and in the other a copy of *Minstrel in the Gallery*, by Jethro Tull. It is highly unlikely that anyone of the opposite genital grouping has wanted to copulate with him since he last saw his feet. This is, of course, hugely unfair. I eat a lot of pork pies, and I don't have a beard.

The main reason, however, is that most pork pies sold in this country, like so many of our traditional foods, are made to as low a specification as the manufacturers can get away with and taste like cardboard-covered vomit. They are solid lumps of stodge filled with greying meat and slimy jelly. Even I would not eat them, and I have been known to take tasty titbits out of the bin if I am hungry and the bin is within reach. The real pork pie is a thing of beauty, a filling of well-spiced lean meat encased in a protective jelly and surrounded by a casing of crisp pastry made from a hot-water paste. A good pie has only six ingredients: pork, salt, pepper, flour, lard and water. Not an additive or an E-number in sight.

The very best pies come from Melton Mowbray, which now has geographical protection status akin to champagne and stilton. The best pies in Melton Mowbray come from one small company, Mrs King's Pork Pies, now owned by the irrepressible Hartland family.

I encountered their pies on my very first visit to London's famous Borough Market. I had one bite as I was walking around the stalls and almost went back and hugged the owner, it was that good. Over the years few weeks have passed without me, or TGS, buying one of these beauties and enjoying it at home with a glass of shudder-making bitter, a slice of cheddar and a large spoonful of sharp piccalilli. The initial crunch of the pastry giving way to the soft jelly and then the spicy meat, which requires effort to bite, is one of the greatest sensations in the world.

Watching the Hartland clan making pies is like walking onto the set of a Three Stooges film. They bicker, as all families do, with Ian, the oldest, playing mediator and his son Adam seemingly doing all the work. Despite the arguments and the tea-break every twenty minutes without fail, they still manage to turn out 1,000 pies a week, all of which are snapped up by right-thinking people across the country as quickly as they can make them.

Ian gave me a history lesson. The pork pie was the snack of choice for the hunting set in nineteenth-century England, primarily because the tough pastry casing protected the meat as the riders jumped over hedges in pursuit of some poor fox. In the same century the law required that horses be changed exactly one day's ride from London on the routes up north. That point was Melton Mowbray, which is why it became the most famous home for pork pies. Over the years little was done to protect the name or the reputation, and anyone – no matter where or how bad their product – was allowed to call it a Melton Mowbray pork pie, which is why so many people's opinion of them is so low.

Now, however, there is a body called the Melton Mowbray Pork Pie Association, which sets a standard for a pie to carry the famous name, including a minimum of 45 per cent meat. Mrs King's take it a notch higher, to 50 per cent. Lean leg and fatty shoulder meat are mixed to ensure enough moisture, then simply seasoned with a little salt and pepper. The pastry casing is made with lard and flour, and the two are combined using a pastry press and a meat press.

Traditionally, of course, they were hand-raised, which involved using a block of wood called a 'dolly', lifting the pastry around it until it was high enough to take the pastry. The Hartlands used to do it this way when they first started, but, as the business grew, it became increasingly impractical and they had to resort to 'modern' methods. I use the term 'modern' loosely, though, as their pastry press is over 200 years old and operated manually by whichever brother's shift it is to press and pack the pies. It is, along with a whippersnapper of a flour mixer at a mere one hundred years old, their only concession to the industrial process. Once packed, the pies are cooked at about 200°C before being topped up with a jelly made from boiling pig's trotters in water; then they are allowed to set, before being released to a waiting world.

I was not up there just to watch, and Ian soon had me unloading shelves full of heavy pies from the hot oven as they bubbled fiercely with the natural juices from the meat. He then showed me how he filled them with jelly, with the aid of nothing more than a pouring jug and a knitting needle. That's all there is to it. But by God they are good and, thank heavens, becoming increasingly popular not just in the UK but across Europe, where artisanal products are treated with a great deal more respect than we can seem to summon up in the UK. Spain, in particular, Ian told me, has developed quite a craving for God's good pie. Which, given their love of all things pork, is hardly surprising.

They are under no illusions about their audience. Unless Madonna suddenly decided that a Mrs King's Medium Pork Pie is going to be on her rider for every concert, their market is still going to be predominantly, if not exclusively, male and, of that demographic of the nation's men, it is still going to be enjoyed most by those of a larger girth and with an unhealthy interest in progressive rock of the early to mid-1970s. 'Thank God, there are still enough of them around for us to sell as many of the things as we can make', Ian remarked.

It was time to leave the Hartland clan. I deposited my overalls with a little regret and left the family to resume their good-natured arguments. Ian insisted on giving me a pie to take with me for the walk back to the station, which may well have been prompted by me pointing at one and saying, 'Can I have a pie?'

I thought about bringing it home to London and sharing it with TGS. Such thoughts lasted until about ten minutes after I had begun my hike. As I walked, I passed a small pub in the nearby village. The sun was shining in a cloudless sky, and I couldn't resist stopping for a pint. As I sat outside, looking at my notes from my visit, the pie called to me and I took it from the bag. 'One small nibble', I promised myself. Ten minutes later the pint pot was drained, and the pie was no more than a dribble of jelly down my chin, with enough crumbs on the floor to attract a small group of birds. What TGS doesn't know won't hurt him.

Research told me that the United Kingdom and its Irish neighbours now have, combined, nearly as many artisan cheese-makers as France, if not more. It is a remarkable fact, given that the British cheese-making industry was more or less destroyed during the Second World War, in part by rationing and in part by laws prohibiting the making of anything but hard, long-lasting cheeses which could be stored to help the war effort.

The fact that cheese-making in this country is now in a much healthier position is down almost entirely to one man, Randolph Hodgson, owner of Neal's Yard Dairy and acknowledged god-father of the British and Irish cheese industry. The two Neal's Yard stores in London are now part of the landscape for any food-obsessed person either living here or visiting.

My first visit to the original shop, near Covent Garden, changed my life. To this day I can recall walking in and my nostrils being filled with an array of smells the like of which I had never encountered. Before I had the chance to utter the words 'Laughing Cow' the staff, in their blue hats and starched white coats, had given me tastes of about ten cheeses and I had handed over £10, a considerable sum for me, for slices of Cheddar, Caerphilly, goat's cheese and sheep's cheese whose tastes I can remember to this day. Neal's Yard has had thousands of pounds of my hard-earned over the years, and I don't begrudge them a single penny of it.

When I decided that I wanted to go and meet some cheese-makers, it made sense to spend some time in the Neal's Yard branch at Borough Market and see who could be likely candidates. Could it be Montgomery's Cheddar, Mrs Kirkham's Lancashire or perhaps even, Gorwydd Caerphilly? I got into conversation with one of the approachable staff and told him what I was doing. 'What about Ireland? There's some great stuff there, and you get to drink Guinness.' As he spoke, he handed over a thin sliver cut from an orange disc of a cheese from Milleen's, which I had tried quite a few times before, and then moved to a larger round of blue cheese before handing me a sample of that too, saying, 'You could go and see them making Cashel Blue too'.

One taste, and I was going to Ireland. I bought some cheese, obviously – about £30 worth, if I recall – and headed home, where I made a lunch of them with some oatcakes and a glass of organic cider. As I ate, I booked a flight and made a few phone calls. The makers of the two cheeses in Ireland I had chosen to visit, Milleen's and Cashel Blue, were both very receptive, and I soon had the dates written in large black letters in my diary.

Milleen's is based just outside Castletownbere, west Cork, which involved a three-hour drive from Cork airport, during which every slow-moving vehicle and tractor seemed to have been rolled out just for my benefit. It did, I guess, give me the chance to admire the scenery, which is breathtaking. Eventually I found myself in Castletownbere and at my B&B. As I was not due to meet my first cheese-maker until the next morning, I dropped off my car and decided to go for lunch and a hike.

It will come as no surprise if I say that Ireland offers some of the best walking anywhere. I was perfectly happy spending a few hours wandering through fields and along clifftops with breath-taking views, stopping to drink in the history of any number of mysterious stone circles. By mid-afternoon I was ready to drink in something altogether more fun and set off back to town for a pint of stout.

While the rest of Ireland may come under the spell of Guinness, this was Murphy's country. In many ways I prefer the latter's richer, darker, more roasted flavour to that of its well-marketed rival. They do have one thing in common, however: they both take an age to pour properly. In the current climate of immediate gratification it is a welcome change to have food or drink that is not, nor was ever meant to be, served quickly, and here they certainly followed the age-old traditions to the letter.

As I entered McCarthy's Bar on the High Street, at about 3 p.m., it was almost empty and the old dear running the bar and its attached grocery shop was busy sweeping the floor. I ordered my pint of the good stuff and watched as she began to pour, the chilled liquid cascading against the side of the glass to produce that legendary head. When the glass was about a third full, she sat it down on the counter, picked up her broom and continued on with her sweeping. Three minutes later she returned to the glass and filled it to the half-way point before setting it down again and returning to her work. A final few minutes later she topped of the glass and set it on the counter with strict instructions to 'Let it rest a while, dear'. Good things, it would appear, cannot be rushed.

When I finally got a quick nod from her, I lifted the glass to my lips and took a long, slow glug. It was worth the wait, a welcome cold bite with a slight bitterness at the end which made me shudder agreeably. I had two pints, which meant that I did not leave McCarthy's Bar until an hour and a half later and with a slight stagger caused by the strong, dark, black beer and the lack of anything to eat for over twenty-four hours. Lunch by now would be an early supper, and I went in search of something to eat.

If the views in the town were breathtaking and the stout sublime, then the food offerings were shameful. Another example, I thought, of a country with some of the best raw materials sending it all abroad and leaving its own population to eat dreadful bilge. After walking disconsolately up and down the high street looking for somewhere that was actually open, I found myself entering a brightly lit café and taking a seat at a corner table. The place was packed and, as I entered, conversation stopped and all faced turned towards me. None of these particular Irish eyes seemed to be smiling, and my mind turned to scenes from *Straw Dogs* and *The Wicker Man*. I hid myself behind a menu and the local paper. The front page was celebrating the return of a local dog whose disappearance had obviously formed the substance of the front-page headlines from the week before. The owner came over to take my order. I had barely looked at the menu, but when I did, I saw it mainly consisted of 'something and chips', so I pointed at the word 'chicken' and left it at that.

'It comes with the vegetable of the day', the owner said. 'Do you want that?' I nodded, assuming that, at the very least, it would be some greenery, and returned to the story of the missing pooch's joyous return. Five minutes later a plate was plonked in front of me. Next to a piece of breaded chicken, baked until cindered and rock hard, was a pile of soggy oven chips and a large mound of grey mashed potatoes.

'I don't think I ordered mashed potatoes', I said politely.

'Mashed potatoes is your vegetable of the day', he countered and wandered off to deliver another plate of food.

His logic was, of course, faultless. Even in my hardest-hearted moments I can't argue potatoes to be anything other than a vegetable, but for God's sake! On its own the appearance of four types of carbs on my plate, counting the breading of the chicken and the four slices of cheap white bread covered in margarine that he had brought over with my plate of food, would have been enough to make me quail in terror. But that was nothing compared with what sat ominously at the side of the plate daring me to look at it. At first I was unsure, taking it for a slightly misshapen piece of chicken. I prodded it, and the way it yielded to my fork told me it was some thing that had never clucked. I prodded it again and then, my heart in my mouth, cut it open. Mother of God, it was a whole, deep-fried, breaded banana. I recoiled in terror like the victim in a Victorian melodrama and very probably let out a little whimper. I was hungry enough to eat the chicken, a few of the chips and even a mouthful of potato, but I could not bring myself to go near the banana again as it sat there challenging me to try and eat it. When the owner came back to collect my still pretty full plate, he looked down and said, 'Will you not be wanting your banana then?' before carrying it away with a disapproving sigh as I slunk out of the café and back to my B&B.

The farmhouse producing Milleen's is situated in the small hamlet of Eyries, about four miles from the town, and when I arrived, Quinlan Steele was hard at work making the cheese that I make a point of buying at least once a fortnight. Norman, his father, dragged a couple of kitchen chairs out into the sun-dappled farmyard and gave me a brief history lesson while we waited for his son.

There are, I am told, sixty-five farmhouse cheese-makers in Ireland, and Norman and his wife, Veronica, started making their now famous cheese to use up the excess milk of their one cow, Brisket. The following thirty years saw large chunks of both good and bad fortune as, on the one hand, their cheese found its way to the table of Ireland's only Michelin-starred chef at the time, Declan Ryan, and on the other hand, their entire herd of cattle was wiped out by foot and mouth – something from which Norman still has not fully recovered. He now prefers to buy in his milk from neighbouring farms because he just doesn't 'have the heart' any more.

Norman was eccentric, garrulous and everything I expected a cheese-maker to be. He had a seemingly inexhaustible supply of anecdotes and, as we waited for Quinlan to finish in the work shed, he told me about the time he caused a postal strike when sending out mail-order deliveries of high, runny cheese and about the time a Health & Safety official came to visit and invited him to shave off his long, straggly grey beard, a request that was given shrift that is as far from long as it is possible to get. Quinlan Steele, however, with his lanky, slightly awkward good looks and bookish mentality, was completely different.

After about thirty years Norman and Veronica were, quite understandably, exhausted and felt the business was going backwards rather than forwards. Enter Quinlan Steele, with a name more suited to a super-spy than a cheese-maker. At twenty-six, an IT graduate, he came back home from Dublin and moved production from his father's intuitive, self-taught methods to one he supports with internet research studying the latest papers on microbiology: a technology-based approach that he feels helps the consistency of Milleen's without robbing it of its identity.

It is this slight quirkiness, reflected in its makers, that makes Milleen's one of my favourite cheeses. Quinlan gave me a tour of the cheese-making shed. It was much smaller than I imagined. It does turn out only ten tons a year of the small wash rind discs, and there is no great desire to increase that. Afterwards Quinlan

selected a particularly good example and wrapped it up for me
to take back to the B&B. Frightened of what other food horrors
the town might offer up if I braved another supper, I stopped off
at a supermarket and bought some fruit, oatcakes and a bottle of
beer and had a picnic in my room before falling asleep with the
pleasing scent of this little cheese filling the air.

The next morning, over breakfast, the owner of the B&B
gave me a rather suspicious look as I ate my bacon and eggs.
Later, as I was packing my car, I saw her peering into what had
been my room and having a deep sniff. I was running late, so I
didn't have time to explain my meal of the night before. To this
day she probably still tells people about a short, bald man who
came over from England and performed some unholy ritual in
one of her rooms which left a smell that she has not been able
to remove despite a couple of bottles of Fabreze and a visit from
the local priest.

I pointed my car north towards Cashel, a small, historic town
close to Cork. Three hours later and after about half a dozen calls
to the farm to get directions, I found myself pulling up in the
driveway of the J. & L. Grub Farm and being greeted by Sarah
Furno, who, like Quinlan Steele, has taken over the running of
the family business from her parents. That, however, is where the
similarity with Milleen's ended. Although both would claim to
produce 'farmhouse' cheeses, they could not be more different.
Where Milleen's produces ten tons, at Cashel, I was told, nearly
270 tons a year are produced. Where Milleen's was the work of
one dedicated cheese-maker, Cashel Blue is the work of a team
of close to twenty; and where, despite Quinlan's devouring of
biochemistry papers, Milleen's is still a cheese made as much
by intuition as by technology, Cashel Blue is a cheese made for
consistency, which is assured by rigorous and carefully annotated
tasting.

Inevitably I found myself being offered overalls and Wellington
boots to wear and being invited to dip my feet in regular baths
of disinfectant as I was given a tour of the impressive facilities.

Cheese-making is pretty similar wherever you go and whatever the style of cheese. Coagulating milk with rennet splits it to whey, which is drained, and curds, which are collected, pressed, shaped and aged. It sounds straightforward enough, but it is the possibility for endless variety at each stage that makes cheese such an interesting food, from the animal chosen to provide the milk – cows, goats or sheep – to the pasture and feed on which they graze, to the type of rennet used to the flora of the environment in which the cheeses are stored.

It is this potential for variety which Sarah is most concerned to monitor, and after the tour I joined her and husband, Sergio, for what they consider the most important part of the whole process: tasting. For well over an hour she plucked long cylinders of cheese from different batches from different milks, and we tasted them for acidity, fat content and for the spread of the blue, which had been injected after the curds are collected and pressed.

As with wine, the real skill of the taster is not just in the ability to taste but in the ability to articulate that taste. It is about developing the vocabulary. It does not take long, though, and by the end of my time with the Furnos I was tossing around words such as 'length' and 'graininess' with abandon. After the tasting I said my 'goodbyes' and left them to their real lives before heading back to Cork for my plane to London. The next morning I headed back down to Borough Market and Neal's Yard to recount tales of my journey to the young man who had served me before.

'Sounds good', he said as I told him about my visits. And then, of course, he sold me £50 worth of cheese.

3

Sydney: Underwhelmed Down Under

If you are going to spend a year or more travelling around the world eating, it is inevitable that you are going to spend some time in Australia. The Australians are exceptional self-publicists and have persuaded many that Australia is the 'best country in the world™', even if the ones promulgating this fallacy are usually living in Earl's Court as they speak and show little inclination to return.

It is the same with Australian cooking. Cookery programmes across the globe are populated by bronzed, healthy-looking Aussies extolling the virtues of Australia's new cuisine, which has taken its lead from the immigration explosion in the country of the 1960s, '70s and '80s, particularly from South-East Asia. Plus, of course, Aussies just love to travel. As an Aussie friend once said to me, 'It's our world, mate. The rest of you just live in it.' TGS was less charitable. 'If you came from Australia, you'd want to travel too.'

It is easy to see how adventures in far-flung places such as Thailand, Malaysia and Vietnam would have a profound impression on a new generation of Australian chefs brought up on the previous national diet, a British legacy of pies and Sunday roasts. Sydney and Melbourne, in particular, have worked hard to persuade people that they are top-notch cities in which to eat, so I felt that I would scarcely have been considered to have eaten my globe if I did not head off to visit one or both of them. A friend from a food website invited me to come and stay with him and his family in Melbourne, and trawling the net had provided a likely source of cheap accommodation in Sydney. I was all set.

Nothing quite prepares you for the horrors of flying to Australia, literally the other end of the world. My cheap ticket meant that, apart from a twenty-minute stop in Singapore, I spent the best part of twenty-five hours sitting in a flying tube, travelling at 400 m.p.h., breathing recycled air with all the health-giving properties of sucking through a sumo wrestler's loincloth before landing in Sydney, not knowing what day it was and smelling like a sheep shearer's armpit.

People of Sydney, I hate to ruin things for you, but Sydney is not, never has been and never will be 'the greatest city on earth'. No matter how many times you tell people and add the word 'mate' at the end. No matter how many of those fiercely unimpressive opera houses you choose to build, and definitely no matter how many times you choose to let fireworks off that sodding bridge and expect the whole world to give you a round of applause. No one ever, in any industry, has ever asked 'Will this play in Sydney?'

Now that I have said all that, I can also say I actually like Sydney rather a lot. It is hard not to. It's certainly beautiful, and the weather makes visiting there better than a weekend in Whitley Bay in January. Actually, just about anything I can think of, including recent root canal work, is better than visiting Whitley Bay at any time. It is just the constant and slightly desperate bleating of every person from Sydney I ever meet that their city deserves to be up there with the best of them, including London and New York, which is a little bit silly. Once you get over that little obstacle, Sydney is an agreeable place to spend some time, and I had little over a week of eating on my or with like-minded souls to look forward to.

Given my limited budget, my expectations on accommodation were markedly different from when I used to travel on business. I actually found myself using the word 'hostel' for the first time in over thirty years and, as it had done then, it brought me out in a cold sweat. But if my savings were to last, I had no choice.

I set myself some guidelines. I was happy to share a bathroom. Whether anyone else in the accommodation who saw me in the morning was quite so happy, you will have to ask them. But I was not prepared to share a room. Quite apart from not wanting an audience for some of my more unsavoury nightly activities, I considered this an act of altruism, to protect people from the fact that I snore and, when I snore it can apparently be measured on the Richter scale. I am told that my midnight emissions could knock down the walls of Jericho. This may explain, alongside the fact that I am, apparently, and I quote from an ex-partner, 'a selfish, self-absorbed, self-righteous pig', my current single status. Whatever the reasons, a single room it had to be, and at a price that would allow me to spend the rest of my budget for the trip on food.

Which is how I ended up at a hostel in Surry Hills, lugging a 90 lb rucksack on my back and looking like the dodgiest back-packer in town. As the owner showed me around, I suddenly realized that I was the oldest person in the place by at least twenty years. As soon as I was in my room, I locked myself away like Charlton Heston in *The Omega Man* and took a look around. You don't get a great deal for AU$22 a night in Sydney, but my room was clean and tidy and would suit me down to the ground. In the corner was a bunk bed, the lower half of which looked pretty inviting. I threw my bag on the top bed, lay down, fully clothed, and promptly fell asleep.

The only thing that woke me from my jet-lagged slumber the next morning was the sound of a young German couple having wild, monkey sex in the room next door. In fact, they seemed to do this most mornings, and their Teutonic grunts, groans and spanky noises became a very dependable alarm clock. I am many things, but I am not a killjoy, so I left them to their squeals of pleasure and dragged myself to the showers to clean away the filth of the previous day's journey. Showered and shaved, I sat on the edge of my bed and consulted my notes for my first day's eating around the city.

Although I had made plans to meet a few people when I was in Sydney, for the most part I was going to be eating on my own. A lot of people find solo dining an unpleasant experience, and it is certainly true that many restaurants can make it intimidating as they lead you through a crowded restaurant to a seat so conspicuous that you should have a large neon sign above your head reading 'Sir William of No Mates'. Others in the restaurant will stare at you, many will compose their facial features to express pity, others contempt, and all will be hugely glad that it is not them in the same situation. I rather like eating on my own, sitting with a book or a magazine to keep me company, but usually perfectly happy to sip on a chilled Martini or glass of wine as I watch other diners come and go and try to catch snatches of their conversation. I love eavesdropping. It is a family tradition.

My Welsh grandmother would have been, if there were an award for such things, a world champion at the sport. She could pick up saucy gossip at a hundred yards, and in any social situation her ears would be twitching. A particular favourite location was the beach; if juicy titbits were not forthcoming, it was not unknown for her to move the whole family *en masse* to a more favourable location. In later life, as her hearing faded, she still tried her best but often found herself spending a fruitless day next to a family without one whiff of scandal, only for us to point out that the family in question was German. Her response was an undeniable, if quirky, 'Typical of them to be German. They are like that.'

Being on your own also gives you the opportunity to mooch. Mooching, to put it at its most basic, is the ability to pass hours of time wandering around with no particular purpose or destination, looking at whatever happens to cross your path. It sounds simple, but it is in fact an art form. It takes a great deal of work to get to the point where you can mooch, apparently without effort, for hours on end.

Suffice to say I give good mooch, and my first day of mooching around Sydney saw me have breakfast at a local institution, Bill's, the restaurant of Australian *Überchef* Bill Granger. Granger is what I would call 'the acceptable face of modern Australian cooking': blond, blue-eyed and perma-grinned, he sums up everything Australia wants its cooking to stand for in the pantheon of cuisines – simple ingredients of high quality, not screwed around with too much – and he succeeds. Certainly he did so with a breakfast of scrambled eggs run through with a creamy, home-made ricotta and served on a slice of crunchy sourdough toast. Just the job to fuel me for my day and a long walk around Sydney, luxuriating in the autumn weather.

You will by now already know that I love pie in all its forms, but meat pies in particular are a constant source of wonder. Everywhere in Australia pies are available. As the genre has developed, they have tried to finesse things a bit with new and unusual fillings, but the truth is that the traditional Australian meat pie, in its unadulterated form, is a thing to be treasured.

In Sydney there can be only one choice: Harry's Café de Wheels, a pie-dispensing caravan set close to the naval dockyards of Woolloomooloo (yep, I had to check the number of Os too). It has been around since the 1930s and to this day attracts a diverse crowd of late-night revellers, politicians and celebrities, who turn up at all hours to sample the legendary pies. As I ordered a standard meat pie, I looked at pictures they had pinned on the wall. Unless someone in the 1940s had developed a primitive version of Photoshop, then it is pretty safe to say that both Frank Sinatra and Robert Mitchum had enjoyed the same meal as me. Not bad company, although there was no one old enough behind the counter to tell me what Ol' Blue Eyes made of this Australian speciality.

Sometimes a pie can be 'all filler no killer', but this pie was a perfect example of the art, packed with thick chunks of meat in a rich gravy topped with a covering of good, flaky pastry. On top of the pie a large mound of mushy peas cooked down until thick had a taste that took me back to my own childhood days in Rotherham, when my parents would bring home pie, chips and peas for a Saturday lunchtime meal spent in front of the TV. It really was a lovely thing and fortified me for the long walk back to my hostel, to brave the stares of the young folk in the communal area and to catch up on some much-needed sleep, which may well have involved a dream about the legalities of marrying a meat pie.

I needed to sleep it all off anyway for what I anticipated would be one of the highlights of my time in Sydney: the umpteen-course tasting menu at the eponymous restaurant of the now legendary Tetsuya Wakuda. Among gastro-tourists, those people who travel the world solely for the purpose of visiting every fine dining establishment they can, Tetsuya's is regarded as one of the very best in the world, and in 2008 it again found itself voted into the top five of the world's best restaurants by the 600-strong panel of the trade journal *Restaurant Magazine.*

This being one of the eating world's hot tickets, they don't make things easy for you. Faxed confirmations, telephoned confirmations, reconfirmations and vials of blood to be deposited at a secret location (OK, that last bit is a fib, but you get the picture). But for AU$300 you get to experience a meal that justifies its position in the pantheon of fine dining. It is far from flawless – in a meal of that many courses you are bound to get dishes that misfire – but it would have been worth the money for one dish alone: Tetsuya's signature dish of ocean trout confit in local olive oil and served with daikon and baby fennel.

This was one of those memorable dishes, not just for me but obviously for the whole restaurant, as table after table went from noisy chitter-chatter to complete silence as each diner in turn lifted their first taste to their mouth. The fish is poached in barely bubbling olive oil to a point where it is still medium-done and then topped with konbu seaweed and served on shreds of baby fennel and daikon radish. It ranks as one of the great tastes of my life: I wanted to ask for a scalpel so I could slice the fish so thinly it would last for ever. If I close my eyes, I can still see and taste a dish that would be on the menu if the good lord decided to create a tasting menu in heaven. Other dishes came and went, but this was the highlight and the rest of the meal is a blur – a pleasing blur, but a blur none the less. It would be fair to say that the next morning I was feeling a little bit under the weather. Fourteen courses with matching wines will do that to a man.

Through my fug I realized that, the day before, I had booked myself on a coach trip up to the Hunter Valley, one of Australia's primary wine-growing areas. I have no idea why I did this. I loathe organized coach trips at the best of times, let alone when I have a thudding hangover. Added to which, I was no great fan of Australian wines. Well, that is not fair. Let's just say that I am no great fan of the Australian wines that find their way to the UK. Cheap, mass-produced 'plonk' price-promoted so heavily by the UK supermarkets that most people would come out in hives if they were asked to spend more than £5 on a bottle.

Every Aussie has built into them a concept they call 'Fair Goes', which means that you have to give people and things a chance. It would have been churlish of me, then, not to give Australian wines a chance now I was in striking distance of where some of the better ones were supposed to be made. An organized trip seemed to be the option, given the fact that Australia's police apparently take a dim view of bald men in hire cars hurtling through the countryside swilling enthusiastically from open bottles of Shiraz. But when I reached the departure point for the coach, my heart sank down to my walking boots. I was the only single person on the trip.

The rest of the group was made up of young couples holding hands and whispering to each other, elderly couples doing much the same and a group of seven Filipinos who had never had a drop of wine between them but were on the journey because one of their number had watched *Sideways* on the plane over from Manila. They seemed particularly perturbed by my solitude and kept on pointing at me during the journey. Points were followed by whispers and then, rather disconcertingly, suppressed giggles. Steve, the driver, took pity on me and invited me to join him in the front of the van, which at least meant I had someone to talk to, even if I knew the others were all staring at me behind my back as though I was the Elephant Man.

I am not quite sure what I was expecting. Perhaps lush, green, sun-dappled rolling vineyards set in idyllic surroundings, where I would be at liberty to wander around the fields before having a sample of some of the area's finest wines served to me by rose-cheeked young women desperate for my considered opinion of the latest vintage. What I got was a little different. First of all, the Hunter Valley is not that nice a place. People from Sydney refer to it as 'The C*nter Valley', and to its main town, Cessnock, as 'Cesspit' because of the amount of violent crime. Second, the weather was appalling: it poured almost from the minute we set off to the minute we arrived back in Sydney.

The tour itself was harmless enough, in reality a buying opportunity where visits to two small boutique wineries book-ended a few hours in a wine resort, where five wineries had come together to create a destination with restaurants, shops and hotels encouraging people to stay longer and spend more. There was a passable lunch thrown in, and I got to sample enough wines to give even my jaundiced liver a bit of a buzz. But therein lies the problem. The wines were just not any good – awful, in fact. By 4 p.m. I had tasted enough over-oaked Chardonnay and figgy Sémillon to last any number of lifetimes, and if one more person had offered me a 'fruity red', my trip would have ended in ignominy there and then as I drowned them in a barrel of reprehensible 15 per cent ABV slop.

I slept soundly on the way back to the city, as did most of the rest of the group, and when we got close to the nearest drop-off point to my hostel, Steve gently nudged me awake and let me off the bus. What can I tell you? I still think Australian wines are lousy.

As a result of massive immigration in the 1960s and '70s

Australia's Asian community has had an enormous impact on the country, not least on its food. In Sydney I found offerings of excellent quality from all corners of South-East Asia at prices that made me shed a tear of pleasure. Many of these places are to be found in food courts, another of Sydney's treasures. Unlike the dreadful slop-houses found in malls in the UK and the USA, food courts here take their lead from places such as Singapore and Beijing, where dishes from many Asian regions are served from small stalls for a few Australian dollars a time.

I met food blogger Helen Yee for lunch in Sydney's impressive Chinatown, and she introduced me to bahn-mi, the crunchy and delicious Vietnamese sandwich, and as we ate she pointed me in the direction of many other places I should try: restaurants specializing in food from Xi'an province at the beginning of the Silk Road and Cantonese places serving traditional roast meats. I returned more than once to my own favourite, Barbecue King, for a portion of their crispy pork, the crackling skin supported by a creamy layer of fat.

Outside the enviable array of Asian food I found Sydney's dining scene to be vibrant but small. I had some enjoyable meals, but the arguments I heard and still hear from Australians about it being one of the great places to eat on earth rang a little hollow. The top restaurants in Sydney do not disappoint. Tetsuya is deserving of its place in anyone's list and provided me with one of the great tastes of my life in that dish of ocean trout confit in olive oil. But in the mid-range, while there is consistency and talent, there is too little originality to suggest a city close to finding its own culinary identity.

I was also not convinced by the new wave of cooking, particularly as young, recently travelled Aussie cooks are eager to show off their chops. They have created what I dubbed the 'Hey lemongrass is on special offer' school of cookery, where ingredients from disparate places are flung together with little thought, to create dishes of jarring flavours and inappropriate tastes. I couldn't help but wonder why, just because they have been around Vietnam on a motor-bike, the rest of us should have to suffer. It was a view exemplified by a meal I shared at Bentley's with Simon Thomsen, the coruscating food critic for the *Sydney Morning Herald*. The cooking was more than competent, drawing influence from the Ferran Adria school of foams and fancies, but there was little about it to suggest that I was in Sydney, as opposed to a mid-level restaurant in any other city of a decent size.

Where I expected Sydney to be good, it excelled. There are, as they like to keep reminding you, few more pretty cities on earth and few places with as many ways to enjoy yourself. There are also few people in this world who know how to enjoy their city as well as the people of Sydney. You name it, they do it: jogging, kayaking, windsurfing, diving, cycling. No wonder they are so bloody fit, and they know how to live a bloody good life. They can probably teach the world a lesson or two on that subject.

Now all they need is someone to teach them how to make wine, create their own cuisine and to stop trying to convince the rest of the world that Sydney matters and I might head back there. Lights blue touch paper and retires.

4

Melbourne: Eating with the Devil

Children like me. Don't laugh. It's true.

I may look like the child-catcher from *Chitty Chitty Bang Bang*, but for some reason children seem rather taken with me. At dinner parties I am inevitably the one sitting in the corner with my hosts' kids playing games rather than indulging in serious adult conversation, and on occasions when I am invited to christenings or weddings I invariably plonk myself down at the children's table to talk to them rather than listen to some stranger tell me all about his career in accountancy while covering me in spittles of cold poached salmon.

Eric Balic, however, hated my guts.

One of the first invitations I received when I put out the word about my trip was from two friends in Melbourne, Adam Balic and Rebecca Hewlett. Rebecca is a normal, well-adjusted type with a proper job. Adam is a brainiac scientist with a passion for food history. We had only met a handful of times, but we had swapped countless mails and indulged in long arguments on food websites.

By the time I started my trip, Adam and Rebecca had moved back from the UK to their home town of Melbourne, with Adam acting as house-husband until he found a job involving test-tubes and dissecting animals. He extended an invitation for me to come and spend a week seeing what Melbourne had to offer, with him as my guide.

The city has a reputation as one of the great eating cities, primarily because of the bewildering number of nations whose citizens have washed up on its shores: people from all regions of

China, Indians, Turks, Jews from Eastern Europe, thousands of people from southern Italy and more Greeks than in any other nation apart from Greece itself, all of them bringing with them their cuisines and techniques. No trip with my lofty ambitions could possibly be complete without a visit to the city.

I arrived in Melbourne after a long flight from Perth, where I had spent a few pleasant but unmemorable days. Adam was waiting at the door. In his arms was eighteen-month-old Eric, for the period of my stay my nemesis. From the look on his round, freckled face, partly hidden by a shock of pure ginger hair, it was obvious that no one had explained to the poor mite that for the next week he would be sharing the loving attention of his parents with a visitor.

After a hearty handshake with his father, I turned my charms towards Eric and went to give him a peck, which would, of course, win him over to my side. It always does. As I leaned forward, whispering all the required 'coochee-coo' noises, the little sod delivered a swift right cross to the bridge of my nose, a punch that carried unexpected force and made me utter expletives that no eighteen-month-old child should have to hear.

That set the tone for the week. I tried, I really did. I considered it a bit of a challenge. I mean, after all, kids love me, remember? They cry for weeks after I leave, refusing to sleep, eat or listen to bedtime stories. But Eric was having none of it. I tried all my best moves. I smiled, I made normally irresistible faces and I even tried bribing him with biscuits when his parents were not around, all to no avail. Fortunately, for much of my time there he was at kindergarten or confined behind the bars of a playpen, which I could not help thinking would give him valuable experience for later life.

Adam, being the methodical type, had my week all planned out. He had treated it like a scientific experiment and had a methodology that would see me cover every ethnic cuisine in Melbourne, along with a significant number of cafés and restaurants, in seven days. Although I did not see it, I suspect he had a chart somewhere. It began the next morning, as I emerged from the shower and deftly dodged Eric's attempt to do me harm with a toy tractor.

'Hurry up and get dressed. We're going to the market.'

I needed no prompting. I love markets. The proper ones, mind you, not the newfangled farmers' markets, filled with baby-strollers and stallholders who think they are doing you a favour by being there. Real markets, where rough-looking men with calloused hands shout things at you like 'lurvelytomsapound-abowl' and who shovel fruit into brown paper bags with a well-practised twist before saying 'That'll be £1.50 in English money, Guv', being the only people apart from London cabbies who can say 'Guv' without deserving a good slap.

It was a short tram ride to the Queen Victoria Market. After the relative disappointments of Sydney, Melbourne was immediately appealing. Whereas Sydney seemed hell-bent on comparing itself to London and New York and competing on a world level that it would never quite reach, Melbourne and its laid-back inhabitants seemed content for it to be a great Australian city – and it really is a great Australian city.

The Queen Victoria Market is the real deal. Alongside the stalls selling all the usual fruits and vegetables are pitches piled high with mounds of fresh, glistening Asian herbs. Next to these, the varied communities of the Mediterranean are represented in splendid arrays of tomatoes of many hues, purple heads of plump garlic and mild onions to form the base of dishes from countries where wine and good conversation flow in equal measure. German butchers with more ways of making sausages than you ever thought possible sit next to Chinese fishmongers with live carp flapping around in their buckets waiting to become brightly spiced wok-fodder. The market was everything I wanted. Well, not quite everything. In my rush to get out I had declined the offer of breakfast and was now close to a dead faint. Adam obviously had it covered. In the section housing the German butchers was a Melbourne institution: a stall serving hot bratwurst, sausages so plump the meat was almost bursting from the skins and served in crunchy rolls topped with the sweetest sautéed onions. It took just one bite for me to think that being in Melbourne could just turn out to be a very good thing indeed, a feeling that was compounded as Adam made more use of Melbourne's fantastic tram system to take me on a week-long gastronomic tour. It was a tour that included grilled meats from the Middle East, dim sum from Hong Kong cafés, Jewish cakes, and fiery dishes from Vietnam that put to shame any of the examples I had tried back in London.

Before all that, however, we needed a bit of sweetening up, and we met up with Rebecca before heading over to Lygon Street, one of the centres of Melbourne's considerable community from southern Italy. Rebecca appeared pushing Eric, who was feigning sleep while glowering at me through half-open eyes.

As we approached Brunetti's, another Melbourne institution, he sat bolt upright and started howling, a howl that meant that, if he did not get cake and get it soon, there was going to be trouble. For once I was in total agreement, and we squeezed our way into an already crowded shop while I went in search of pastries. I came back laden down with some specialities of the house, including flaky 'lobster tails' – the local name for the Neapolitan sfogliatella pastry, piped full of sweet cream, and cannoli so authentic you could hear the theme tune to *The Godfather* as you ate them. I even picked up some mini-versions for Eric. Everyone was a winner.

On the food website where I first encountered Adam he would post graphic accounts of attempts to prepare dishes gleaned from the pages of the hundreds of cookery books in his collection. From multi-course dinners taken from the pages of Epicurus to puddings from the pages of Mrs Beeton designed to sate an Edwardian appetite, nothing seemed to stem Adam's passion to recreate classic dishes of the past. As well as descriptions that brought me out in a sweat reading them, Adam took stylish pictures, which he posted to universal acclaim from all the other obsessive food types. Like me, Adam soon tired of the internet forums and set up his own site to showcase his search for the great meals of the past, which he called The Art and Mystery of Food. To Adam, cooking is akin to alchemy. Go and look it up: I think you will agree he is a genuinely scary individual.

When I dragged myself out of bed the next morning, Adam was long gone and had taken Eric kicking and screaming to kindergarten, where he would no doubt be happily overseeing his protection scam for the one-year-olds. We had agreed to meet at Flinders Station, a Melbourne landmark where courting couples for decades have met up 'under the clocks' before heading off to do what romantic couples do.

Adam had our day organized down to the minute, as usual. First, a walk through the Botanical Gardens (boo!) followed by some lunch (hurrah!). This was not just any lunch, however. This proved to be one of the top ten tastes of the whole of *Eat My Globe*.

Another short tram ride brought us to Chapel Street, the Greek enclave of Melbourne. Adam wanted me to taste the souvlaki at Lamb on Chapel Street. To all intents and purposes the Greek souvlaki is similar to a Turkish doner kebab, not that I would ever say that to a Greek person for fear of being separated from my manhood quicker than you can say 'Nana Mouskouri'.

I had tried these before. There are few meat and bread combos I have not tried in my forty-four years: from the lowliest ballpark hot dog to the clubbiest sandwich in all of clubdom, I have done the lot. But this little beauty was something else. Thirty whole shoulders of lamb, boned and threaded onto a large skewer above smouldering hot coals. As the skewer rotates, the thinnest layer of the meat cooks until it is crispy before being sliced off with a blade that would make a samurai blush. The slivers of crispy meat and fat are cocooned in fresh, warm pitta bread with a few extraneous bits of crunchy salad added before the lot is doused with a pungent garlic sauce. The first bite is good, as the pitta is ripped apart to release the combined flavours of meat, garlic and lemon juice, but it just gets better. That the cook was a large, hairy, pot-bellied man in a sleeveless undershirt and I still wanted to kiss him tells you just how good this was, or that I have some serious issues.

It was going to be hard for Adam to try and top that. But God he tried, and Melbourne lived up to its reputation as a city for great food. Over the next few days he planned out a schedule that saw us hurtling all over the city to sample the best that was on offer from simple street snacks to a fifteen-course *dégustation* menu at Vue de Monde, one of the most highly regarded restaurants in the city.

It wasn't all good. The Turkish food we tried was tired and listless compared with what was available back in London, and I will never begin to understand the almost pathological appeal to Australians of dim sim. A grim, ersatz version of Chinese dim sum, dim sim is the snack *de choix* of every hungover Melbournian. Based on the few I tasted, I would rather have the hangover. But for the most part what I experienced was of a quality, variety and price that make it perfectly understandable that the citizens of Melbourne apparently eat out more than anyone anywhere else.

A week in Melbourne passed very quickly, and before I knew it, I was stuffing my clothes back into my large rucksack, which I had now christened Big Red because it was, er, big and red. My taxi arrived bang on schedule, and I prepared to say my goodbyes. Another hearty handshake from Adam, whose glazed eyes showed that he had already forgotten my existence and was thinking what to cook for supper. Eric ran towards me, his arms open wide and a big grin on his face. Had Uncle Simon finally won him over? Was this the moment we finally bonded, and I kept up my 100 per cent record of child adoration?

As he reached me, he dipped his head and butted me as close to the goolies as he could reach. I guess not.

Little bastard.

5

Japan: Eating like a Sumo from Tokyo to Kyoto

Until 1978 my only knowledge of Japan came from episodes of *M.A.S.H*, where Hawkeye and 'Trapper' John would wangle forty-eight-hour furloughs to this seemingly magical place of sinful abandon. Then, one Christmas, I used £5 I had been given by my grandparents to buy an album called *PS 78*, by the now long-defunct Dutch punk band Gruppo Sportivo. It contained an insanely catchy but irritating song called 'Tokyo'. I sang it constantly for over a month until TGS, quite rightly, beat it out of me with a wet towel. Soon albums made in Tokyo by Cheap Trick (*Live at the Budokan*) and by the impossibly ugly Scorpions (*Live and Dangerous*) joined my nascent record collection, and the notion of Japan began to seem quite hip.

Move on thirty years and, although those records had long been consigned to the bargain bin of my life, I had by now developed a passion for Japanese food. Based more on enthusiasm more than expert knowledge, it was a passion I indulged at every opportunity in London's growing number of Japanese restaurants, and even more often on my regular visits to New York, where every neighbourhood seemed to offer the possibility of decent sushi and sashimi.

Japan, I decided, would make the ideal starting-point for the next leg of the journey, which would also take in Hong Kong, China, Mongolia and Russia. I also decided that, rather than travel independently, I would rather like to do this trip with a group. Not a large group – I had no desire to walk behind someone waving an umbrella in a re-enactment of *If It's Tuesday,*

This Must Be Belgium – but I did think some local knowledge and language would be useful.

I arrived in Tokyo a few days before my official trip began, which allowed me time to explore on my own, and, after depositing Big Red, headed out to search for supper at one of the yakitori bars in the neighbourhood of Ueno.

Yakitori literally translates, as 'roasting chicken'. It actually comprises a range of chicken bits on skewers, grilled to order and either sprinkled with salt or dipped in sauce and served with a cold draft beer or the fierce local spirit, shochu. Yakitori bars can be smart or, as in Ueno, makeshift, with seats made from beer crates and tables from packing cases. They are primarily the haunts of salary men on their way home from a hard day at the office, and, as I chose one at random, I had to squeeze my ample frame in between two men deep in conversation on their mobile phones before gesturing for a beer.

As a huge bottle of Sapporo appeared, the man on my right reached over and took hold of it. Where I was brought up, in Yorkshire, touching someone else's beer is worse that goosing their wife. It will inevitably lead to a fight, and there may well be broken glass and teeth involved.

'Pouring own drink bad luck', said the man as he began to fill my glass, and we began a very faltering conversation. The skewers I had ordered appeared quickly, and so did those of my new friend, Koji. The inevitable swapping followed, along with more orders as he wanted me to try crispy chicken skin, chicken hearts and livers, gizzard, roasted garlic, leeks and many more. The sauce was thick and sweet, and the salty chicken skin was crunchy, working perfectly with the cold beers Koji kept in constant supply. At the end of the meal, despite my protests, he insisted on paying the bill and then walked me back to my hotel, both of us swaying happily until, after dropping me off at the door, he headed into the night.

Once you get over the initial chaos, Tokyo's subway system, its main method of public transport, turns out to be an absolute delight. Even, as is always the case, when it is heaving with people and despite the fact that the map looks like an eighty-year-old woman's knitting basket after the cat has got at it. It is air-conditioned, which for someone from London is enough to make you pack a picnic and refuse ever to get off. It is also impossibly punctual, as indeed are all the trains in Japan. I spent the next couple of days taking advantage of the fantastic system, whizzing from district to district trying to cram in as much as I could.

Just about every department store in Tokyo devotes its basement floors to food: on one floor a food hall, and below that a range of restaurants that would make any foodie swoon. Tokyo Food Hall in Shibuya was a perfect example, about the size of a couple of football pitches. The range of products on offer was staggering, from stands selling smarter versions of yakitori to glistening steamed and grilled unagi eel served over rice and Japanese and Western cake stalls, all staffed by fiercely polite young women who would call out as you passed their station. I spent over an hour walking around in awe, heart-broken that I did not have the opportunity to buy more than a few bits and pieces to eat on the hoof.

Later that morning I headed up to Kappabashi, the area of Tokyo where stores supplying the restaurant business ply their trade – not with food but with kitchen equipment, menu holders, place mats and just about anything any self-respecting place would need, including, I was delighted to see, a human-size model of the Statue of Liberty. Best of all, however, my notes told me there were the two stores specializing in the supply of plastic models of food for Japanese restaurants to display outside their premises as a guide for potential customers. The practice began during the occupation after the Second World War, when local restaurant owners needed to explain what was on offer to British and American soldiers. Originally they were made of wax, but they are now made of plastic and can be found everywhere, from high-end sushi restaurants to fast-food stands all over the country. They are fabulously realistic, offering everything from plastic dumplings to complete bento boxes with miso soup, rice and noodles. If I had not been on the road for another three months, I would definitely have purchased a plate of egg and chips as a keepsake.

I had to rush back to my hotel to meet the small group with whom I would be travelling. They turned out to be an agreeable mix of Australians, New Zealanders, Belgians and Brits, with one unfortunate American, Adam, drawing the short straw and getting to call me 'roomie' for two weeks. After the initial tour briefing our guide, Yuka, took the assorted throng out together for a local supper. I had other plans. I was going to eat like a sumo.

The Ryogoku area of Tokyo is known to everyone as the sumo district. There, surrounding the large stadium, are streets of shops selling everything any self-respecting stable of sporting heavyweights could need. Just as retiring footballers in Britain used to open a pub, so retiring sumo often open restaurants specializing in chanko nabe, the one-pot stew responsible for building and maintaining their impressive girth.

The chanko restaurants are dark, and the sliding doors prevent you peering in, so all but the most inquisitive might pass them by. One place looked promising and, recognizing the word from the Japanese script Yuka had scribbled on a piece of paper, I slid back the door and stepped hesitantly inside. A rather severe-looking man came from around the counter and barked at me.

'Chanko?' I said hopefully. He looked at me as though it was the first time he had ever encountered the word.

'Chanko', I repeated.

'Chanko?' he countered, with no more sign of recognition. I tried again more in hope than expectation, this time thinking to thrust Yuka's note in his direction.

'Ah, Chanko', replied the owner, as though the scales had fallen from his eyes. 'Chanko, chanko, chanko.' He said it a few times more, smiling, as though the word was getting good to him and then he gestured for me to take off my shoes and pointed to a table in the corner.

He brought over a menu all in Japanese and pointed to three vertical lines of lettering with the word 'Chanko'. He obviously just loved saying that word now. You could hardly stop him. I pointed at random and he disappeared, looking pleased now we had broken the communication barrier.

An elderly lady appeared with a large steel cooking pot filled with broth, over-sized cooking chopsticks and a ladle. She went off and reappeared with a plate the size of a satellite dish filled with seafood, fish, vegetables and a mound of white cabbage and began to place them gently into the pot of bubbling broth with the cabbage on top before leaving it to cook slowly. Five minutes later she began to serve me, filling my bowl with a little of the soup and a small amount of each ingredient.

It is meant to be shared by at least two people, a fact reflected in both the size of the meal and the price. It is little surprise that sumo are so huge, eating like this every day. I could barely make a dent in it, and the elderly woman looked disapproving when, after about half an hour, I gave up the ghost with chanko sweat beginning to pour from my brow.

As I left, the owner, whose pictures of his sumo heyday lined the walls, gave me a cheery wave, a thumbs-up and a hearty goodbye 'Chanko'.

For those coming from the UK, where it is worse that a visit to a dentist with the shakes, train travel in Japan is an unending delight. The journey to our next stop, Nikko, was relatively short, but, as we would be arriving at our destination rather late, we were advised to pick up some supper at the station to eat on the train. Every station offers a wide range of shops selling great things to eat, including fabulous bento boxes that would make even upmarket London Japanese restaurants blush with shame. On occasions it was suggested we should eat on the hoof, we were able to return with trays containing rice, pickles, eggs, katsu, sushi and shashimi of very decent quality to keep hunger at bay. The Japanese railway station bento box is definitely one of the world's great foodie treasures.

Nikko is a couple of hours out of Tokyo, and we were soon settled in our traditional Japanese inn or *ryokan*, with its tatami mat floors, slippers and robes in the rooms and large, private, hot spring bath overlooking a tumbling river. We had already eaten, but we all needed a long, cold drink, which led me to discover one of the other great pleasures of Japan: the ubiquity of its vending machines. They are everywhere, over 6 million of them in Tokyo alone, I am told, selling everything from books, beer and water to some rather more unusual things, including, and I am not kidding, used women's underwear and whips and chains for that quiet night in.

In London machines like these would be out of order within minutes and covered with the grafitti informing the world in general that 'Kevin is a bummer'. In Japan, where vandalism seems to be almost non-existent, these machines selling a bewildering variety of soft drinks and beers remain untouched.

We stayed for just two nights in Nikko, which, with its pine-covered hills, roaring rivers, shrines and sacred buildings, was a welcome and calm change from Tokyo. The food, however, was unmemorable with the exception of the local speciality of yuba, made from the skin formed when soy milk is boiled, which is then dried and stored to be used during the rainy season. Yuba was first developed as a way of supplying protein to local monks, who were, of course, vegetarian; it provided a welcome boost of energy for me as I slurped up a bowl in a light broth before lugging Big Red to the station for the long journey to our next destination.

Hakone is one of Japan's primary holiday resorts because of its pleasant climate and extraordinary scenery. It attracts the rich and famous, and the surrounding region is filled with stunning housing complexes and smart restaurants, ranging from upmarket French to, more bizarrely, a handful of German wurst shops. The weather is cool, and there are enough attractions to keep a family occupied for their extended vacations. However, I found little to beguile me about the town itself and felt slightly heavy-hearted when we set off to hit the tourist trail first thing the next morning. But I was heartened by the fact that, the previous night, Yuka had promised me a visit to the Gyoza Centre of Goza, a small town not far from Hakone.

'The best gyoza in Japan', she promised.

Gyoza are small dumplings, which came to Japan with the migration of thousands of Korean workers after the occupation of the Korean peninsula in the first half of the twentieth century. They are steamed first and then fried on one side with a little water added to the pan to create a surrounding pancake so the order can be served in one piece. I don't know whether those at the Gyoza Centre were the best in Japan, but they were incredibly delicious and I ate more than my fair share just to make sure. Later, with Yuka's help, I was able to meet the owner, who showed me the kitchen, where he had been making the gyoza for over twenty years. I was told later this was the first time he had ever let a visitor into the kitchen.

After Hakone another arduous journey followed, this time to Takayama, a small city best known for its beautifully preserved neighbourhoods of seventeenth-century houses and for its morning markets. As before, we were staying in a traditional inn, but this time perhaps the nicest of the whole trip and the most traditional, requiring soft slippers and silk robes to be worn for much of our stay. It was comfortable, with lovely rooms and a well-appointed bathing area, which I made full use of despite my fellow male travellers complaining of receiving an all too regular sighting of 'the last chicken in the shop' as I paraded around gleefully in the altogether. The town itself was pretty but unremarkable and would have been quickly forgotten but for three things.

The first was two stylish meals prepared at our inn by one of the best-regarded chefs in the region. Sitting cross-legged at low tables, we were each served individual small portions of over ten dishes made from the very best local ingredients: hand-harvested mountain vegetables and herbs braised gently in miso, locally caught river fish fried on a hot plate and doused in sweet soy sauce, and more of the exquisite yuba I had first tried in Nikko.

The second reason was one of the courses: thin slices of the local beef known as hida. Although kobe beef has become well known around the world, appearing on menus everywhere, few people outside Japan are aware of its cousin hida. From the same Wagyu breed of cow as kobe, hida beef is regarded by locals as its superior because of the impressive marbling of fat. I can't claim enough expertise to make a true comparison but, when cooked slowly over a tea candle with a small amount of broth so that it melts away on contact with the tongue, it is a taste that stays with you for a long time.

At the other end of the scale I shall remember Takayama because of a small izakaya, a kind of Japanese-style pub, located in an alleyway near our guesthouse. On our first night, after supper, I was still hungry. Our meal at the hotel was pretty and tasty, but not that filling, so I persuaded most of the group to come with me on a bar crawl. After a couple of nondescript places with nondescript food, we wandered into our last bar of the evening, and I spied a bowl of glistening pork belly marinated and braised overnight in sake, soy, sugar and star anise before being grilled until crispy on the outside while still soft on the inside. I tried one piece and then another, then another, before commandeering the whole bowl for our group. It was like crack in pork form. That's why I remember Takayama, and I have to admit to having dreams about that pork on the next long train journey, to Hiroshima.

The devastating effects of 6 August 1945 and the after-effects of the A-bomb obviously inform every person's conception of what Hiroshima was and, indeed, is. They inform every aspect of this amazing city too, from the understated monuments to peace and in the memory of the dead to the shape and nature of a city where great effort has been put into rebuilding it along its original lines.

Hiroshima was my kind of town, the sort of place you think of when imagining modern-day Japan, which was little surprise given that it had to be entirely rebuilt after the end of the Second World War. Lively, bustling and frenetic, it still has an air of civility about it and also offered some of the best food of the trip. Among its many claims to fame, Hiroshima is the spiritual home of okonomyaki, an omelette-like snack which, while being cooked with great skill on a hot plate, is layered with a huge range of fillings including noodles, meat, vegetables and seafood. It is not fine food by any manner of means, but for hungry travellers it is everything you could need: filling and delicious.

So well known is Hiroshima for this delicacy that it even has an okonomyaki district, which houses the greatest density of restaurants serving the dish in the whole of Japan. We decamped to Yuka's favourite and watched in awe as the serious-looking chefs prepared our meal in front of us. A thin layer of batter spread out like a crêpe was layered with ramen noodles; shredded white cabbage was then sprinkled on top, strips of pork, shrimp and vegetables too, before the whole lot was topped with an omelette and flipped one last time. Served with a hot sauce and a cold beer, it is little wonder that it is the snack of choice for the wage slaves of Hiroshima.

The Japanese attitude to the A-bomb is an interesting one. In many ways they are quite matter-of-fact about it and openly put the war and its tragic ending down to 'mistaken domestic policy'. Their view of the Americans too is quite understated, with little blame attached – merely a view that it should not happen again. Whatever one's views about the dropping of the bomb, the human reality is hard to avoid and provokes incredibly strong emotions. The A-bomb Dome was the only building in Hiroshima to survive the blast, now preserved as a monument to the dead. I will not deny holding back a few tears as I walked around the city and stood before the memorial to the 140,000 who died on the day itself. Walking down a small side-street, I found a tiny monument marking the spot 600 metres above which the bomb exploded. But by now I needed to forget about the war and all its horrors for a while and see what the rest of the city had to offer.

Fast food in Japan is huge business, and the high streets have filled with chain restaurants, which have arisen to feed those who need to eat and leave in the space of fifteen minutes. In many you choose from a menu outside and buy a ticket for the corresponding meal from a vending machine inside the front door and hand it to the server when you sit down at the counter. About a minute later your meal is in front of you with some free water and green tea, and you are all set. I chose a particularly peculiar Japanese speciality, kareh riasau, which apparently traces its roots back to British naval visits in the nineteenth century. This is a sweet curry containing soft chunks of meat and sometimes fruit, and the Japanese adore it. It is their comfort food, their hangover food and their chicken soup. It sat like a lump in my stomach all the way to Kyoto.

I am not going to lie to you. By the time we got to Kyoto, I was all shrined out. Which is a bit of a shame as Kyoto is officially 'The Home of 2000 Shrines'. It is littered with them: everywhere you look, you will find the tell-tale red signs that something or someone is being revered. They range from the truly magnificent to the tiny and discreet. Not that I found out about any of that as I was at the point in my trip where, if I had been asked to see another temple or shrine, remove my slippers and bang a bell one more time, I would have done a 'Mishima'.

After another rapid train journey Yuka sat us down in the lobby of the last *ryokan* of our journey and began to explain all the shrine-filled excitement that lay ahead in the next two days. She must have noticed me glazing over and when, after the meeting, I sidled up to her and asked if she minded if I did my own thing, she did not seem the least bit surprised. The next day, while the group headed for the bus stop for a day of visiting famous and important sights, I had a bit of 'me' time.

Yuka had recommended for lunch a kai-ten sushi restaurant – a restaurant where you select your food as it trundles around on a conveyor best – called Moshashi, which she described as the best of its type in the city. I squeezed into a spot at the counter and, as the conveyor belt moved around at a stately pace, helped myself to ten or eleven plates, including one which I found out later was a sashimi made of horsemeat. To my right an elderly man was ordering a dish not on the belt from one of the chefs working at the counter. He wolfed it down with considerable enthusiasm and ordered another. It was obviously good stuff, so with the help of much pointing I ordered one for myself.

The chef looked less than convinced when he placed before me a plate carrying a small, blubbery sac on top of the normal vinegared rice. I put it in my mouth in one bite and almost threw up over my neighbour before spitting the rest into a napkin. He howled with laughter and then, with his hand, made the sign of a fish swimming followed by what I am convinced was the sign for masturbation well known to every football goalkeeper in the UK. Later I showed a picture of my dish to Yuka. Her laugh was louder than his.

'You ate cod sperm, Simon.'

On our last day I had arranged to meet a Kyoto housewife, Tomoko Osashi, a member of the Women's Association of Kyoto, whose aim was to form links with other groups around the world through their love of cooking. She was to give me a morning of cookery lessons, and during the course of my time with her she demonstrated much deft chopstick twirling as I attempted my own shambling efforts.

I learned the correct way to make miso soup – 'It is all down to the quality of the dashi', Tomoko instructed, showing me how she created the stock using seaweed, before adding miso paste and small, neat squares of soft tofu. We made maki sushi, the rolls so familiar to us in the West. After the maki sushi has been made, Tomoko showed me how to make chirashi sushi, to all intents and purposes a salad of the left-over rice mixed with egg, off-cuts of fish and herbs. It is presented in the wooden dish into which cooked rice is poured to be cut and fanned before the sushi is made.

But best of all, she gave me the secret to perfect tempura. According to Tomoko, few housewives in Japan make their own batter any more, for two reasons. The first is that it can be a bit of a pain in the backside. The other, more importantly, is that the end-result, according to most people, is better, crispier, when made with tempura powder. I must have looked sceptical and a bit crestfallen, because, she suggested we do a comparison. She, of course, knew how to whip up her own tempura batter with the prerequisite lumps, and we took the same items – raw ingredients of prawns, scallops and vegetables – and fried them in each type of batter before we did a taste test, which entirely proved her point. The version made from powder was crispy and delicious, whereas the one made in the traditional manner soon became soft and limp.

After a few hours of cooking we sat down to enjoy the fruits of our labours. Between us we had created a meal that she announced would not disgrace the home of a Japanese house-wife, and my tastes of my first attempts at cooking Japanese food were as good as anything I had eaten on the trip.

It was not the end of my time in Japan, but it was the end of my time with this particular group of travellers. I went to bed early for my train to Tokyo the next day. I had one more important place to visit before leaving for Hong Kong.

The Tsukiji fish market is one of the most remarkable places I have ever visited But unless you know exactly where to go and the rules involved, it can be confusing and intimidating. I had arranged to meet Aaron, my Australian guide, for a 5 a.m. start so that we could be sure to see the auctions in action. I was exhausted, but it was worth it as, apart from fluent Japanese, Aaron counted among his skills an amazing capacity to retain facts and, as we walked around, he gave an incredible insight into the market, its history and how it works in more modern times.

The fish market has been in existence for over 350 years, having originally been set up to sell off the fish not eaten by the nobility. The same eight families who were in charge when it opened are still in charge now. They rank among the wealthiest in the country, owning the fishing fleets, the auction houses and the distribution network of the fish from the market to all parts of Japan. As Aaron explained, the fish bought in the market can be in Osaka or Kyoto by lunchtime, and on any given day one person in every seven in the country will eat fish sold in the market that morning. It is an incredible feat of logistics and also explains why both the buyers and the sellers of fish have to be there from one o'clock in the morning.

Everyone knows about the incredible tuna sold in the market, but to see the auction in process was an extraordinary sight. Frozen fish from the Japanese seas are brought in by small shuttle ships that go from trawler to trawler, allowing the larger boats to stay at sea constantly. The fish is brought in by one of the eight families and then examined by licensed buyers who buy from the same auctioneer. They buyers have contracts with numerous clients from upmarket restaurants, department stores and even convenience store chains to provide fish, so the pressure is really on them to buy the right product at the right price. With tuna going for nearly ¥5,000 a kilo, it is little wonder that they recently beat the $1 million mark for a single fish.

After we had been to the auction area, Aaron led the way to the inner market, which is normally open only to wholesalers. Unlike most of Japanese society, this is not a place where the men hold sway. Here the women are in charge. As the men cut fish, the women sit in small wooden cubicles, and it is they who do the deals and keep track of all the cash. The array of fish is beyond staggering. Abalone and eel sit alongside tuna that would cost more than an arm and a leg back in London – if, that is, you could get fish of that quality. In addition to the types of fish that I recognized there must have been about one hundred other species, possibly even more, that I had never set eyes on before and which Aaron said had no English name that he had ever been able to find.

Over 30,000 people work in the market. It is, in effect, its own town within Tokyo, which means it also houses a vast network of support services, from restaurants to feed the workers to shops selling razor-sharp knives and a general market to supply the public.

After a stroll through all the areas of the market, we went for breakfast at Jiro's. Kujiro's family have been running a restaurant at the fish market for over 300 years, serving primarily the local porters and fish cutters. He spoke good English and explained that the morning's assortment of sushi fish had not yet arrived, which was a real disappointment but offset by a bowl of rice topped with more of the unagi of which I had become so fond during my stay. It is not to everybody's taste, as the oiliness of the skin and the fatty nature of the flesh are unusual, to say the least, but glazed with the slightly sweet sauce it proved to be the perfect breakfast.

That was Japan: a little over two weeks in which I got the impression I saw a lot but saw only a fraction of what this country has to offer, in which I tasted amazing things but sampled only some of the extraordinary variety that is available, in which I met friendly people but did not even begin to get beneath the skin of what makes the Japanese people tick, and in which, just when I thought I had the culture and the country sussed, something else popped up to throw me for a loop and make me realize that I understood the country not at all.

I ate incredibly well, from the simplest skewers of bits in the yakitori bars of Ueno to the formal setting of our *ryokan* meals in Takayama. But, most of all, as *Eat My Globe* was meant to do, the food brought me in touch with people. People like Koji in Tokyo, who treated me to my first meal in Japan, Tomoko in Kyoto, who stood patiently by as I made a pig's ear of my attempts at maki sushi, and Yuka, our guide, who stood equally patiently by as I stumbled off a bullet train with all the grace of a drunken elephant and who guided me to some of the best food of the trip.

I had expected great things of Japan, and Japan certainly did not let me down.

6

Hong Kong: Feast Meets West

Hong Kong has a reputation for great food to equal that of anywhere on earth. From Cantonese street food to the very best examples of Western fine dining, Hong Kong's got the lot, representing its colonial past, its Chinese future and its current economic strength, which make it a home to expats from many nations. It would, I thought, make the perfect staging post before I hit mainland China.

Francine and David Holden are a true Hong Kong mix: Francine, Hong Kong-born and -bred, David a relatively new interloper from New Zealand. They were friends of friends and had generously agreed to put me up for a few days as I ate my way around the former British colony. Their home was set in one of Hong Kong's gated communities, with security guards, live-in maids and all the other accoutrements I assumed were the luxuries of the expat. I was soon put straight when Francine told me that over 80 per cent of the population in these communities was now Chinese and the expat population was on the decline as Chinese mainland influence began to exert itself. Whatever the demographics, they are welcome havens of peace and quiet compared with the rest of Hong Kong, as I was to find out in the next few days. But for now I just wallowed in the comfort of a family home and an incredibly hospitable welcome.

The next morning I set out on Hong Kong's efficient public transport system to my first planned port of call. Mong Kok is everything you imagine Hong Kong to be: bustling streets of restaurants and shops selling just about everything alongside stalls selling everything that the shops may have forgotten to stock. It's also a fantastically seedy area, with rows of strip clubs and girly bars nestled unapologetically alongside other shops. They are not subtle about it, with large neon signs advertising hourly rates at the hotels and lists of the services provided. As I walked, I noticed that there were lots of hairdressers with their unmistakable signature of swirling candy-striped poles extending over the pavements. Hundreds of them. Did people in Hong Kong really have their hair cut that often? It was not until later, when talking to David, that I found out that they were split into two very different categories: those which offered a cut and blow-dry and those which offered a cut and blowjob. Apparently, you can tell which is which by the direction the pole is swirling.

The main artery through Mong Kok, in fact through the whole of Kowloon, is Nathan Road, and I used that as a reference point as I wound my way through the backstreets, past the Po Street Bird Market, the Flower Market, the Ladies Market and Temple Street Night Market until I hit the southern tip of Tsim Sha Tsui.

The travelling, the walking and the heat had worn me down by now, however, and, after a restorative lunch of beef tendon soup I headed back to the New Territories to have a nap and a much-needed shower before the night's activities. David and Francine had invited me to join them at The Crown wine venue, a former Second World War bunker set high up near the top of Hong Kong's towering Victoria Peak. It had been converted into a restaurant and a cellaring facility for the fine wine collections of Hong Kong's great and good. Tables were communal and, as people ordered their own food, they brought out bottles from private collections to share with others at the table.

It made for a fun evening, and Francine, who is in the wine business, opened some memorable wines. By the end of the night we must have each had twenty glasses in front of us, which had contained everything from gentle Old World Pinots to jammy

Australian fruit bombs. We didn't drain them all, but enough for me to know I might regret it in the morning.

I am sure, however, that I shall not be invited back. I am never backward in expressing my opinion, as you may well have gathered by now, and when I have had a drop, there is no stopping me. One woman offered us a glass each of her favourite Pinot Grigio, a thoroughly nasty little grape in my opinion. I let her have both barrels, announcing to her and the world in general that 'I begrudge the five minutes of my life it took me to drink that horrid little wine'. It is little wonder that I used to get beaten up so regularly as a child.

To the bewilderment of my hosts, I decided to work off the next day's hangover by returning to Mong Kok and walking the whole length of Nathan Road, about 12 kilometres, before crossing over to Central, the business district, for lunch. Among the stupid ideas I have had, this ranks pretty high. The temperature was approaching $30°$ and the humidity meant that I was soon dripping like a leaky tap, but like all mad dogs and Englishmen I carried on regardless, ducking down side-streets, stopping at the food stalls for sticks of fried dough or steamed buns filled with char su and snapping away with my digital camera until I reached Tsim Sha Tsui.

The Star Ferry has been crossing from Kowloon to Hong Kong Island since 1888 with only a short break during the Second World War. Until 1978, when a tunnel was built, it was the only way to cross between the two points and also another glorious symbol of British colonialism, with only whites being allowed to travel on the breezy top deck and the local Chinese being confined to the diesel-fume-smogged lower decks. Even today, when anyone can sit anywhere, you still have to pay a whole HK$0.30 more to sit on the top deck. Me? I am a man of the people, so I took my place below stairs with the common herd as we crossed over the water to Hong Kong's business hub.

I arrived at Lan Kwai Fong, the area of Central that houses most of the cafés and restaurants, to find that most of the workers in the business district were leaving their offices for lunch. It was mayhem. Every storefront food stand was six deep with people slurping bowls of noodles or shovelling rice into their mouths at a furious pace with chopsticks. I forced my way to the counter of a place called Dragon Roast Meat and ordered a typically Cantonese plate of crispy goose with rice. As I ate it, I noticed an article on the wall about Anthony Bourdain, sitting where I was sitting and eating more or less what I was eating. What little delusions I had of myself as a culinary Magellan flew out of the window in a puff of goose-flavoured steam.

In my next 'discovery', Mack's Noodles, I fought for a space at a communal table and ordered a plate of chewy noodles topped with crispy roast pork. This at least, I was convinced, was virgin territory. A real find. The man next to me finished his own plate of noodles, stood up collecting his newspaper to reveal another picture of Mr Bourdain, under the glass, sitting at the same table eating the same meal. Both places, I found out later, were local institutions and have been featured in his television show *A Cook's Tour*. I walked back to the subway with the sounds of my application to the Explorers' Club being ripped up in my ears.

It was my last night in Hong Kong and the eve of Francine's birthday, so David had planned a special celebration at one of Hong Kong's most notable venues, the Derby Restaurant at the Hong Kong Jockey Club, where both were members. The restaurant had been recently refurbished at a huge cost, and part of that had been spent bringing the award-winning chef Donovan Cooke from Australia to take charge of the kitchen. Originally from the UK, Donovan had worked with notable chefs such as Marco Pierre White and Gordon Ramsay.

It was a memorable meal of more than ten courses of classical French cuisine combined with a New World flair for the ingredients. Ravioli injected with egg yolks and poached in a pork knuckle broth, lobster tail cooked 'sous vide' and a 'linguine' of squid tail all featured among the ten courses. Each came with a perfectly matching wine, and at the end of the meal we sat back with large glasses of our chosen *digestifs* and waited to thank the chef.

'Now then, how was the meal?' A recognizable accent came around the corner. Donovan Cooke, it turned out, was originally from Hull, close to my own home town of Rotherham. We had a long discussion, and I told him the purpose of my visit.

'Eating around the world, eh? Like my mate Anthony Bourdain?'

My heart sank.

'Aye, he was in here not so long ago. I think I get a mention in his book.'

There was the sound of that application being ripped up again.

7

China: Great Expectorations

China is a foreign country. They do things differently there. I became only too aware of this as the crew on my flight from Hong Kong came through the cabin collecting any 'Western media' before we landed at Guilin airport. I was about to join another group for the journey north through China from Yangshuo to Beijing, but I was not meeting them until a few days later, so that I could attend the highly recommended Yangshuo Cookery School.

Yangshuo is easy-access China, and I could immediately see why the travel guides refer to it as a 'backpackers' colony'. Its population of 40,000 is swelled by thousands of foreign tourists and increasingly visitors from China itself, who come to take advantage of the astonishing scenery surrounding the Li River and the recent development of Yangshuo as a centre for rafting, caving and hiking.

Yangshuo's main drag, Xi-Jie, had been renamed 'Western Street' by the locals and was filled with cafés selling an odd fusion of local dishes and Western food alongside shops selling everything a backpacker could possibly need. There is a constant hustle, and everyone has something to sell or a service to offer. I found myself approached by an old woman offering her basket for me to examine. I peered inside, expecting to see local handicrafts or bottles of Coca-Cola, only for her to grab my arm and shout 'Memory cards. 2GB'. Hustling hits the twenty-first century. But it was done in an amiable way, with very little hassle, and I found myself rather liking the town.

My first experience of visiting a market in China was not something I shall forget in a hurry. The sights, sounds and smells were a full-scale assault on every sense, and levels of cleanliness seemed to be variable, to say the least. Alongside baskets of recognizable fruits and vegetables were an equal number of items I had never seen before. There were live carp flopping around in buckets of water to clean the river mud from their gills before being chopped up to order, their heads tossed on the floor to gasp their few last breaths. There were butchers' blocks caked in blood, where every bit of the animal imaginable was on show; the putrid smell of the meat mixed with the humidity brought a wave of nausea over me. And, of course, there were dogs. There were live dogs cowering in cages and dead dogs hanging from hooks, where their raw flesh was coated in a crispy skin, and where blowtorches had been used to remove the fur. It may be a challenge to everything we know to see markets like this, with their opportunities for disease and different moral perspectives, but this a way of life for much of the world's population and to superimpose Western values on it achieves nothing.

As I had seen the dogs in the market, I thought I should at least try them in the flesh, so I fought my way to a nearby restaurant, where I ordered a small bowl of braised dog with a less challenging side-dish of steamed chicken dumplings. The dog was like a gamey version of pork, but when I was told later that the dogs are beaten before being killed because people believe that adrenalin in the meat makes it taste better, I decided that it would be my one and only dog-eating experience.

Pat Dimmond, an expat Australian, gave me that happy information, but fortunately for me, the food at the Yangshuo Cookery School, which she owned, was going to be a lot less daunting. She arranged for me to be collected at my hotel and taken the few miles from the polluted, bustling city to the serene surroundings of the cookery school, where the classroom opened up to the stunning background vista of karst mountains and rice fields.

Over the next few of days my fellow classmates and I were shown how to cook over a dozen dishes, most of them specific to the region, although there were others that I was to find again as I travelled throughout the country. Carp cooked in beer was a local favourite, as was kung pao chicken, a dish from the Sichuan region but popular here because of the abundance of peanuts. The best dishes of all were also the easiest to prepare. Vegetables stuffed with spiced, minced pork and then steamed were simple and delicious and, best of all a dish Amy called 'egg rope dumplings', which involved making mini-omelettes in a wok and stuffing them with minced chicken before folding them over until they resembled Chinese dumplings. It was a well-organized school and, after cooking, we enjoyed the fruits of our efforts in a small courtyard surrounded by beautiful countryside.

The afternoons were free, and Pat organized a cycle tour for me with Christina, a local farmer, around the rice paddy and peanut fields. Bikes and I are never the closest of friends, particularly when I discovered that the seat seemed to have been specifically sharpened to cause maximum torture to my ample buttocks. After two hours my eyes were watering and my backside was screaming in agony. Christina, noticing my pain and knowing about my interest in food, asked me if I wanted to come and help her prepare a meal for her family. I was off the bike before you could say 'maillot jaune'.

It was a simple meal, but every last bite of food on the table had come from Christina's small farm. She pickled her own garlic and used this to flavour the oil before adding strips of home-cured bacon and green beans. She dug up taro, sliced it into fries, soaked it and then deep-fried it in peanut oil as she steamed some fresh vegetables. We were joined by her elderly grandmother, her husband and her baby daughter as we ate our meal. Much as I had enjoyed the cookery school, it was moments like this I had been searching for. After another two hours on the bike, Christina led me back to the hotel. She let out an unsympathetic chuckle as I gave her the bike back and wandered into the distance waddling like John Wayne.

A food writer's got to do what a food writer's got to do, so that evening I headed out in search of one last unlikely ingredient, one that I knew would challenge my stomach more even than dog. I headed to the night market, where stalls selling food to locals and tourists alike were already busy, with over-sized woks spitting over blazing coals. I chose one and began to point to a variety of ingredients for the cook to stir for me in his already smoking pan. He didn't bat an eyelid when I pointed to the selections of vegetables or the cured bacon. He raised an eyebrow when I pointed to a meaty pig penis but duly chopped it up. It was when I pointed to the last ingredient that he stopped and said, 'You know what is?'

I did. It was a cane rat, killed and dried, laid out head and all, teeth in a rictus grin. I nodded and he shrugged, picked up the rat and chopped it up, head and all. He watched carefully as he served my finished dish. All I can say is that it didn't taste like chicken; it tasted exactly like I imagined a dried cane rat would taste.

Let us never speak of it again.

8

Gorging on the Three Gorges

If you are of a nervous disposition, skip this section. What follows will not only make you sick but will haunt you for the rest of your days, as it is haunting me.

I had by this time met up with my next group and, after spending two days in Yangshuo in order for them to acclimatize, we began a month-long journey that was going to begin with an eighteen-hour train ride north from Liuzhou to Yichang and from there on a three-day boat trip up the Yangtzi River.

If anyone ever tells you that travelling by train in China is romantic, I want you to kill them for me and I want you to do it slowly. It is not in the slightest bit romantic and, when it is combined with the travelling Chinese, it is one of the worst experiences imaginable. The first indication of the horrors came as we were about to board the train. I suspected that the toilets on board might be a little unsophisticated, so I headed to the public bathrooms of the station. This, unsurprisingly, is the point at which the squeamish among you should look away, particularly if you are on public transport and do not want to throw up over your fellow passengers.

I expected squat toilets. I even expected a smell like hell's anus. What I did not expect was half a dozen holes in the ground straddled by Chinese men grimacing and groaning as they worked hard to extrude their daily bread in open view. It got worse, a lot worse. Some of the men thought that this was the perfect opportunity to have supper at the same time and were eating bowls full of noodles. I asked one of my new companions to go and check to see if I had really seen what I though I had seen. He returned a few minutes later looking decidedly green.

'I didn't know which end the slurping was coming from', he reported.

On the train things were little better. When we boarded, the state of the carriage in our chosen class of 'Hard Sleeper' even made our guide, Jackie, blanch.

'This the worst I have ever seen.'

The only challenge to the stifling heat was a spluttering ceiling fan, which did little but move the dirt around. We opened the window as we got moving, only to be covered by a thin film of black goo from the engine and the heavy pollution outside. I climbed up to my middle berth and tried to get to my 'happy place', which for those of you who don't know me is a cocktail bar in a good hotel, where I can at least get a free bowl of nuts.

I managed to doze off, helped by the clickety-clack of the wheels on the track, but was woken up by the sound of the stranger on the bottom berth, voiding his rheum directly onto my sandals. I had already realized that the sound of Chinese men spitting was going to be the soundtrack to my time there but had not yet discovered how little they cared where they spat or on what. In the next weeks I saw them spit in bars, in expensive restaurants, on the streets, in buses and here on trains. I soon learned not to wear open-toed sandals.

By the time we got off the train at Yichang, our moods were as filthy as our clothes and little improved by the bumpy bus journey to join the vessel that would be carrying us up the Yangstzi River. It was described on the trip notes we had been given as 'a basic Chinese-style tourist boat', and Jackie explained that ours was a 'medium-quality' boat allocated to us by the Chinese government. My first impression was that I would be spending the next three days on a floating sewer. The room I shared with my companion, Chris, had sticky carpets, dirty sheets and slime caking the walls of the wet room. The so called 'sun deck' had already been commandeered by the Chinese men, who were washing their baggy underwear in water from the river before hanging it up to form a fluttering, ceremonial bunting of saggy smalls.

Jackie suggested we clean up and meet in the small restaurant for supper before it closed. The water from the caked showerhead trickled out an uninviting brown colour, and I came out feeling dirtier than I had gone in. At least I was able to change clothes before I headed off to eat. Remarkably, the food sent out from the tiny kitchen into the dining-room was delicious. We were now in Sichuan province, and it showed in the food we ordered, which carried the peppercorns and chillies used in every dish, primarily to keep people cool in the humid climate. The peppercorns, actually the dried berries of a local ash tree, have an anaesthetic quality, which starts by numbing the tip of the tongue and works its way back through the mouth, while the chillies, dried on the roadside in the heat of the sun, bring a soft heat and an unmistakable red tinge to many dishes. The menu was limited, but simple dishes of cabbage cooked in beef broth, Chinese sausage with courgettes, tomatoes tossed with eggs and pork with plenty of those chillies at least restored us to some semblance of humour.

The journey did give us an opportunity to see the Chinese in their relatively new role as tourists. Most excursions are as a group rather than solo. All participants are given matching caps and are then barked at through a megaphone by their guide, even if they are only inches away. They stand when told to stand, take pictures when told to take pictures and sit down when told to sit down. There was little sign of anyone showing individual thought or initiative.

In the evening the men would gather on the sun deck to watch their underwear flutter in the polluted breeze, drink vicious-smelling brandy and smoke powerful cigarettes. To keep cool they would roll their shirts up, tucking them under their ample man boobs to expose bellies which they would then sit rubbing as they continued to spit with some professionalism. I didn't go out on the sun deck much.

We made one small stop on the way, at the small town of Fengjie. There was nothing much to recommend the town but for a small market and a local restaurant, which again served terrific food. The market was filled with all the ingredients so characteristic of Sichuan cuisine: Chinese broccoli, potatoes, endless varieties of tofu, dried meats and sausages, fresh chicken and eggs and, on the floor everywhere, the peppercorns and red chillies laid out to dry. The restaurant made full use of all of these, and our table was soon filled with plates of pork with water chestnuts, tofu and shredded taro in a slick of deep red oil, sausage and candied aubergines, with more peppercorns and chillies. It was more than some of the group could manage, but I was in my element, delighted to be presented with delicious new smells from the kitchen and deeply savoury food.

I would have been happy to be anywhere but the floating diesel dustbin after three tortuous days floating along the polluted Yangtzi. When we finally arrived at our destination, Big Red felt light as I hurtled up the hundred stairs to our waiting bus without a backward glance.

We broke our journey to Chengdu with an overnight stay at Chongquing – officially, we were told, the fastest-growing city in the world, with a population of well over 30 million, most of whom had arrived in the last ten years. Not that I saw much of it, in part because we were only there for one night and in part because it is easily the most polluted place I have ever visited. While the hotel check-in procedure was being dealt with, I took a walk outside to snap a picture of the skyline. The fug of smog hit me in the face within seconds and led to a prolonged coughing fit and eyes that were still watering the next morning when we boarded the train for the short six-hour journey to Chengdu.

Chengdu is the capital of Sichuan, and Jackie promised it had 'the best food in the province'. It was obviously worth testing and, as soon as we found our hotel in the Tibetan Quarter of the city, we followed Jackie to 'Snack Street'. All over China,

Snack Streets have been created by local authorities in part concerned about levels of hygiene and standards at the old hawkers'
markets, but even more concerned that they were in the way of
potentially profitable building development. They are astonishing places, the shouts of the cooks and the smells wafting in the
air along with the sounds of sizzling pans making your mouth
fill with watery anticipation. I tried to sample as many vendors'
wares as possible: small cakes of rice stuffed with fiery barbecued
pork, piping hot broths filled with noodles and chicken then
laced with more chillies, and minced beef stuffed into bamboo
canes that cracked open to let the aromas of the contents escape
into expectant nostrils. Sticky rice balls came filled with melting
sweet tofu, and deep-fried pancakes with kiwi fruit were like the
best turnover you can possibly imagine.

Supper too was a triumph: that most classic of Sichuan dishes,
the hotpot. When we arrived at our chosen restaurant, it was
already packed with family and friends enjoying one of the ultimate communal meals. At the centre of each table was a small
burner, and on it was a large dish with two bowls. In the inner
bowl stock bubbled away while the outer bowl shone fiercely
with oil flavoured with fresh and dried peppercorns and, of
course, chillies. From a long list we chose over thirty dishes,
which were brought to the table for us to cook in either pot
depending on how brave we were feeling. Sweet shrimp, tripe,
quails, eggs, beef tendon and lung, slices of bamboo root and
many more were dipped into the hot oil and devoured until we
all slumped back, full to the brim and with sweat pouring from
our foreheads.

We were leaving Chengdu the next day, and Jackie wanted us
to experience a unique lunch before we left. Manjushuri is one
of the most revered monasteries in China and well known for
the food it serves at the restaurant in the quiet grounds of the
temple. It is a set feast, and we sat around a large table with a
lazy Susan in the centre as servers appeared and placed dish after
dish after dish in front of us: plates of thinly sliced pink sausage;

kung pao chicken; sweet and sour pork, crispy and delicious; fish fritters in a lemon sauce, topped off with chives and chilli; crab soup thickened with sweet corn; green beans with quails' eggs. The meal went on and on until I counted well over thirty dishes before us. At the end we could barely get up to walk away from the table.

Manjushuri has a secret, however. Not a single animal was harmed in the making of our meal. Every dish was purely vegetarian, created from fruits, vegetables and tofu skilfully combined to create dishes that anyone would have sworn contained meat. If veggie food tasted this good back home, not a single creature with eyes and a face would ever need to die for my benefit again.

Chengdu was a city I promised myself I would visit again, and it is tragic to think that so much of what I saw has since been destroyed by the huge earthquake of May 2008 and its aftermath. That, however, was all in the future as we began our journey to our next destination, Xi-an.

As we sat on board the bus that collected us at Xi-an railway station after our journey from Chengdu, our guide shared a very interesting fact with us. There are, apparently, 40 million bachelors in China. 'It is because of economic and demographic factors', he announced, as though reading from an approved text. As I thought back to my previous encounters with Chinese men, the spitting and hacking of young and old, the T-shirts rolled up and placed beguilingly under flabby man tits and the rubbing of the sweaty bellies, I couldn't help thinking that there might well be plenty of other reasons Chinese women don't want to go near Chinese men.

There are, however only two main reasons why tourists come to Xi-an. One is to visit one of the great archaeological discoveries of all time, the Terracotta Warriors, and the second, more important from the point of view of my trip, is that Xi-an has some of the most delicious food in all of China.

The capital of Shaanxi province, Xi-an takes its name from the

Chinese words for 'western peace', a throwback to when the city was the beginning of the Spice Route bringing trade between Europe and the Orient. It is still one of the most important commercial centres in the country, but as you walk around the city, its history is apparent everywhere – in the large and imposing Drum and Bell Towers, in its sensitively restored city walls and, most of all, in the faces of its people, who are mainly drawn from the Han majority and the Muslim Hui minority, both of whom bring their cultures and their food to the city.

Xi-an also has the largest Muslim population in China, another fact that has a significant impact on its food, and it was to the Muslim quarter I headed as soon as we were left to our own devices. Naturally, no pork was served, which after Yangshuo and Chengdu, where every possible part of the pig is available, came as a bit of a shock. In this quarter of Xi-an it was mutton that formed the basis for nearly every meal, the most famous dish being the nourishing yang rou pao mo, a soup consisting of braised mutton in a broth thickened with the local wheat bread. This is brought to the table with side-dishes of chilli, pickled garlic and coriander to flavour according to taste. It was warm and savoury, and after twenty-four hours of travel I was ravenous and devoured two bowls.

After a stroll around the city walls and a couple of hours doing inevitable chores such as laundry, I met up with the rest of my travelling companions to head to another famous Xi-an institution, a restaurant called De Fa, which was acclaimed for its dumplings, and more precisely for its dumpling banquet. The locals have a saying, 'If you have not had a dumpling banquet in Xi-an, you have not been to Xi-an at all.' It was certainly an experience. We were seated around a round table to be presented with bamboo baskets containing examples of dumplings from all over China. Fish, chicken, beef, pork, seafood, vegetables were all represented in boiled, roasted, steamed, pan-fried or deep-fried form. The presentation of each was different, as the dumplings were dyed in bright colours as well as being served in a variety of shapes. The stuff just kept coming until, by the end, even I had to turn down the offer of one last walnut and roasted duck steamed dumpling for fear of projectile vomiting.

I had received an e-mail from a friend, when I told him I was in Xi-an: 'Funny, you go all the way there and the Terracotta Warriors are all over here in London.' I didn't have the heart to tell him that, while there may well have been an impressive display of a few examples on tour in the West, at the Museum of Qin they were not going to miss a few Terracotta Warriors because there were thousands, in fact nearly seven thousand excavated so far, in three pits, with thousands more still believed to be underground. The army was created by Emperor Qin Shi Huang to protect him in the afterlife, with each warrior based on an actual person shown in his allotted rank as they were on the day they were first erected – row upon row of them, along with their armour and chariots.

It was one of those all too rare occurrences where the expectation is matched by the reality, and we went our separate ways for two hours to take in the sights of the four main galleries of excavations. The first warriors were discovered in 1974 by four farmers, who have since become superstars in the local community and play the part to the hilt as they sit in to the museum area every day, ready to sign copies of souvenir brochures and posters – for a fee, of course.

Two days was all too short a stay in Xi-an, but as we clambered on board the train for our last journey together, I was filled with genuine excitement about finally reaching one of the world's great cities. My excitement was only slightly tempered eighteen hours later, when we arrived and were faced with an assault of the Chinese in full flow as thousands of people fought to exit the station through the one door that was open. The notion of waiting seems entirely alien to the people of Beijing and, as I had countless times before on the trip, I found myself being pushed to one side by the aggressive locals.

The Beijing city authorities had tried to put in a queuing

system at the station to bring some semblance of order to the chaos, but the locals simply ignored it. As we stood patiently waiting for cabs, people screamed and jumped in front, shoving us angrily to one side. None of our group would be particularly proud to admit it, but we became quite aggressive in return, giving as good as we got until we forced our way into a couple of cabs to our hostel.

Having calmed down and showered, I went for a walk in the area around Beijing's other main railway station. The temperature was in the high nineties, and the humidity meant that I was drenched within minutes of stepping outside. Looking for some respite from the sun, I ducked down a small alleyway and found myself in one of Beijing's famous *hutongs* – small warrens of lanes built around a local water supply (the name apparently comes from the Mongolian word for 'well'). After years under threat from development, many are now protected and the communities within them preserved. They are alive with energy, the streets filled with shops and food carts, steam rising into the air from the dumplings and noodles stored within. I was starving, so for a few pennies I bought a large, round, steamed dumpling stuffed with minced chicken. Enough to keep me full until supper.

The dish most associated with Beijing is, of course, roast duck. Everywhere you look in the capital you see it hanging in the windows of restaurants waiting to be served to tourists and locals alike. It's a dish I had eaten many times in the UK with my family and had been the cause of many an argument as the waiter served the skin and the flesh only to take the bones, my favourite bit, away so they could use them to make soup for the staff.

Duck restaurants in Beijing come in many different styles, from the small family places to restaurants in the grand hotels. Each has its own recipe and its own way of serving. Some serve the skin and flesh separately; others layer one on top of the other. Some make a meal out of the whole duck, offering hot dishes of soup and blood before the main event. All present the ducks to the table first, glistening and golden, before carving and plating alongside baskets of steaming pancakes, dishes of hoisin sauce and shredded crisp vegetables to add texture as well as flavour. Our first choice was one of the family-style places, where we demolished two ducks and plenty of side-dishes. The crispy skin, the melting fat and the moist flesh worked in harmony with the slightly sweet sauce as I rolled more than my fair share of pancakes.

'You need for energy,' Jackie said, rolling herself another dumpling, 'for walking the Wall.'

I had not actually been that bothered about walking on the Great Wall of China, put off by images I had seen of sections restored to former glories, filled with throngs of tourists following obediently behind their flag-waving guides. I had planned to give it a miss and head to Beijing's Snack Street instead.

'No, we not do like that', Jackie argued, explaining that there were still sections of the the wall in total disrepair after years of being plundered for their stones by local farmers and that, if we were prepared to suffer a four-hour ride in a cramped mini-bus to the faraway sections of Jinshanling and Simitai, she would promise us a very different experience.

She was right. What followed was an unforgettable five-hour hike along the wall, where we often had to climb up crumbling parapets on our hands and knees, along ledges and down steep slopes and along parts that had not been repaired, I would imagine, since they were first built. There was barely a soul in sight, and for well over an hour I found myself walking alone. My thoughts turned to my mother and my eyes began to water. I knew it had been one of her dreams to see the Great Wall and, as I stared out in the silence, I offered up a small prayer that she could share this part of my journey.

The following day was my last with this group, and we had one more sightseeing trip planned: to Tiananmen Square and then to the Forbidden City. Both are places whose names resonate through history, for very different reasons, and both are places that depressed me, again for entirely different reasons. I recall blurry images when I was a child of missiles being paraded in front of the Chinese leadership in Tiananmen Square, mainly for the benefit of those in the West. In later years, of course, a burgeoning democracy movement found its spiritual home in the same square and, when it was put down with ruthless efficiency by the authorities, the images were screened around the world and printed indelibly on the minds of all who saw the massacre that took place.

Unsurprisingly, the Chinese government brooks no discussion of such matters, and our official guide denied all knowledge of such events. No mention is allowed in the media, and the internet is scoured for any unauthorized release of images. China may be opening up, but at times like this you sense that it is still very much a closed country. As a visitor, you are allowed to see what they want you to see and allowed to hear what they want you to hear.

The square is impressive. Built on the gardens of the original city of Beijing, which was destroyed by Mao Zedong, it has a capacity to hold over a million people and is still the centre for many celebrations and concerts. Topping and tailing the square are reminders of China's hardline past and its most significant leader, with a mausoleum containing the mummified body of Mao at one end and the instantly recognizable portrait at the other end.

To the majority of Chinese Mao is more than just a dead political leader, but his influence is definitely on the wane. The older generation revere him, almost to the point of divinity; to the younger generation, with their exposure to Western culture, he and his school of thought are increasingly anachronistic, a piece of history that had a great impact on where they are now but is of little relevance in their daily life.

My thoughts inevitably turned to the anonymous man with the shopping bag who became a symbol of the failed push for democracy as he stood in silent challenge in front of row after row of tanks. No one is quite sure what happened to him, but it is fairly certain that the Chinese leaders did not give him one of the luxury apartments they kept aside for their cronies.

Our guide led us from the square into the Forbidden City. It was impossibly crowded with tour groups, primarily Chinese, who followed dutifully after their flag-waving guides who were barking at them through plastic megaphones as they moved in irresistible waves through the grounds. Half an hour of wandering around saw me right royally pissed off at being shoved from pillar to post. I decided to take my leave and head off to find something forbidden of my own, in the form of the more unusual snacks offered on the streets of Beijing.

Beijing's Snack Street is certainly not for the squeamish. It specializes in things on skewers – it is just that those things on skewers just happened to be seahorses, silkworms, slugs, live lizards and scorpions, impaled and all wriggling around until they are selected, dipped in oil to meet their death on a sizzling hot griddle. I tried a selection. I do it so you don't have to. The silkworms were chewy, and the seahorses were chewier still. I could not bring myself to eat a lizard but watched in horror as it shrivelled in its death throes to order for eager customers.

Across the road I saw a sign saying 'Gourmet Street', pointing down under one of Beijing's huge modern shopping malls. Following the arrows, I found myself in an enormous food court, stretching hundreds of yards into the distance, filled with stalls selling food from every part of China: spicy Sichuan hotpots, Cantonese roast goose, Silk Road noodles and mutton soups, fiery Hunanese fish, stir fries, dumplings and braised pork knuckles. Payment was made by a pre-paid swipe card, and the quality was exceptional. The stallholders filled the air with amiable banter persuading you to come to their stalls rather than their neighbour's.

'Eat this. Good. His stuff smell bad, very bad, make you sick.'

It was enormous fun, and large plates of food with the inevitable 'bin pijou' cold beer, costs little over £1 a time.

One day later I was ready to say my goodbyes to my companions, but I still had one more treat in store, thanks to Jackie, our guide, who offered to show me what she considered the best street snack in Beijing. She led me to a small stand where a man was busy cooking on a hot plate.

'Juanping', she told me.

It was a thick crêpe brushed with hoisin sauce, lined with a crispy dough stick then sprinkled with chilli, dried chicken and spring onions before an egg was broken into it and the whole thing was folded over for easy eating. We stood outside the market eating our snacks. Jackie smiled. 'Something to remember China by.'

I thought of eating dog and rat in Yangshuo, of the train journeys and the boat trip up the Yangtzi. I thought of the spitting and the men who ate noodles while using the bathroom. I thought of the mêlée at the train station and the horrors of the pollution. Then I thought about the cookery school, the simple meal I had helped Christina prepare for her family, the Sichuan hotpot, the Snack Street of Chengdu, the yang rou pao mo and the dumpling banquet in Xi-an and, of course, the roast Beijing duck here in my last port of call.

'Don't you worry, Jackie,' I said, 'I have plenty to remember China by.'

9

Into and Outta Mongolia

I used the thirty-six-hour train journey from Beijing to Ulan Bator to make the acquaintance of yet another set of companions, this time joining me as I travelled on the Trans-Siberian Railway to Moscow. We got to know each other over many bottles of cold beer provided by hawkers at the regular stops and by becoming embroiled in a series of hard-fought card games.

It was a small group, a mixture of singles and couples, with the youngest being only twenty-four and the oldest well into their seventies – not a bad feat considering that this had all the hallmarks of an arduous journey. By the time we reached Ulan Bator we were all acquainted and slightly dishevelled after a day's journey through the Gobi Desert, which filled the whole train with dust for over five hours.

The recent history of Mongolia is one of subjugation and tyranny. Since the time of Genghis Khan and the decline of the Mongol empire, this small country has been under the control of other nations: first the Chinese and more recently the Soviet Union. For nearly seventy years Ulan Bator was a Soviet out-post, with all that that entails: the economy was governed by strict Soviet socialism, religious observance was outlawed and all places of worship, including centuries-old monasteries, were destroyed or turned into municipal buildings.

In the early 1990s, when the Soviet Union shattered into nation-states, Mongolia was cut loose and left to fend for itself. With no apparent source of income and no ready-made export market to the USSR, it quickly descended into poverty and would have also descended into chaos but for one factor: the incredible resilience of the Mongolian people. Brave, passionate, proud of their country, intensely close to their families and unendingly hospitable, there were few people I encountered on my travels quite like them.

Although the majority of the 3 million-strong population of Mongolia live a classic nomadic lifestyle, Ulan Bator, whose population just topped the 1 million mark, sums up the state of the nation perfectly. With no funds to support infrastructure, the city's pavements are crumbling and road surfaces almost non-existent. Medical services are negligible, and there is horrendous poverty apparent everywhere. It is one of the most ugly cities imaginable and I understand why guidebooks describe it as a carbuncle on the face of the earth. The majority of the architecture is a legacy of its Communist days, and there are high levels of pollution. In a remarkable contradiction to this tale of gloom, Mongolia also has a very stable education system, levels of literacy are high and many people speak excellent English. The country has some of the most advanced communications networks in Asia and, because of foreign investment in the mining of Mongolia's rich deposits of minerals, it now has large expat communities from all over the world, which, inevitably means equally large numbers of restaurants, cafés and bars to serve them.

By far the largest group are the Germans, and whither go Germans there goes beer, which means that UB is also filled with pubs and bars primarily selling the local beer, Chingis. The bar at the Chingis Brewery was a fully decked-out German Bierkeller, with all the Mongolian waitresses looking uncomfortable in dirndls, the traditional Alpine costume seen in Munich's beer halls.

Food in UB is hardly of the delicate kind and has a lot in common with that of its former Soviet overlords: lots of smoked fish served with heavy, stuffed pancakes called kushur. It is also the only place outside France and Japan where I have been offered horse to eat. For our first meal I ordered a horse rib. What came reminded me of the opening credits to *The Flintstones*, where Fred orders a Brontoburger at the drive-in so big it tips his car over to one side. This was about the same size, and I tucked into it with about the same gusto. It was very high in flavour, quite gamey and stringy but perfectly acceptable, and after many hours on a train eating Pringles I gnawed it down to the bone.

We were only staying one night in UB before setting out into the Mongolian wilderness to spend the next couple of days at a *ger* camp, in the traditional tents of the Mongolian nomads. The passion of our guide, Nemo, for Mongolia was tangible and, as we drove, he took time to show us things that we would otherwise have missed: small pyres of stones, topped with flags around which you walk three times to invoke a blessing and wish for a safe return; men at the roadside with their arms extended to carry hooded eagles used for hunting; and, best of all, an encampment of Mongolian nomads with whom he was acquainted. He pulled our van into their camp and led us to one of their tents with a promise that we were going to sample some of the traditional nomadic food.

One of the great fallacies accepted over the years is that Mongolians drink yak's milk. They certainly keep yaks, thousands of them in great herds over the plains of the wilderness, but for their wool only. Yaks produce very little milk, though, and airag, the fermented drink so associated with the country, in fact comes from mare's milk. Nemo showed us how it was produced. The milk is poured into a bag made from a cow's stomach, which holds nearly 80 litres. About 10 per cent is kept back each time as a master culture, and it is refilled each day with fresh milk. The bag is stirred vigorously with a paddle every time someone passes, to incorporate the new milk with the old. If children misbehave, they are punished by having to paddle the milk for an hour, and any visitor entering the tent is also expected to give the bag a good stir as a thank-you for the hospitality. It reaches a strength of around 5 per cent and remarkably, Nemo told us,

Mongolians can drink as much as 5 litres a day. It is little wonder that they also have one of the highest rates of liver cirrhosis in the world.

He passed round a bowl so we each got to try some. It was a noxiously dreadful drink, tasting as you would imagine a musty bowl of white horse piss should taste. Other products we were offered, all made from horse milk, were equally unpleasant: a tough, sour curd biscuit; a 'vodka' distilled from horse-milk yoghurt; and a couple of hard cheeses. One item, however, seemed to meet with universal approval: orum, a cream with a thick skin like clotted cream and made in a very similar way, by heating the milk in a pot over simmering water.

We headed off for the camp and pulled up to the small lines of tents murmuring sounds of approval. It was a small space, with about twenty circular *ger* tents, often used by Mongolians from UB when they want to get away from the chaos of the city and return to a more idyllic existence. Idyllic it certainly is, and after dumping my kit I wandered off on my own for a short while into the hills behind the camp.

After the chaos of Beijing and the grime of UB, the clean air and the tranquillity came as a welcome relief, and when I returned to the camp, I could see it had the same effect on the others in the party. The next twenty-four hours passed very gently. Some people went riding. (Not me – I eat horses, I don't ride them.) Some tried their hand at archery, and others went for long hikes. It was good to be out and about in the clean air and to have the opportunity to see the Mongolians doing things that have been part of their culture for centuries.

They say Mongolians are born in the saddle and die in the saddle, and it's true, they are incredibly at ease on horseback. The next morning I awoke at about six o'clock and dipped out of my tent to enjoy the chill morning air. As I sat contemplating, I heard thundering hoof beats. Climbing a hill, I looked out and saw two men on horseback out herding their cattle. Hurtling along at full gallop, they were both standing up in the stirrups hands on their hips as though the horse was simply an extension of their bodies. A magical sight.

When it came time to leave the camp, we all felt a little deflated. It was such a beautiful place to be, and the quiet and calm were so welcome that we wanted one more night. However, we were heading back for one more night in UB before the beginning of the next stage of the journey: the beginning of the Trans-Mongolian/Trans-Siberian Express, which, after all, is what the trip was all about.

The Trans-Siberian Express: Riding the Rails from UB to St P

It's a big place, Outer Mongolia. So big that the next stage of the journey would see us travel for over forty hours and across two borders before we even hit our first stopping point in Russia, Irkutsk.

We stopped at Ulan Bator's state-owned department store to buy snacks for the journey, having been warned that there was precious little food on board the train. Even though there was a dining car, we would be dependent on what we brought and what we could buy from the housewives who lined the platforms selling pastries at each stop.

We boarded the train, stowed the bigger luggage under the seats and soon settled into the rhythm of a long journey, with games of cards or Scrabble, reading from the floating library of books or simply sitting with a bottle of beer or glass of vodka and watching the world go by outside. Those who had seen my misery on that first train journey in China would laugh to hear me say that by now I was beginning to enjoy these extended train rides. I had figured out a routine to keep reasonably clean, and the enforced periods of inactivity with nothing to do but listen to the rhythmic rattle of the train over the tracks was strangely pleasing.

Not so pleasing was the interminable wait at both the Mongolian and Russian borders. Five hours at the former challenged both patience and bladder as our carriage attendants decided it was a good idea to lock the toilets. The delay at the Russian border was more tolerable, and after we cleared customs and our passports were taken away for visas to be checked, we were at least able to get down from the train and walk into the nearest settlement to top up on supplies.

Our first aim, obviously, was to buy Russian Baltika beer, available in grades from 3 to 10 with the lowest being the light, refreshing beer that Russian men like to drink during the day and the highest being a dark, rich, black beer akin to stout. But we also needed food and handed over roubles for some weird and wonderful snacks including tubs of dehydrated mashed potato with croutons, an odd mixture that became strangely more palatable as the trip progressed as we reconstituted them with hot water from the samovar in each carriage.

Cleared to go, we settled once more into our routine for the next twenty-four hours until we reached our first stop in Russia, Irkutsk, the capital of Eastern Siberia, where we immediately boarded a bus to take us the short journey to Listvyanka, on the edge of Lake Baikal.

We were split into smaller groups and billeted to spend the night as the guests of local Russian widows who rented out rooms in their apartments to raise extra income. I paired off with another single traveller and, joined by Andrew, our guide, we found ourselves in the home of our hostess, Ludmilla, who for reasons I never quite figured out spoke to us only in German. Whatever the language difficulties, she was incredibly welcoming and soon had us sitting in her kitchen enjoying cups of strong black Russian tea, plates of fresh vegetables and bowls of pelmeni – small dumplings in broth. Despite the slightly forbidding appearance of the apartment blocks, remnants of Soviet times, the homes themselves were comfortable and warm, and much restored, we left our luggage and walked down to the edges of the lake to meet the others.

Lake Baikal is the largest freshwater lake in the world and contains over 20 per cent of the earth's total, so pure that it is pumped from the lake straight to the surrounding homes. It also provides a ready supply of fish, in this case sig and omul, to the local restaurants, and just about every meal had fish in some form – be it smoked, in pâtés or freshly grilled. At the local market every stall was attended by plump, stern-looking women selling fish, which they were smoking themselves. Hanging from hooks above them, the fish swayed gently giving off a wonderful smoky scent in the breeze. I just had to try some. They were still warm and bubbled with the oils released during smoking. The flesh fell from the bones and was deliciously sweet as it dissolved on the tongue. It spoiled me for other smoked fish.

Tradition dictates that visitors to Lake Baikal must indulge in one of Russia's favourite pastimes, the *banya* or sauna, which in this case meant sitting in a hut at the edge of the lake, slowly being boiled alive by steam coming from a wood-fired burner, drinking vodka and then throwing yourself in the ice-cold lake. There are no written statistics of fatalities, but I suspect the bed of the lake is littered with the bodies of middle-aged men clinging to vodka bottles. The combination of heat, cold, vodka, heat, cold, vodka was an interesting one and made sure that, when we all congregated the next morning, there was little noise except a few gentle moans as we boarded the bus back to Irkutsk.

Irkutsk is a growing city of nearly one million people and clings fiercely to its place in Russian history as the home of exiled revolutionaries from the Decemberist movement of the nineteenth century. It is also proud to declare itself a city 'built by women', in honour of the wives of the exiles who chose to give up their lives of comfort in Moscow and follow their husbands to such a bleak outpost. The term 'Decemberist wife' is still used in Russia to describe a woman who shows loyalty to her family in the face of extreme adversity.

Alongside the modern buildings of the city's recent rapid rise, the side-streets remain lined with the wooden buildings of its first incarnation, and it made a pleasant interlude before our next, longest part of the journey. It also provided me with my first close encounters with the Russians themselves.

For centuries the people of Russia have had little or no individual freedom. During feudal serfdom and then under harsh Soviet rule they were told what to do, say, think and believe. They compensate for this lack of influence by now clinging to any scrap of personal power life may offer them and by making life miserable for anyone else who may need them to perform a service. They have an ability to appear exasperated at anything and everything. Buying anything inevitably involves eye-rolling, shrugging of shoulders and the distinct impression that it is a terrible inconvenience and an insult from which they may never recover.

A favourite drink in Irkutsk is kvass, beer made from fermented bread. On just about every street corner elderly women sit by large barrels dispensing glasses for a few roubles a time. Buying some, of course, is immensely hard work.

ME: 'Kvass please.'

OLD CRONE: 'Kvass?' (Looks mystified, as though she has never heard of it before, despite the fact she is sitting next to a barrel with the word KVASS written on it in letters two feet high. She makes sure to turn to anyone passing to show how unfair life is expecting her to deal with people like me.)

ME: 'Kvass.' (Points to two-feet-high lettering.)

OLD CRONE: 'Ah Kvass.' (Looks at me as though I had spoken gibberish and why was I wasting her time. Wearily pushes small button to dispense beer into plastic glass as though it pains every bone in her elderly body.)

ME: 'Thank You.' (Hands over exact change.)

OLD CRONE: (Stares at exact change as though I had given her a $1 million note, rolls her eyes, looks around again to make sure everyone knows just how miserable her life is, then gives me one more look of withering contempt.)

Unfortunately, the beer is not worth all that effort. It is cloyingly sweet, and I poured most of it away. Out of sight of the old crone, of course.

If Siberia were a country in its own right, it would be the biggest country in the world, which explains the length of the journey from Irkutsk to our next stop, Vladimir. But I was actually looking forward to it. I didn't even mind when confronted by the two terrifying female attendants who would watch over us for the duration of the trip, or when instructions were barked at us as though we were prisoners on the way to Stalin's gulags. I slightly uncharitably christened them Kong and Mighty Joe Young and, at the advice of Andrew, our guide, went to try and buy them off with a bar of Russian chocolate, which they snatched without the hint of a smile. There is a reason why Russian men have a life-expectancy of only fifty-four and almost always die before their wives. They want to.

I had been told that people become institutionalized when travelling on the Trans-Siberian Express. Until I made the journey myself I thought this was absolute tosh, but they were right. After nearly four days of riding the rails to Vladimir, a few hours' drive from Moscow, with little to break the routine other than a leg-stretch on a station platform or a walk down to the dining car, I had quickly become used to the rhythm of train on tracks, the water bottle showers in the morning and the diet of dumplings, crisps and pasties washed down with beer and vodka. I had become used to reading, playing cards or board games, listening to music and, as the guidebooks advised, just staring out of the window for long periods of time. After almost fainting with misery on my first train journey through China, I really enjoyed the ride, and getting off the train in Vladimir was indeed a shock to the system in more ways than one. Not only did we all experience serious 'wobbly leg' syndrome, but we had arrived in the cold winds of Europe in the same clothes we were wearing in the warmth of Asia and stood shivering on the station platform until our bus came to collect us.

We spent our first night in the pretty town of Suzdal, capital of Russia in the eleventh century and famous for having the highest density of churches in the country, and for being where the Tsars sent their wives to live in convents when they got fed up with them. After a huge breakfast and a good night's sleep everyone, me included, was in good spirits as we boarded our bus for the drive to Moscow.

It was not my first visit to Russia's capital. In 1998 I had attended the Moscow Book Fair. I was accompanied by my company's Russian literary agent, who not only translated for me but guided me through the complicated etiquette of doing business Russian-style, which seemed to consist mainly of drinking umbrella stands full of vodka or whisky before, during and after every meeting. By midday on the first day I was horribly drunk and, in fear of alcohol poisoning, had to leave the conference hall to go and be violently sick at the feet of a large statue of Lenin. I had not been back since and knew that Moscow had changed considerably since then. A friend who had been there more recently told me that the change was not for the better, that it was a dirty, ugly, corrupt and dangerous city.

It is all of the above, of course, but it also has elements of a frontier town and of a city that, rediscovering itself after years, centuries even, of deprivation and struggle is alive with the good and bad effects of capitalism. A city where you have to admit anything can happen.

I adored it and wasted little time setting out to explore, which gave me a chance to marvel at one of Moscow's great treasures. The stations of Moscow's underground railway are like nothing else on earth, glorious tributes to Soviet power housing towering bronze statues of Soviet heroes that stand guard over the platforms. They are cheap and efficient, and we were soon blinking in the autumnal sunlight of Red Square, where we split up and headed off in our separate directions.

I was glad of the opportunity to be on my own. I'd had enough of eating junk for a few days and knew that if I were with any of my companions, they would baulk at my plan to go for a budget-busting lunch. I spent the late morning working up an appetite with a long walk along the Moskva River, past the impressive monument to Peter the Great and through the grounds of the Red October chocolate factory, where production left a permanent sickly sweet haze hanging in the air. Then I headed up to Ostozhenka Street, where I had chosen a restaurant called Tflis for lunch.

Considered the finest Georgian restaurant in Moscow, it was also the lunch venue of choice for the country's oligarchs. It had suffered recently with the sanctions levied by President Putin after a spectacular fall-out with the Georgians and, because of this, it was not able to offer any Georgian wine or beer. But it was an agreeable place to have lunch, even if the prices brought water to my eyes. Georgian breads stuffed with suluguni cheese, soft rolls of curd in yoghurt, a salad of pomegranate seeds with chopped walnuts and an expertly grilled shashlik lamb kebab. After the privations of the train it was everything I needed, although my heart missed a couple of beats when they presented me with the £100 bill, which, to be fair, did include a small cup of tea.

We had considerable time to ourselves in Moscow, and I gladly took the opportunity to mooch. After buying a bowl of bortsch from a roadside stand, I found a small park filled with neglected statues of Soviet heroes. I sipped my bowl of soup with its fragrant beetroot steam wafting up into my nostrils, watched silently by my dining partners, Lenin, Brezhnev and Andropov, before heading back to meet my companions for an overnight journey. After our recent travels this was an unchallenging eight hours, allowing us two full days in Peter the Great's capital, an astonishing work of construction and rightly compared to Venice for its beauty and network of canals.

As with Moscow, this was not my first visit. After the literary agent, had poured me into bed after a few drunken meetings at the Moscow Book Fair, she had poured herself in after me and we had become more than friends. I readily agreed to spend a week in her company in St Petersburg over new year. I had enjoyed the city, but Russia in winter was, unsurprisingly, slightly chilly and we had spent quite a lot of time in our comfortable hotel room. That was no bad thing, but I did not see anywhere near as much as I wanted to and what little I did encounter was through the thin gap left by a woolly hat and a thick scarf.

Now, in autumn, however, it was a different matter, and I could see St Petersburg in all its considerable glory. Its court-yards, churches and gardens looked impossibly beautiful in the watery sunlight, and I had big plans to catch up on lost oppor-tunities. The Russians, though, had different ideas. I had pur-chased a train ticket to take me from St Petersburg to Helsinki in Finland for the next leg of the journey and had arranged with the tour company to have my tickets delivered to the hotel. Once we checked in, I asked politely if they had arrived.

'No', the woman at reception barked at me. 'If they were here, I would have told you.' She gave me that now all too common look of withering contempt.

I decided to give it until the next day and headed off with the others to spend time in the Hermitage, but found myself unable to concentrate on the wonders in one of the world's greatest museums. I called my travel agent, and they assured me the tick-ets had been delivered, so I headed back to the hotel to ask again. The same woman was behind the reception desk.

'Are you calling me liar?' she snarled, looking across at her colleague. 'He is calling me liar.'

A slight air of panic began to set in, and Andrew suggested that I should consider alternative travel options on the overnight buses, which ran between the two cities every day.

Next morning the staff remained obdurate, and I headed out to buy a bus ticket, only to realize when I got to the station that I had forgotten my passport. I headed back to the hotel, angry and frustrated, and stomped to the lift.

'You', a familiar voice snapped. It was the receptionist. 'Do you not want your package?' She waved an envelope at me.

'What?'

'Do you not want package? It has been here since yesterday', she added with an innocent look.

I took the envelope and opened it, hardly surprised to see my tickets come tumbling out onto the counter. 'But, but, but I asked you about these yesterday', I stammered.

'You never asked me. It must have been some other person.' She glanced across as the same nodding colleague for support.

I almost cried, but at least I had the tickets. I could go out and enjoy my last evening. For the last few months I had been a backpacker. I may have been a lousy one, who moaned a lot and was generally a bit useless, but I had been a backpacker. My companions, being experienced travellers, had all helped me along the way, but now it was time to drag them into my world, a world of smart bars, well-mixed cocktails and plush leather seats. I gathered a willing handful together and led them the short walk to St Petersburg's famous Grand Hotel Europe, where I commandeered a circle of seats in the corner of their lavish bar. I called over the manager.

'Six Beefeater Martinis up with a twist, very, very cold. Very, very dry. Oh, and some crisps.'

The drinks came soon, and we raised them, by the stem of course, never by the bowl, and made a toast. I had been grateful to all of my companions, and the others on the previous trips, for their support. But now, with my first shuddering sip of Martini, I was back in my world and all was right with it, and not even the Russians could ruin that.

II

Pertti and the Prinsessa

Sitting in my train carriage as it chugged away from St Petersburg towards Helsinki, I experienced an agreeable shiver of pleasure as the Finnish customs official took a cursory glance at my battered British passport, smiled and then said, 'Enjoy your time in Finland'. After passing through the Chinese, Mongolian and Russian borders accompanied by bladder-bursting waits on locked train carriages and unsmiling men with guns, it felt good to be back in the EU.

I had added Finland to my itinerary because of a friend in London, Martina Rydman. When she heard about *Eat My Globe*, almost inevitably as I was buying her dinner, she suggested I should go to Finland. I actually laughed so hard that I snorted a rather good Argentine Malbec out of both nostrils.

'Finland?' I shrieked. 'That is the only country with a worse reputation for food than England.'

Martina began to wear me down with descriptions of how good the food was. Not an easy task because my only experience had been something called korvapuusti, a doughy breakfast bun more suited to hand-to-hand combat than to eating. She finally won me over, however, when she announced that she could arrange for me to go hunting with a family friend who only knew two words of English, one of which was 'vodka' and one of which wasn't.

Details of my visit were placed in the hands of Martina's family, and I arrived in Helsinki to be greeted by her older sister Paola, who helped me lug Big Red into her small car and pointed it in a northerly direction. I had no idea what was ahead of me. With so much of the past two months having been organized down to the last detail, it was good to have some surprises. Paola explained that we were heading up to Juupajoki, where the family shared a holiday home.

After a two-hour drive we turned off the road and into the pages of a storybook. Their picturesque house sat on the edges of a lake whose surface shimmered a golden reflection of light from the low sun. The welcome from the Rydman family too was like something from a storybook, their immediate and genuine hospitality in stark contrast to many of my experiences in Russia and China.

Baggy, comfortable sweaters were provided to combat the chill in the autumn air, and my footwear was quickly replaced by a large pair of Wellington boots padded out with thick Finnish socks. They sat me, snug as a bug in the proverbial rug, at the kitchen table and made sure I finished off at least two bowls of thick pea and ham soup, mopped up with large chunks of bread, while they padded around making sure that my makeshift bed was prepared on a very welcome-looking couch. After my early start I could have dived under the covers right then. But Paola likes to plan, and she had plans for me. I was instructed to wrap up against the chill as we were heading out to forage in the local woods.

Foraging is not so much a pastime for the Finns as a way of life. For them it takes on a spiritual quality born of the fact that an abundance of wild food was responsible for keeping the nation from starvation in the dark days after the Second World War. So sacred is the right to forage that it is enshrined in Finnish law that any person is allowed to go picking fruits and mushrooms on any land in the country beyond a given distance from any house.

The woods surrounding the Rydmans' house had a thick carpeting of sharp, tangy lingon berries, which the Finns revere for the vitamins they provide. Alongside these, but much more scarce, were clumps of meaty chanterelle mushrooms, and I was warned to watch where I was treading in case I put my size 10 on a patch of fungal goodness. In a short space of time we had filled up two buckets with prime specimens, and Martina's mother, Maija, headed back to the house to start preparing them for supper while I was shuttled to the next stage of my adventure: hunting.

I was heartbroken to find that, because of my schedule and the short season, I was going to miss the elk-hunting season by a matter of days. Over 50,000 of these moose-like creatures are culled and then butchered and prepared to provide meat for the rest of the year. Martina's brother-in-law Henri and friend Niko told me that we were going hunting anyway, for wild duck and grouse.

Hunting in Finland too is a way of life. These are not people who think that their meat and fish come in choice cuts wrapped in cellophane. The birds we shot that day, if indeed we killed any, would end up in a pot, not as a trophy. Of course, when I say 'we', I don't mean that there was ever going to be a circumstance where I was going to be let near a gun – a very wise decision for all concerned. I was briefed to stand perfectly still when we reached the hunting site and not to do anything that might make them think I was a bird. I strongly suspect at this point they were taking the piss. I can just see the headline: 'Bald, 180 lb man with large ears, wearing highly decorated sweater, shot when Finnish man mistakes him for small game bird.'

We met up with our hunting partner Pertti, who owned the land on which we were about to hunt. Well into his seventies and with a face marked with a crease for every year, he had been hunting since his childhood and had probably killed more birds in that time than I had eaten. We split into pairs, and I headed off in pursuit of Henri, who was striding through the brush towards a small copse. Niko and Pertti went in the opposite direction, towards a spot overlooking an open field.

Then we waited and waited and waited. Nothing. Well, not for us, anyway. Not a thing. We had more chance of catching pneumonia than a bird. I didn't mind. The scenery was indescribably beautiful and the air clear and crisp as I placed my rear on a welcoming tree stump. Henri seemed less sanguine about the whole thing. He moved around a bit with weary sighs expressing his general dissatisfaction with the birds' failure to land in front of his gun sights and then decided to make some peculiar noises. They were meant to sound like a lady duck with loose morals, but really sounded like a desperate Finn making cartoon duck noises in the middle of a forest. Eventually Henri gave in. With another sigh he broke his gun and called me over just as I was having a pleasant daydream about Sichuan barbecue.

'Did we catch anything?' I asked innocently, already knowing the answer but unkindly looking forward to the sheepish reply.

'No, but Niko and Pertti did', he replied, a mite too tersely.

How did he know? I hadn't heard any shots ring out. Perhaps there was an intuitive connection between brother hunters in Finland, built up over centuries. Perhaps, after years, he could smell a mixture of cordite and death in the wind. Perhaps this particular group of hunters had developed their own form of communication involving hoots and squawks that a novice like me would have mistaken for animal sounds.

'They texted me', he said, holding up his Nokia.

The others had indeed caught a couple of beauties, plump and ready for hanging. Pertti, who was sitting on the bonnet of his car with the ever-present cigarette dangling from his mouth, posed for a picture with his prize as his two young disciples looked on. He set off home to his wife so she could prepare the birds for a meal to which we were all invited the next day, while we headed back to the Rydman house with Henri and Niko talking about just how close they had come to shooting some beauties of their own. Course you did, boys, course you did. That night it was fish on the menu.

Loimu lohi is one of the most simple dishes you can imagine, but it tasted impossibly delicious. A whole side of salmon was nailed to a plank of wood and left to smoke gently over the embers of a fading fire. Dishes like this appeal to me. Get a great ingredient and then don't screw around with it too much. When supper was ready, I cut a large slab of oily fish and ladled a spoonful of the mushrooms we picked earlier on to my plate. They had been cooked in a little cream. It was a truly sumptuous meal in the surroundings of a welcoming group of new friends. It is little wonder that, as soon as I dived under the covers of my put-me-up, I was asleep and dreaming of duck noises.

The next morning it was time to meet Pertti's wife, Kiti, known to one and all as the Prinsessa. It is hard to know how to describe a woman who, like so much I had experienced in Finland, stepped straight out of the pages of a fairy tale. A plump woman with a face brightened by a constant smile, her entire existence seemed to involve making sure that everyone she met was eating all the time.

When I arrived at their picturesque house, she was already hard at work baking, and as I sat down, she poured me a large glass of fresh rhubarb and ginger juice that she 'just happened' to have made. She gave me a tour of her house, filled to bursting with a lifetime's collection of bric-à-brac, before settling me down to talk about her greatest passion, food. I fell in love immediately. She was a kindred spirit, and as we talked, we cooked together. We prepared more of those meaty mushrooms, we stuffed wild mallard that I had collected from the cellar where they hung, with apples and garlic, we made salads and we laughed. A lot.

I never really spent that much time with my own mother cooking. The kitchen was her domain, and I just enjoyed the end-results. Now she's gone, I have added it to the long list of regrets I have. But sitting there with the Prinsessa, I got just an inkling of what it would have been like. By the time people began arriving for lunch, the Prinsessa had already laid out enough food to cause her dining table to sag under the weight of all the dishes. Alongside the mallard, which had been braised in cream, were rolled herrings, wafer-thin slices of cured elk, a whole poached salmon and the chanterelles served three ways: pickled, in cream and tossed with apples and walnuts. There were also salads and loaves of hot, crusty bread to be smothered with butter.

Pertti, as tradition required, read a passage about the joys of sharing the harvest of the land, and then we all tucked in to a memorable meal with almost everything served coming from their land or the skies above. Among all the abundance was a small dish of new potatoes from their garden. I popped one in my mouth. It was the best potato I had ever tasted. Needing no accompanying salt or butter, it was sweeter than candy, and I returned time and again to sneak more. We ate until we had to be rolled away from the table and then moved to the parlour to take tea with a slice of apple cake. While everyone tucked in, I am not too proud to admit that I sneaked back to the dining table and stole the last potato. If *Eat My Globe* was about anything, it was about moments such as this – sitting with people who were, until recently, complete strangers, sharing their delicious food.

At the end of what would prove to be one of the hardest legs of the trips – China, Mongolia and Russia – to be cocooned in the welcoming arms of a loving family, even if it was not my own, was a very special thing. I shall never forget it. That night, as I went to bed, however, my mind was on other things. I had already turned my attention to the next stage of the journey.

I was off to look for America.

12

Fed, White and Blue

I fell in love with the United States on my first visit to New York City, in the early 1980s. Most of all, I love the people: extraordinarily engaging, frighteningly open and the most passionate and loyal friends any man can have. I count myself fortunate to have many.

I adore eating in America too, and not just the fine dining scenes in major cities such as New York, Los Angeles or Chicago, where the restaurants can be staggeringly good but can also be as mediocre and over-rated as anywhere in the world. It is the food Americans seem most apologetic about and loath to admit liking that attracts me most. Dishes that, when made well, are simple but stunning: barbecue, a legacy of German butchers; baking, a legacy of Jewish immigration from Eastern Europe; and simple delights such as meatloaf and hamburgers, which can be entirely delicious. It was this food I was in search of. Of course, somewhere along the way I was sure to poke my curious nose around the entrance of a few smart restaurants, but that is not where the great stuff is, that is not where the great people are and it is certainly not where the real America is.

Kansas City, Missouri, is an odd place to begin an eating tour of America. In fact, it's an odd place to visit anyway without a reason. It is a pleasant city, with a vibrant community spirit and bags of culture paid for over the last century by cattle, rail and lumber magnates, but there is still a feeling that it has never quite recovered from turning down the chance to be the central hub for the cross-country rail lines back in the nineteenth century, an opportunity grabbed by Chicago instead.

My friend Mark Cordes is the most wholesome man I have ever met. He uses phrases such as 'Gosh darn it' with no sense of irony at all and calls so many people 'sir' or 'ma'am' that I keep thinking we are on the set of *Little House on the Prairie*. We became friends through business, and for years he had been inviting me to join him at the American Royal, arguably the biggest barbecue competition in the world, where, my research told me, nearly 400,000 lb of meat were cooked and consumed in the space of two days every year.

With the exception of my sister, who never touches the stuff, meat is rather important to the Majumdar clan. From the gargantuan roasts on Sunday, where inevitably we would have heated discussions about what animal would provide the centrepiece to the following week's lunch, to the Welsh stews and Bengali curries prepared by my mother, meat was at the centre of every meal and remains so to this day.

TGS and I have even predicated entire holidays around our search for meat. We talk about meat a great deal, love pressing our noses against the windows of local butchers, watching in awe as they use their skills to produce glistening cuts of things that once made cute little animal noises, and have even been known secretly to rub the fat on joints of beef, pork or lamb making sounds usually heard from honeymooning couples.

Of course, I was interested in coming to an event where thousands of Midwesterners cooked and ate vast amounts of meat while drinking beer, and there was nothing stopping me this time. I turned up at Mark's house two days before the event and made myself comfortable in his guestroom before he even had the chance to say 'That's swell'.

The American Royal barbecue competition is part of a bigger event bringing together people from all over the Midwest to celebrate the cattle industry. There are rodeos and farm shows in events lasting a few weeks. The barbecue competition is the centrepiece, with over 500 teams competing in two events: the Open, for anyone who can afford to rent a space, and the

Invitational, for the serious professionals who already have a championship under their belts. It is hard to explain the scale of the event, even if I tell you that it covers a space at least the size of ten football fields. It is immense.

Barbecue is serious business in America, not even closely related to the UK notion, which usually means lots of rain, lots of swear words, bits of supermarket chicken charred on the outside and life-threateningly red on the inside, and inevitably plenty of tears as what should have been a nice family occasion goes tits-up in withering blasts of accusations and botulism. In America, barbecue involves huge hunks of meat being smoked over different woods for hours on end, in smokers the size of a small European car, so they are cooked to succulent perfection. It involves slabs of pork or beef ribs marinated in secret rubs and cooked until the flesh begins to fall off the bone. It involves chicken cooked until the skin is crispy and the flesh moist, and it involves links of plump, spicy sausages with the juices bubbling under the skin ready to release their flavour at the slightest tooth pressure. It varies from region to region. In Texas it is all about the cow. In Kentucky you may even see mutton on the menu. In Kansas it's a combination of fatty beef brisket cooking alongside pork butt and baby back ribs. Everyone in the different states of America thinks that their barbecue is the best. They usually have guns, so I tend not to express an opinion.

I had been invited to join Burn Rate, a motley assortment of Mark's friends who use this as an opportunity to do a bit of male bonding, barbecue being very much a male event. The women-folk were left at home looking after the children while the men set to work erecting a marquee and preparing two large smokers for the days ahead. It was hard work, lugging hay bales to mark our patch and erecting fences to create a perimeter, but cooled by cans of beer pulled from tubs of ice and fuelled by some ribs that had been thrown on the smoker to test the heat, we were able to turn what had originally been an assortment of cases, freezer boxes and off-cuts of wood into an attractive party space with a working kitchen.

I was happy to be set to work hefting boxes, putting up fences and doing whatever I was told, not only because I wanted to earn my corn but also because it gave me the perfect opportunity to get to know my fellow team members and to thank them for their extraordinary generosity. After we had more or less finished, Paul Diamond, one of the team, tossed me a nice cold one and said, 'You wanna rub some butt?'

I am not normally that kind of boy, but in this case, yes I did, I wanted to rub some butt very much indeed. We headed over to the kitchen, and I was handed a tube containing plastic gloves of the sort that make me want to run and hide when my proctologist puts them on, before Paul opened one of the freezer boxes and produced a large piece of pork.

'About five pounds', he announced proudly. 'We have about fifty of them, I am not sure it will be enough.' He was deadly serious and passed me one to work on.

We smeared each of them with French's mustard to hold the rub on. Then we heaped dry rub on to the mustard and began massaging it into the meat, which I am ashamed to admit was an unnervingly sensual experience. Americans love to explain their ingredients at great length. 'There's oregano in there', Andy, another team member, explained. 'A little rosemary, garlic, lemon, pepper', the list went on longer than the credits from a *Star Wars* movie. I didn't mind, I was just happy rubbing away, grinning like a buffoon.

'I can't ever recall seeing you look so happy', Mark beamed.

He was right. Buzzed with a couple or three beers and cheerily giving a foot rub to a dead pig, I was rapidly coming to the conclusion that this was one of the happier days of my life. It got better as the first rack of ribs was taken from the smoker for us to try, and the whole team gathered around the table grabbing hands full of succulent pork and moaning in pleasure as they took their first bite.

'The rules say that the meat should fall from the bone only where you are biting and not off the whole rib, or it is over-cooked', explained another team-mate. 'These are good, but they are not good enough for the competition.'

By now it was beginning to get dark and, our set-up complete, we prepared more meat and began to chill out after hours of hard work in the hot sun. Someone produced the biggest bottle of Jack Daniels I have ever seen in my life, poured me a three-finger slug and then the same for himself which he topped off with Coca-Cola.

'We've earned this', he sighed, taking a long draw from his plastic cup.

We were all set up for the following night, and most of the team members looked as though they were ready to drop. Some, in fact, had already begun to flag and were draped out over hay bales; others had retired to the back of the van, where they had placed sleeping bags and pillows. I can take male bonding only so far, and Mark, thank God, felt the same. We left them to it and drove back to the comforts of his flat for a good night's rest.

By the time we arrived the next morning, the team were already hard at work preparing the meat both for the competition and for the night's party. The two smokers were stacked to capacity with brisket, pork butt and chicken, and ribs were marinating happily in freezer boxes on the floor. There was not a lot to be done. Most of the team were having breakfast, which from the appearance of ribs and whiskey on the table seemed alarmingly similar to supper. I was not quite up to this breakfast of champions at 8.30 a.m., so I took the opportunity to wander off with Mark to see the rest of the showground.

All the teams were getting ready for action. They ranged from small 'Mom & Pop' teams out to have a weekend's fun to serious contenders with large marquees, enormous smokers and even stages for live music to be played during their party. Best of all were the names. I thought our own, Burn Rate, based on the term used for the speed at which new companies get through their start-up capital, was good, but it was tame in comparison with Motley Que, The Master Basters and, finest of all, hats off to Morning Wood.

The taste of what we had done at Burn Rate was good, but when I got to sample the barbecue from some of the teams in the 'pro' section, I realized that they had taken things to a whole different level. Pulled pork came with a fabulous char created by adding brown sugar to the rub; brisket had fat that just melted on the mouth like savoury candy floss; and the ribs, my God, ribs with just enough bite to make the hunt for meat worthwhile. It is little wonder that some of these people spend every weekend of the year competing and can earn up to $2 million in prizes and endorsements.

By the afternoon country music was already blaring from speakers all over the campground as I threaded my way back through the crowds to the Burn Rate marquee, where our party was just getting under way. The wives of the various team members were gathered, staring in horror into the back of the truck, where their husbands had been sleeping, a space that now looked like a cross between *Lord of the Flies* and something Alexander Solzhenitsyn might have written about.

'We are barbecue widows', Paul's wife, Kathy, sighed. 'The boys do this, and we take care of the kids for a few days. But next month all the girls get to go to Cancun or up to Chicago for the weekend, and the men look after the children.'

Their children had already begun to dive headlong into the food we produced. Nearly 400 lb of meat, I was told, alongside salads, coleslaw, beans, bread and desserts. It was easily enough to feed 500 or more, so I was glad to see a steady stream of people arriving.

'You're grinning again', Mark nudged me, and I realized I was just standing there with an overburdened plate in my hand and a huge smile on my face. I was still trying to take it all in. Not just the scale of the event, the amount of work it had involved or even the unbeatable taste of barbecue. It was more about the people. Over the course of the day each one of the team had come up to me and personally invited me back again any time I wanted. Some had offered accommodation if I ever got fed up with staying with Mark, and others had said just to come over any time anyway, just for the hell of it. It was moments such as this that the whole trip had been about. The chance, through food, to meet people whom I could genuinely call 'friend', and here in America's oft criticized Midwest I had found a whole group of them.

I forked a large mound of pulled pork into my mouth, turned to Mark and just nodded.

13

Dog Eat Dog in Chicago

I am slowly beginning to develop a theory about American food. It is by no means fully gestated but goes along the lines that the USA's greatest contribution to world cuisine is ... the sandwich.

Before all the amateur food historians pop out and buy a ladder to climb on the highest horse they can find, I know the Americans didn't invent it – the British did – but like football, we sent the sandwich out into the world for everyone else to do better. It is in America that the concept of slamming incredible ingredients between slices of bread has reached its highest point. Americans, in fact, have raised it to an art form.

I am talking about portable food originally designed to feed honest, hard-working folk on the go for small amounts of money. I am talking about the Po'Boy and the Muffuletta I was hoping to see in New Orleans. The cheese steak I had marked out in Philadelphia, the pastrami on rye, which New Yorkers cannot live without, the barbecue brisket sandwich I had eaten in Kansas and was looking forward to in Texas and, of course, hamburgers and hot dogs, perhaps America's biggest contribution to the culinary landscape of the world, exported to and copied in every corner of the globe.

This theory began to find fertile soil in my brain as I headed off to one of my favourite cities anywhere. Chicago is to my mind one of the truly great American cities. New York, like London, is a city of the world: it operates on a different level. Chicago, on the other hand, could never have been imagined or built anywhere but America. Its architecture, its location and, of course, its food make it stand out from any other city in the USA. Every time I walk its streets, I find myself staring open-mouthed at a skyline that represents some of America's greatest achievements, from the towering Gothic splendour of the Wrigley Building to the International-style high-rises of Mies van der Rohe. The people too offer a uniquely American combination of brusque charm and brashness, all mixed with a childlike enthusiasm for their home town.

I had been particularly pondering the evolution of the sandwich because, as I get older, I find myself underwhelmed by so many restaurant meals. It may be that, after thousands of them, I am jaded, or it may be that, after years of eating food that has been messed around with by chefs keen to show their skills, my taste buds just crave the simplicity of good ingredients not screwed around with too much. So it was in Chicago. Admittedly, I did not trouble the very highest end of their dining offerings by visiting Charlie Trotter or Alinea, but the restaurants I visited came well recommended by locals and were packed to the rafters with diners who seemed happy enough. The meals, however, were ordinary and fitted neatly into the identikit mould of mid-range American dining. A bit of tuna here, a strip steak there – you could write the menu in your sleep. I found myself much happier eating stuff between bits of bread and particularly, in Chicago, the hot dog.

The first was at a legendary joint, The Wiener's Circle, famous not just for its hot dogs but also for the abrasive nature of the staff, who are, shall we say, not the sort of people you would take home to tea. I had just had a 'blah' lunch at a place called North Pond and was feeling miserable and, even more shamefully, still hungry. On the way back to my hotel I passed The Wiener's Circle and popped inside.

'What the fuck d'ya want, big ears?' shrieked a large African American woman through the serving hatch.

'Er', I stammered, 'I am not sure.'

'What the fuck kind of accent is that?', she hollered. 'Are you retarded?'

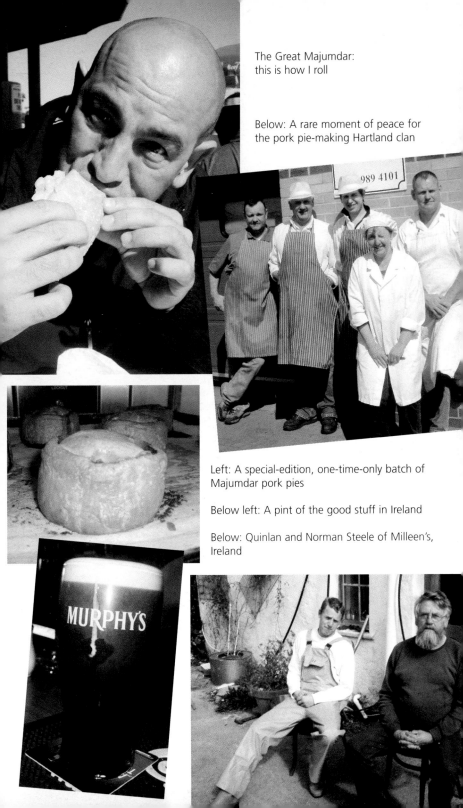

The Great Majumdar: this is how I roll

Below: A rare moment of peace for the pork pie-making Hartland clan

Left: A special-edition, one-time-only batch of Majumdar pork pies

Below left: A pint of the good stuff in Ireland

Below: Quinlan and Norman Steele of Milleen's, Ireland

Eric Balic: evil in eighteen-month-old human toddler form

Right: Tsukiji Fish Market in Tokyo

Below: Chanko: enough to feed three people, one sumo or me

Making maki sushi with Tomoko in Kyoto

Everyone helps with the harvesting and shelling of local peanuts in Yangshuo, China

Dog and rat at Yangshuo Market. Well, I did say, 'Go everywhere, eat everything'

Fulfilling an ambition of my mother's, visiting the Great Wall of China

Hunting eagles in Mongolia

Below: It's good manners to stir the *airag*

Out of my comfort zone on the Trans-Siberian Express, and back in my 'Happy Place' once we reached St Petersburg

Above: Pertti the victorious hunter

Right: Pertti and the Prinsessa

Above: The Great Majumdar rubs
butt at the American Royal Barbeque

Right: BBQ connoisseur and true
Texas gentleman, John King

Above: Even at 1 a.m., you have to
queue for a Philly cheese steak at
Geno's

Left: Showing commitment to the
product at Zingerman's

Toy skulls for the Day of the Dead, a uniquely Mexican experience

Below: Perfect *taco de tripa* in Guadalajara

Left: If your dinner stares back at you, you're probably in Iceland

Right: Chatuchak market, Thailand

Chef Ismail, guardian of traditional Malay cuisine

Claude Tayag in the kitchen of his *bale dutung* in the Philippines

Below: Cooks slaving over a hot charcoal grill at Bade Miyan, Mumbai

Left: Eating like a true Bengali in Kolkata

Right: Women picking the delicate leaves from the tea bushes, Darjeeling

Emil Den Dulk, Master of the South African Braai

Below: *Teranga*, true hospitality from Bath in Senegal

Left: 'But is it Spain?' TGS muses on sherry and seafood in Jerez

Above: Food labels are not necessary at the markets in Casablanca

Left: With Big Red and a restorative cup of tea, at the end of the road

'No, I'm British.'

'Same thing', she countered, before turning to a hidden colleague in the kitchen. 'We got the goddamn Queen of England out here.'

Slightly shaken by this interesting approach to customer care, I ordered quickly. 'A Red Hot ... with everything.' I had no idea what a Red Hot might possibly be, but I wanted to get the experience over with.

'That's $5.40, big ears.' She extended a chubby paw in my direction.

I handed over $10 and waited for my change. Instead, she put it in a large jar marked 'IT'S FOR THE TIPS BITCH' and glared at me.

'That OK with you, big ears?'

'Yes, Ma'am', I whimpered and stood to one side to wait for my hot dog like a good little boy. It is all *shtick*, of course, but that only matters if the hot dog is no good. I need not have worried. It was a great hot dog and worth all the abuse and the 90 per cent service charge extracted from me for the pleasure. Perhaps I am just funny that way and just like being abused.

If that hot dog was good, the next proved to be one of my most memorable tastes of the whole trip to date.

I was lucky in Chicago to have contact with Adam, the poor chap who had shared a room with me as I travelled around Japan and who had seen me parading in little else but a variety of short silk robes. He lived close to my hotel and joined me for a number of meals. While he was working, he put me in the charge of his girlfriend, Saritha, who seemed happy to wander around with me as I looked for things to eat. I did what any gallant chaperon would do when accompanied by an attractive young woman. I made her walk with me through one of the rougher parts of town in search of another hot dog, in this case at the legendary Hot Doug's.

When I did my research, Hot Doug's was the name that came up most regularly. A little bit more research showed that Doug was a bit of an old punk rocker and had named some of his offerings after the members of my favourite band of all time, the Buzzcocks. It was obviously kismet.

When we arrived, Doug himself was seated behind the counter and, as the line shortened, I took in the menu. The Pete Shelley was a temptation until I realized it was a vegetarian option. I just couldn't do it. Saritha, however, was a vegetarian, which probably explains the whining when she realized we were going to a hot dog joint for lunch. I went for a standard Frank with everything, some fries and a diet Coke, and we took a seat in the cheerful little dining-room and waited.

Three minutes later our food arrived. On one of their windows they had hung a sign that, to paraphrase, said that there are few things better in this world than an encased meat sandwich. They are not wrong. This was fabulous stuff as the skin of the dog popped to let the meat inside escape in a waft of meaty steam. I ate quickly, too quickly, which led to lots of hot-dog-scented burps for the next few hours. I approved of this, considering it the gift that keeps on giving. Saritha did not and made 'eieew' noises after each regular expulsion.

I had only a limited amount of time in Chicago, as I was squeezing in a couple of days between Kansas and another invitation in Ann Arbor. So I did not really have time to explore the bewildering variety of food Chicago has to offer. I did not even have time to visit one of Chicago's legendary steakhouses.

I could tell you about the other restaurants I visited, about Avec, where the service was so charmless you would have thought they had brought Hillary Clinton in to give lessons, and about the West Town Tavern, where they did things to a plate of crisps that must be illegal in at least thirty states. But what I really want to tell you about was a hot dog, a simple sandwich, which made me begin to form a small, unimportant theory of my own about what makes America such an amazing place to eat. For that alone, I am glad I went to Chicago.

Oh, I did have 'a burrito as big as your head' before I left town. Well, you are forced to, aren't you?

14

Ann Arbor: The Cult of Zingerman's

Gauri Thergaonkar is another of those people unfortunate enough to have made my acquaintance via a food website and is a long-time resident of Ann Arbor, Michigan. As soon as she heard about *Eat My Globe*, she extended an invitation for me to spend time with her.

A campus town for the University of Michigan, Ann Arbor is filled with bright, young idealists still waiting for life to come and beat the living crap out of them and with lots and lots of coffee shops for them to sit around in while waiting for that to happen. It may seem strange to cut short a visit to Chicago, one of the great eating cities in the country, to head up to Ann Arbor, but I was going for one reason only: to visit Zingerman's.

Zingerman's styles itself as a Jewish deli, and in fact the name is a composite put together by the founders to make it sound the part. However, to call Zingerman's a deli is like calling Fortnum & Mason's a corner shop. It is an extraordinary collective of food-related businesses in orbit around the main store, which all pride themselves on the superlative quality of their products and their levels of customer service. Alongside the deli there is a creamery, a bake house, a vast mail-order business and a number of restaurants.

Founded by Ari Weinzweig and Paul Saginaw in 1982, Zingerman's has rapidly built up a reputation nationwide, not only for the quality of its food but also for levels of service, which border on the pathological.

When I first met Gauri she was, like so many people in Michigan, working for one of the major car companies. Food was her obsession, and she found herself spending so much time and money in Zingerman's that she decided to have a total career change and take a job as a line worker in the deli. Over the next few years her enthusiasm and ability saw her rise to become one of their managers and, because of her own big career shift, she understood completely when I told her about *Eat My Globe*. She sent me a supportive mail and at the bottom wrote, 'I'll organize for you to hang out at the deli'.

This alarmed me slightly. The enigmatic leadership and management style of Zingerman's engenders a loyalty among its customers and, even more, its staff that is almost cult-like. Gauri, however, is used to getting her own way, and on a Saturday in mid-October I found myself reporting for duty.

Gauri had decided that the best way for me to understand the deli would be to undergo one of the trial shifts they give potential employees to see how they interact with staff and customers alike. I would hang out in each section of the store and, if the general reports at the next staff meeting were positive, they would tell me whether, if I had been eligible, they would have employed me.

My shift began at 8 a.m., but before that Gauri had arranged for me to meet Ari Weinzweig in the Zingerman's coffee shop so I could get some background about the company. As always, he had arrived as soon as they opened and was sitting with half a dozen cups of their different coffees in front of him, doing a tasting. 'So what do you want to know about Zingerman's?' he said, slurping on a rich, dark brew.

'Well, how do you get your staff to drink the Kool-aid?' I asked in a slightly clumsy reference to the Jonestown Massacre. Ari looked up and gave me a thin smile. I was obviously not the first to make the comparison.

'Well, you'll just have to ask them when you are working today', he replied. 'All we try and do is find people who are committed to achieving the same vision that Paul and I have for the company and its future. Some can fit in, and others can't.'

He explained how Zingerman's runs an open-book finance policy, so that every employee is able to view the accounts, and about other policies, official and unofficial, that they use to support their staff, from help with sometimes serious personal issues to promotions on merit and a definite recognition of individual abilities. He also explained about 'preferred futuring', a vision creation method they had used from the very beginning of the business. For a hugely cynical Brit like myself, it was all a bit hard to believe, but, as I spent more time with Ari and the staff of the company, I could see it was genuine.

As I found out when I went to take up my position behind the counter, the level of staff loyalty is incredibly high, as is the level of service – not just to the customers, who were already flooding through the doors, but also to each other and to me, the odd, middle-aged man who had been dumped in their midst and who they made feel immediately welcome.

Jess Piskor, who was looking after the cheese and meat counter, where I was to spend the next couple of hours, explained: 'It is the double whammy. It's homecoming, and U of M have a game today.' I didn't understand a word of that, but I gathered from the crowds, even at this early hour, that it was a big deal.

The staff were swamped. One of them handed me a plate of Montgomery's cheddar and told me to head out into the store and hand out samples. 'Give it your best British shit', he ordered.

One of the few benefits of being British is the accent, which, particularly in America, can help you get away with anything. I played the card to the full, wandering around for the next eight hours giving it my 'best British shit', trying on a range of accents from the 'Cor luv a duck' *faux* Cockney of Jamie Oliver to the plummy tones of David Niven.

I moved from the cheese counter to the bread counter to the dry goods area, where I sold, as the Americans might say, like a Mo'Fo. I persuaded people to buy $50 bottles of vinegar, loaves of bread stuffed with chocolate (admittedly that did not take so much work) and enough British cheese to keep the industry going for another year or so.

At 4 p.m., during a lull, Gauri came onto the sales floor. 'You look shattered', she said. It was true; I was knackered. I caught a glimpse of myself in a mirror. I was covered from head to toe in flour (note to self, black is not a good colour when working with bread), and my face was lined where beads of sweat had attractively cut tracks through the caked-on flour.

Gauri was clutching a package. Inside was a black Zingerman's T-shirt, my reward for helping out. 'You deserve it', she said, giving me a hug, and she was right. But it made me realize how much effort went in to giving the levels of service Ari demanded and how much I had enjoyed being part of it. I was a convert.

Now, where's that Kool-aid?

15

Don't Mess with Texas

I can understand why Texas gets a bad rap. It does precious little to ingratiate itself with the rest of the USA, and you get the impression that signs reading 'Don't Mess with Texas' studded alongside the freeways are not just talking about litter. It is a warning not to get on the wrong side of anybody in a state where it is easier to buy a gun than an apple.

I spent two weeks in 2002 driving around this vast state with TGS in search of amazing barbecue. He, of course, had done his research and had a large map of the state with the word 'MEAT' scribbled on it at places of bovine interest. We both came under Texas's spell and thought we might never leave when we drove into a gas station outside Tyler called Billy Bob's, which sported a large sign announcing it sold only three things: 'Gas, Cracklin' & Ammo'. Ever since, TGS has been known suddenly to giggle quietly and mutter 'gas, cracklin' & ammo' to no one in particular.

I had pretty much the same barbecue intentions this time as on my previous visit, but I was resigned to the fact that I was going to have to make the journey alone. This was a double shame because there are few people who are better company when in search of meat than TGS and obviously, having only one stomach, there was only so much I was going to be able to take on. Fortunately, the food websites came to the rescue again and, via mutual friends, I was put in touch with two locals, Jane and John King.

On my last visit I had fallen in love with Austin. I liked its quirkiness and the laid-back vibe, which meant that everything happened at its own steady pace. I liked its independence and the demand on its inhabitants to 'Keep Austin Weird'.

Five years later there were signs that chains were taking over from the independent shops, but the old Austin spirit still seemed to be intact, particularly at the utterly fabulous Austin motel with its sign, a middle finger extended to 'The Man' and its declaration that it was 'So Close Yet So Far Out'.

After an unmemorable lunch and a short walk to see the shabby titty bars and dreadful restaurants of infamous Sixth Street, I was ready for a nap and returned to my hotel room, only to receive a call from my new chum Jane, arranging to take me to her house for a Tex-Mex feast she and other members of the food website were arranging in my honour. When we arrived, her husband, John, was busy unloading beer from his car into the porch.

Dressed in shorts, a grey T-shirt over his rounded stomach and a straw Stetson worn without a hint of irony, John was almost impossible to dislike. This impression was reinforced when he handed me the first of far too many shots of tequila with the words 'Welcome to Texas'.

I knew almost nothing about Tex-Mex cookery. My experiences of it in London have always verged on the disgusting, and I assumed that it was basically just an excuse to use up residual amounts of any bad cheese that you might find in the back of the fridge. It is certainly meat- and cheese-dependent, and there is no way you would ever call it a refined cuisine, but on the evidence of what was put in front of me, it is entirely delicious.

'Armadillo eggs' were particularly good, made of jalapeno peppers stuffed with cheese and wrapped in bacon. I shovelled down about six of them before I realized that everyone else in the porch was staring at me with a look mixing horror, disgust and nausea in equal measure. I moved quickly on to chilli con queso, a dip made with ground beef and yet more cheese. I did not give the Kings a chance to tell me not to stand on ceremony as I stood right by the table with all the food on it and helped myself until they began to stare again. These were just the starters, and soon a huge dish of enchiladas stuffed with pulled pork and a large bowl of beans appeared. Jane produced a pico de gallo in a vain attempt to keep things on the healthy side, but it was too late. The enchiladas were so good it was all they could do to stop me stripping off and smearing the sauce over my chest.

After making a pig of myself, I flopped down on a pretty pink rocking chair and helped myself to yet another shot of tequila. There is a saying that 'Texas is just a state of mind'. Well, I was in a hell of a state, and no one seemed to mind.

I spent the next day with Jane as she went about her day at work in Central Market, one of the best food shops I have visited in a long time, and we spent the evening cooking Indian food together for more of her family and friends. After supper, as I flopped back into the same rocking chair on their porch, John came and sat on the couch next to me.

'When do you plan to go and eat barbecue?' he asked.

'Tomorrow, my last day before heading to New Orleans', I replied, fighting back a dahl-flavoured burp.

'Do you mind if I come with you?' he asked gently. Mind? I was thrilled. Not only did it mean I would have a dining companion but also I had just seen John eat. Few people can put stuff away like my dear older brother, but John looked more than up to the task of operating *in loco Salami*.

The next morning I met John, as planned, at the café next to the motel. He wandered in as I sipped on my hot chocolate, Stetson very firmly on his head, and looking ready for the fight.

'Big day ahead of us, my friend', he drawled. 'I want us to hit four barbecue pits before we head home. Are you game?'

Lordy, I had never been more game. I love barbecue anywhere, but Texas barbecue is special because it comes without sauce. 'If you need sauce,' John intoned wisely as he drove, 'then there is something wrong with your barbecue.'

We were heading to a small town called Lockhart, some thirty minutes' drive from Austin, considered by many to be the barbecue capital of the world – a legacy of its past, when German butchers would smoke meat to sell alongside fresh meat to local farmhands and cowboys. We had plans to hit three pits there and then move on to another small town, Luling, to visit one more joint.

'We are going to have to pace ourselves,' John warned as we pulled up outside Kreuz Market, our first stop, 'or we won't be able to manage all four.'

Kreuz was the most famous barbecue pit. As we entered, it was filling up with a lunchtime crowd queuing quietly while elderly ladies sliced huge slabs of brisket from large joints or beef ribs to be sold by the pound. The smell was incredible, and John guided me through the ordering of meat along with sides of pickles and white sliced bread. I liked it, but John, the pro, was harder to please.

'It doesn't quite have that smokiness going through to the centre as it should', he nodded seriously. 'Not bad though, not bad.'

We headed back to the car for the short drive to our next port of call, Black's, a small place whose original clientele, I understand, were the black community of Texas. As John headed up to collect more brisket for our experiment, this time supplemented by some meaty sausage links, I went to claim a table. It too was beginning to fill up, and you could see that barbecue really is the great equalizer. In the small dining-room wealthy men in expensive suits sat next to Hispanic farmhands, students and ordinary stiffs like us. Good Q knows no boundaries. The sausages were spectacular, with a sufficient bite and the right amount of spicing.

John was still not happy with the brisket, however. 'It's a little dry, and there is not enough fat.' He is a hard man to please. I would kill for any place close to this quality in London.

A short hop across the road was Smitty's Market, on the original site of Kreuz. It changed its name because of a feud between the surviving relatives of the original owner. The wooden walls are ingrained with the smell of a hundred years of smoke, and so too, it seemed, were the people serving. We ordered more brisket and some ribs and found a space in the long dining-room, where generations of Texans had come to eat exactly the same meal. The ribs were spot on: strips of fat had rendered to leave crispy strands to chew while you worked your way to the meat. The brisket was good too.

'This is the best yet', John said, giving his seal of approval. But I could sense that all was not yet right in his world, brisket-wise. We wrapped up our remains in the butcher's paper in which it had been served and headed to our last port of call, City Market, in the nearby town of Luling. I was suffering by now. Already beads of meat sweats were trickling down my face, and I was not sure if I would be able to face another slab of dead cow. John, however, was made of sterner stuff and ordered an extra-big slab of brisket for us to complete our day.

'Now I am going to show you how to construct a proper barbecue sandwich', he said, laying slices of brisket and pickles between two pieces of bread. I tried to keep up with him, but it was no good, I had to sit back and admire the master at work. He soon polished it off, licked his fingers and said, 'Let's head home'.

I had really hit it off with John, and we talked non-stop on our short drive back to the motel. He parked the car and walked me to my room. As he reached the end of the parking lot, he turned, his body suddenly a round silhouette against the declining sun.

'Thanks for a great day and thanks for the barbecue', he said with one last wave.

No, John, thank you.

That night, when Jane had finished at work, she joined me for a last drink and a dish of ice cream from a shop across from the motel. The saddest thing about meeting people on the road is that at some point you have to say goodbye. I was more sad about saying goodbye to Jane and John than just about anyone I had encountered so far. But, as Jane rightly put it, 'You'll just have to come back and eat more barbecue'.

Damn right.

16

Simon is Big, and Simon is Easy

Abandoned by its government and much of its population after the apocalyptic events of 2005, many other cities would have crumbled. Not New Orleans. Not the Big Easy. It may be a struggle, in the face of federal indifference and public fear, but New Orleans is dragging itself out of the swamps and the flood-waters of Lake Pontrachain and rebuilding itself all over again. I knew that no visit to the USA could possibly bypass this resilient city on the banks of the Mississippi.

Chris Mcmillian is a fourth-generation New Orleans bar-tender and one of the directors of the Museum of the American Cocktail, dedicated to preserving the heritage of mixed drinks in the USA. He is a mountain of a man but softly spoken and polite in the way that only people from the Southern states of America can be.

'You'll just have to come to see me in New Orleans', he instructed when I met him at a bar show in London. 'I make a pretty good Sazerac.'

Three months later, as I sat across from him in the Library Bar of the Ritz Carlton, he was busy living up to his promise. 'New Orleans in a glass', he said in an accent that could not have come from anywhere else.

Drinking a Sazerac is a very pleasurable history lesson. Arguably the oldest of all cocktails, its roots lay in the French origins of the city, when it was made with cognac. Now, it is made with rye whiskey, sugar and local Peychaud bitters before being strained into a chilled, absinthe-washed glass dressed with a lemon peel. The first sip is a great joy. The slight burn of the whiskey followed by the sweetness of the sugar and the citrus of the peel. Chris McMillian at the Library Bar makes the best in the world.

I had plans to visit quite a few restaurants while I was in New Orleans, but, wanting some local advice, I asked Chris for more recommendations. 'Well now, I'm not working until late tomorrow', he said, wiping the bar. 'Why don't I give you the tour?' There was nothing more to be discussed.

When Chris pulled up in front of my hotel, the next morning, the bonnet of his big old American car arrived about five minutes before the rest of it. I could already hear the unmistakable sounds of New Orleans jazz filtering through the windows. Chris opened the door, leaned out and drawled, 'Mornin' y'all ready to eat?'

I climbed in, reclined into the luxurious leather seats and let Chris take charge. He loves New Orleans, with a love I had not seen from any person for any city so far on the trip. He loves it in a way that a father who has almost lost his only child can love. He loves it because of and despite Katrina, and he will love it until he finally keels over and is laid to rest in one of its famous cemeteries.

We took the long route to our first destination so he could give me a tour, pointing out the staggeringly beautiful houses on the edges of the French quarter, dating from when the city was still under Spanish rule. Eventually we drew up alongside the waters of Bayou St John and into the parking lot of the Parkway Bakery, famous for serving one of New Orleans's greatest sandwiches, the Po'boy.

As the name suggests, the Po'Boy, or Poor Boy, sandwich was created as a cheap, filling meal for those down on their luck. It consisted of a long roll, dressed with lettuce and tomato and then filled with deep fried chunks of cheap local fish and seafood such as catfish, shrimps and oysters. Nowadays, of course, those ingredients are not exactly cheap any more, but the sandwich has remained a New Orleans classic. I warned Chris of my aversion to oysters and let him amble up to the counter to order. He returned moments later with two huge cylinders wrapped in kitchen paper.

'I went for oysters, I got you a mixed catfish and shrimp with all the dressing. I hope that's OK?'

I had already torn the wrapper off and had taken my first bite. There's no denying, this is one of the great sandwiches. The soft roll, the crunch of the fish and seafood, which I had drizzled with lemon juice, and the bites of salad to give a semblance of health. We ate in that silence which only middle-aged men can manage, when they know there is something better on offer than conversation. We finished our Po' Boys and headed back to the car.

'I think you need to see what happened', Chris said in a more solemn tone as we climbed back in and headed in the direction of the infamous 9th Ward. I had been surprised by how normal everything looked in New Orleans in my short time there. The Charles Street car was not running and some buildings in the Garden District were boarded up, but on the whole it all looked in a good state of repair. As we hit the 9th Ward, I saw the real story: row upon row of houses in block upon block of streets all deserted and crumbling. Every fifth house or so there was an empty lot where the floodwaters had extracted the building like a rotten tooth. Roads had turned to mud tracks, and all the local businesses were shut.

'It's a dead area. Even if people wanted to live here, there is no infrastructure left to support them. No schools, no shops, no hospitals.'

Chris parked the car and stared out of the window. The sounds of WWOZ, New Orleans's radio station, provided an eerie soundtrack as we looked out at the devastation of the city he adored, not repaired even two years after the event. When we finally drove on, a new tune blared through the speakers – a hybrid of New Orleans jazz and Latino rhythms, the result of construction workers arriving in the city to help with rebuilding joining with young local musicians to create a new sound.

'This is what makes me confident about the future', Chris smiled. 'Whatever they throw at us, New Orleans finds a way to come through it. Now let's go eat some more.' We drove back to the French quarter and pulled up outside Central Grocery.

'Another sandwich?' Chris asked. 'Italian this time.'

The Muffuletta, unique to New Orleans, shows yet another side to its heritage. This time, the influences are not from France or Spain but from Italy or, to be more precise, Sicily. A ten-inch loaf of Italian bread layered with meats, peppers, cheeses and, most important of all, a dressing made with olives, pickles and enough oil to soak into the bread. It's tasty all right but just too messy for my liking. Impossible to eat without getting oil into places where oil really shouldn't get. Chris seemed to have the knack, though, and polished his off in easy order, wrapping up half a sandwich to take home to his kids.

Chris had to go to work. It had been a fantastic morning, despite the depression of the drive through the 9th Ward. I had only a couple more days left in the city and, enjoyable as they were, New Orleans has a lot more to offer the food-obsessive than just these two sandwiches.

I certainly crammed a lot into those two short days, with breakfast at Brennan's filling me up with turtle soup and eggs benedict before I slurped up a bowl of Susan Spicer's mind-blowing garlic soup at Bayonna. Bags of ultra-light beignets from Café du Monde came dusted in powdered sugar that you had to lick off your fingers as you walked and took the fire out of a bowl of crawfish étouffé I had bought to eat on the hoof. Three days in the city was hardly long enough. You could eat three meals a day in New Orleans and not even begin to scratch the surface. But I had limited time and, on my last night, just about enough room for one more meal.

Upperline, in the Garden district, had a menu filled with the sort of Creole food that made New Orleans famous, and I put myself in owner JoAnn Clevenger's hands, leaving her to order.

A large plate of fried green tomatoes appeared, topped with a shrimp remoulade spiced up with grain mustard. Half a roasted duck came with sauces made of garlic, ginger and peaches and, just when I thought I could eat no more, JoAnn carried out a large plate of profiteroles on to which a bitter chocolate sauce had been ladled. This was my sort of meal – well-made, unapologetic food that, because it has never striven to be fashionable, has never gone out of fashion.

I hopped in a cab back to the French quarter and had it drop me off at the beginning of the infamous Bourbon Street. I had avoided it until now, remembering the vile perfume of piss and vomit from a previous visit. My memory had not failed me and, even despite the effects of Katrina, it was still filled with drunk frat boys and college girls.

I hurried towards my hotel. As I turned into the street, I heard music, great music. I followed the sound and saw a parade of people, young and old, of all races and colours playing instruments, dancing and having a ball. I joined the party and followed along for a while until, exhausted, I returned to my bedroom an hour later than planned. As I got ready to hit the hay, I knew they would still be outside partying for all they were worth, not knowing what the future holds for them or the city.

I may not know the future, but I do know one thing. New Orleans may be down, but New Orleans is most definitely not out.

17

Stan and Lisa, Pat and Geno

As I drained my second powerful Martini of the evening, a gruff but not unfriendly voice came from the person on the stool beside mine at the bar of the Smith & Wollensky steakhouse in Philadelphia.

'You in town on business?'

'Sort of', I replied, barely looking up. It had been a long, hard day of travel and the juicy, rare T-bone I had just polished off, with its strip of fat and salty, charred crust, was the only thing between me and bloody murder. Few things can cheer me up when I am in this sort of mood and, since I did not have the latest Victoria's Secret catalogue to hand, a steak and a couple of Martinis would have to suffice.

I turned from my empty plate to be faced with a man in his fifties, with greying hair and the sort of strong features that made me think I ought to be a little more polite. He introduced himself as Stan Cohen. He was a regular at the steakhouse, as his wife worked at the hotel above and he was waiting to take her home. I began to explain about my journey, just as she appeared.

'Lisa,' he turned to his wife, 'this is Simon. He's travelling around the world to eat.'

She turned to me. 'So, are you going to have a Philly cheese steak?'

It was the only reason I had come to the city. I knew there was a lot to like about Philadelphia, I had been before. I knew that it was the home of soft pretzels and the Italian hoagie. I also knew that the Philadelphians were proud of the Reading

Terminal Food Market, with its stores selling the produce of the Pennsylvania Dutch. But I had one full day in town, and I had set that aside to go in search of my first ever Philly cheese steak.

Stan bought me another Martini and Lisa gave me a history lesson. The first cheese steak sandwich was created by Pat Olivieri, who sold a sandwich he made for his own lunch to a passing cab driver, who was so impressed he brought his friends back to try them. His store, Pat's King of Steaks, opened in the 1930s and had the monopoly until Joe Vento opened Geno's, directly across the street, in 1966. Battle commenced, and they have been rivals ever since.

'So, when are you gonna go try one?' he barked.

'Tomorrow lunchtime', I replied.

'Nah', Stan replied. 'You have to go at night time when they are all lit up.' He looked at his watch, looked at Lisa and then back at me.

'C'mon. We'll take you now.'

It was approaching 1 a.m., on top of which I had just eaten 26 oz of T-bone steak and was buzzing from three Martinis.

'Sounds good', I replied, despite the possibility of exploding at the thought of more beef. My trip was not going to get any more real than having a couple of locals drive me across Philadelphia in the small hours in search of a cheese steak.

'If you don't know how to order, they won't serve you', Stan shouted over his shoulder as he drove through the streets of south Philadelphia.

'You gotta order "whiz with", which means a sandwich with cheez whiz', Lisa explained.

'And you want to get it "handicapped", so they cut it in half', Stan added.

Even in the small hours both Pat's and Geno's had long queues and, while Stan went to park the car, I was sent to get in the queue and collect our order. By the time they reappeared, I had our sandwiches wrapped and ready to eat. We took a table on the pavement, and I went to add a little hot sauce to half my cheese steak.

It may have been the context, eating a meal not only in the town in which it was created but also in the very restaurant, but that soft Italian roll, filled with sweet onions, wafer-thin strips of good beef and topped with cheese, was as good as anything I had eaten on the trip.

'They are never as good anywhere else', Stan mumbled between large mouthfuls. 'It's the water we use to make the rolls.'

As I sat in the glare of the large neon Geno's sign, with two people I had met barely an hour earlier, I was as happy as it would have been possible to get, unless, of course, someone produced that Victoria's Secret catalogue.

18

That's so New York

However good New York is, it will never be quite as good as New Yorkers believe it to be. Nothing will ever be quite as good as New Yorkers believe everything in their city to be. If it is good, it is 'the best'; if it is high, it is 'the highest'; and if it is old, it is 'the oldest'. They deal in superlatives and have an enthusiastic capacity for hyperbole.

It is a childlike enthusiasm, which finds its final expression in that wearisome phrase 'That's so New York', a demand for uniqueness that springs from the city's and the country's relative youth. It's a phrase that would never find a home on the lips of the residents of its elder European siblings, who have had thousands of years to, quite frankly, get over themselves. It may be tiresome, but it is this enthusiasm which makes New York what it is and makes New Yorkers what they are.

Few cities are predicated on eating in the same way that New York is, and few people spend as much time eating and arguing about food as New Yorkers do. Every block of the city, be it in Manhattan or one of the other four boroughs, will provide multiple opportunities to stuff your face with great food from all corners of the globe. The same childlike approach is true when they describe restaurants, and I have regularly heard ethnic places described as the very best of their type in the world without a thought that there may well be some half-decent examples in the countries they represent or that the person saying it may never have been further than Queens. Mind you, go to Queens and you could probably eat the globe right there, with just about every race and nation represented in the shops, storefront diners and restaurants. The often blind, black-and-white passion for things and people can be hard work, but it does also make New Yorkers among the most loyal friends you can have, and I am lucky to count many of them among mine. But if I have many friends in New York, I also have some very special relatives.

Sanjoy, my father's cousin, and his wife, Evelyn, are contemporaries of my mother and father. They have become my second parents, and it is with them that I always stay when I am in the city. Sanjoy is a typical Bengali male, whose life seems to involve sitting beatifically in the centre of a maelstrom of his own creation. Bengali men feel that it is the duty of the rest of the world to make their life comfortable and their duty to point out the failings of others – for their own benefit, of course.

When I arrived from Philadelphia, Sanjoy had just returned from work, changed into his loose Indian clothing and was already creating havoc as Evelyn prepared supper for guests who were arriving shortly.

'Sweetie, can I have a soda?' Sanjoy asked, sitting less than a metre from the fridge.

Evelyn rolled her eyes and walked across the kitchen to hand it to him. She is nobody's doormat, but, in the years since they were married she has recognized the fact that Sanjoy would starve if he were left to do anything for himself. He popped open the soda and read his newspaper, circling random words with a pen, something he has always done, although why I have never quite figured out.

Evelyn, although originally from the Philippines, is one of the great cooks of Bengali food, another thing she had in common with my mother. She had prepared a simple but delicious meal of dahl, chicken and vegetables, and invited a group of friends over to share our food. The meal went on until midnight. Both Sanjoy and Evelyn were happy: Evelyn because everyone declared the food delicious, and Sanjoy because he had offended everyone at the table and prompted a political argument that had us at each other's throats while he just sat and watched with a smile on his face. I had a big smile on my face too. It felt like I was home.

In many ways New York does feel like home. After London, it is the city I know best, having visited it countless times for business and pleasure. I know its streets, I know how to get around and I keep up to date with its restaurants and bars. I had based my first day on visiting three places I knew and loved and which represented the incredibly diversity of the city.

Katz's Deli, down on the Lower East Side, has been an institution in New York almost since it opened in the late nineteenth century and is most famous for one thing: a sandwich stuffed with pastrami – beef which has been spiced, brined and smoked before being steamed and then cut into thin slices and piled high between slices of rye bread. The bread itself is nondescript and acts merely as a delivery system for the incredible flavours and textures of the meat. With a little Deli mustard to dip it into and a plate of pickles at the side, each bite is like a taste of New York; it would never taste the same anywhere else in the world.

It is a hefty lump of protein, however, and as I had lunch reservations, I took the opportunity to walk from Katz's, on Houston Street, up to midtown Manhattan. By 1.30 I had walked sufficient miles to make space for lunch and sat in awe at the sushi station of master chef Naomichi Yasuda, one of the great eating experiences of New York, as Yasuda's hands move at lightning pace preparing piece after piece of nigiri or maki sushi for the five or so lucky people.

I particularly requested uni (sea urchin), unagi (freshwater eel) and onargo (saltwater eel) but was also presented with fatty tuna, scallop and salmon roe marinated in a blend of different soy sauces, which led to a mouthful of popping, mildly salty, fish eggs, which is hard to describe. I racked up a small bill of around $60 before heading off into the afternoon sunlight for a good long walk to prepare for what I knew was going to be a major supper.

The Kebab Café may be only a short hop by subway, but is

as far away from Yasuda as it is possible to get. On Steinway Street, in Astoria, Queens, it has, since I was first taken there in 2002, become one of my favourite restaurants anywhere, not just because of its food but also because of its Egyptian owner, Ali El Sayed.

It's a tiny restaurant, with a kitchen the size of a small soap dish, in which Ali produces some of the most delicious food I have ever tasted, with influences from across the Middle East. One of my oldest and best New York friends, Cathy Loup, had warned Ali that I was coming and, knowing my tastes, as I arrived, he came around the counter, put his huge arm around me and said, 'Here, Indian boy, have some brains'.

He handed me a piece of veal brain that he had just breaded and fried. It melted away on the tip of my tongue. This was only the beginning, and, as I caught up with Cathy, he began to bring out dish after dish from his Lilliputian kitchen. Roasted aubergine and beets, calf's brains, tripe soup, stuffed hearts, tongue dumplings, roasted marrowbone and, of course, some testicles. New Yorkers may be prone to hyperbole, but everything you hear about these three restaurants is true, and only in New York could they exist so happily together.

I had experienced two boroughs of New York on my first day. My second day was going to take me to the far reaches of a third, the Bronx. I wanted to get a taste of old-school New York and one of its oldest communities. Another dear friend, Sandra Levine, agreed to show me around, and I met her at Grand Central Station, now fully restored as one of the great landmarks of New York City.

We headed out on the short journey to Arthur Avenue, for many decades the primary Italian neighbourhood of New York. Sandra is the perfect companion: no one knows more than she does about the history of the people and buildings of the city. The area is not what it was, she told me: many of the original Italian families had moved out and were now being replaced with the latest influx, from Albania.

We mooched around for an hour or so, looking at the stores selling pastries, mozzarella and Italian meats, before we found our way to Dominick's Restaurant, one of the old stalwarts on Arthur Avenue. It was already bustling inside, and we squeezed into a place at a communal table.

Just as 'curry house' food in the UK bears little relation to food in India, so 'red sauce' American Italian bears little resemblance to what I was to eat later in Italy. That does not mean that it cannot be tasty, but this wasn't. Overcooked pasta in a heavy shrimp sauce was joined by a chicken scarpiello, which should have been a crispy, garlicky treat, but was stewed and rather nasty. With a glass of wine I did well not to spit across the room, the bill came to $40 – way overpriced. 'Because of your camera and your exotic accent', Sandra assured me. I knew they would both get me into trouble one day.

Italy's other great contribution to New York is the pizza. After I said goodbye to Sandra, I headed back into Manhattan to meet with two other friends, Beth Pizio and her husband, Peter Coughlin. They had been charged with trying to persuade me that pizza is not one of the most disgusting foods in the world, an onerous task because I am very much of the pizza as 'snot on toast' school and have expounded this theory on many occasions to any willing to listen, and plenty who weren't.

They had chosen a well-known place in Spanish Harlem called Pasty's, famous for its use of excellent ingredients. The room looked the part, and it all smelled wonderful. That's the thing, pizza often does. We started with a couple of passable salads, and I left the ordering in the hands of Peter and Beth. Two enormous pizzas arrived at the table, bubbling promisingly. One was topped with garlic, anchovies and basil, the other with fresh ricotta and sun-dried tomatoes. I was aware that two pairs of eyes were watching me expectantly as I helped myself to a slice from each. I wanted to like them, to have a Damascene conversion and to find yummy noises escaping from my mouth despite myself. But I just smiled politely and ate little more than the slice I had taken. Perhaps I am just wired incorrectly, but I don't get pizza, I suspect I never will.

I certainly get steak, however, and there is nowhere on earth like a Manhattan steakhouse – unapologetically masculine, wood-panelled walls, leather booth seating, enormous wine lists and even more enormous cuts of steak. If you ask most New Yorkers, however, they will tell you that the best steaks in New York are to be found not in Manhattan but across the Williamsburg Bridge in Brooklyn, at the legendary Peter Luger Steakhouse, which has been serving steaks from the same location for over a hundred and twenty years.

The Peter Luger porterhouse steak is the stuff of a meat-lover's dreams, dry-aged for at least twenty-eight days and richly marbled with fat to keep it succulent and juicy. There are other things on the menu, but it has never crossed my mind to order them. Strips of sizzling bacon are perfectly fine but just pass the time until the steak arrives cooked, rare to perfection, sliced for you in sizeable chunks, one end of the large plate resting on a bowl so the juices flow to a shining pool at the other. It is not your typical steakhouse – the room is utilitarian, the waiting staff famously grumpy and the wine list appalling – but it is worth it all for the steak.

I shared my meal with two friends from London who were in town. They both like their meat but were still full from break-fast, which left much of a porterhouse for three to me. I did not fail them and cleared the plate, gnawing the last flesh off the bone before mopping up the juices with an onion roll. They looked a little queasy, but steak this good, and its juices, are simply too good to miss.

A meal at Peter Luger could have been the perfect way to end my trip to New York, but my friend Cathy had other ideas and offered to host an *Eat My Globe* party for me. I readily agreed, in part because it would allow me to catch up with a lot of the friends I had not had the chance to see but also, more selfishly, because Cathy is a bloody good cook and, when she turns her attention to the large smoker in her garden, I have been known to do a little dance.

She had procured 40 lb of pork from Flying Pigs farm in upstate New York and, after rubbing it with French's mustard and spices, had left it to smoke gently for fourteen hours. I arrived early and helped her carry it up from the smoker and pull it apart into moist shreds ready to be served, making sure, of course, to sneak regular chunks of the charred crust for myself.

When the others arrived, all had brought wine and most had brought side-dishes or desserts, and there were soon about twenty of us making pulled pork sandwiches with Wonder Bread and pickles and tucking into cole slaw, collard greens and maca-roni cheese before we turned our attention to wonderful pies, cookies, brittles and gelato.

In the end I realized that Peter Luger would never have been the perfect end to my time in New York: this was. I was with some of my favourite people, eating some of my favourite food in one of my favourite cities.

No hyperbole there, it was just 'so New York'.

19

Mexico, Mi Corazón

I was not a fan of Mexican food before I set out on my journey, primarily because my only experiences to date had been of the cheese- and meat-heavy variety in London. I suspected that there had to be more to the cuisine of an entire nation than a handful of dishes resembling raw sewage, and posted about my intended journey on one of the food discussion websites. Almost immediately I received a reply from Cristina Potters, who lived in Mexico, pointing me in the direction of her excellent website Mexico Cooks.

I spent the best part of a day reading it, and it soon became obvious that not only was there a lot more to Mexican food than I had ever imagined but also that Cristina would be the perfect guide. When she suggested I fly down to Guadalajara to meet her and her partner, Judy, for El Día de los Muertos, the Day of the Dead, a major holiday in that region, I jumped at the chance.

We swapped many e-mails in the next six months, so when we finally met at Guadalajara airport, I already felt like I knew and liked her, a fact reinforced as she gave patient and detailed responses to some of my stupid questions about the country and its food as they drove me to my hotel.

The rumbling in my stomach reminded me that I had not eaten for nearly twenty-four hours, so Cristina suggested that we set off straight away for a supper of tacos at one of her favourite stands, Los Altos. It was already swarming with people when we arrived and joined the queue. Cristina instructed me on the etiquette of taco construction. We took our first two, containing shreds of goat meat on top of a double layer of fresh tortilla, layering them with salsa and chillies from communal pots before dousing them with lime juice. My first bite of taco was my first bite of real Mexico and made it pretty obvious that coming here had been the right decision. The combination of crunchy, gamey flesh with the lime juice and chilli was a taste that could not have come from any other country.

'I thought you might like these', Cristina smiled. 'They have a saying in Mexico. *Sin maís, no hay país* – without corn there is no country. You are going to see a lot of tortilla.'

I was already up and in the queue again. I wanted to try two more, this time stuffed with soft, melting goat brains. They were just as good, and I could had squeezed in even more but for Cristina rightly crying 'Enough' at the sight of me eating and distracting me with the thought of dessert from the helado shop next door. There men were busy stirring pots of Mexican ice cream, flavoured with local fruits, in tubs of salt and ice. I ordered a small scoop, the perfect way to round off the meal, and indeed the day.

Jet lag had me awake hideously early the next morning, and because I was not meeting the others until later in the day, I went out to mooch around on my own for a while. Guadalajara is a lovely city – small, with a population of around one million, and filled with charming squares, intriguing alleyways and beautiful churches. It was certainly interesting enough to fill a few hours until my body demanded breakfast. I followed the crowds and found myself in a small, central market, where counters were already crowded with people munching on more tacos, tamales and enchilada.

Above one stall I saw a sign that read 'Tacos de Tripa' and sat down on a high stool at the bar underneath. Tripe has always been a favourite of mine. At sixth-form college, while others played football at lunchtime, I would walk to Rotherham town centre and treat myself to a sandwich from a shop that sold only two things, one of which was tripe and the other slices of roast udder. Here the tripe was boiled and then deep-fried until crispy before being served on the inevitable warm tortilla. Having learned the technique from the night before, I scooped up plenty of fresh salsa from a bowl put in front of me and squeezed lime juice to wake up all the flavours. Another winning combination. I had eight of them, costing well under £1, before heading back to the hotel.

Cristina and Judy wanted to show me a local *tianguis*, a market set up especially for the Day of the Dead. Cristina explained that all over the central states of Mexico the day was taken very seriously. Shrines called *ofrendas* were erected to remember those who had passed away, and these markets were where people came to buy ornaments and food to decorate them. The Mexicans have a unique take on death, which is both joyous and slightly macabre, and the stalls were packed with skulls made of sugar, models of skeletons, known as Katrinas and Katrines, dressed in outlandish clothes and miniature versions of headstones and coffins.

As we walked, the smell of baking wafted towards my nostrils, and Judy pointed towards a man grilling traditional holiday cakes, gorditas de nata, made with cream. I wanted to order straight away, but Cristina held me back.

'Wait until he puts a new batch on', she advised. 'You have to eat them straight off the griddle.'

She was right, of course. When we did buy a batch, they were fresh, hot and rich, with a slightly soft centre that oozed out as we bit into them.

That evening, over dinner at a local restaurant, Cristina and Judy began to map out our plans for the next day's lunch of birria, from their favourite restaurant, El Chololo. Birria is a signature dish of the city and involves roasted meat, usually goat, served with a strong broth flavoured with dried peppers. In the case of El Chololo they braise the meat in the broth first before removing it and roasting to develop colour and a crisp texture, while the broth is served with bowls of hot salsa made of onions and coriander leaf, chillies and lime juice to spark up the flavours.

As we arrived at the restaurant early the next afternoon, a group of mariachi musicians were already unloading their instruments from a small mini-van. Resplendent in uniforms studded with sequins and topped off with wide-brimmed hats, they moved from table to table playing impossibly sad songs.

The restaurant was huge and already beginning to fill up as we took our table. Cristina told me that it was such a popular place that they prepare over seven hundred goats a week. In the huge open kitchen large pots of broth were bubbling and bowls of goat meat were being shredded and placed in the oven to crisp rapidly in the high heat. The moment the food arrived, I could see why the place was so popular. I took a tortilla, smeared it with the salsa and piled it high with savoury roasted goat meat before rolling it up and taking a huge bite. I didn't need any second lesson. In between bites of the tortilla I took sips from the broth, so spicy it brought tears to my eyes.

Cristina waved over the mariachi band and, after a brief conversation, she palmed the bandleader some notes. They gathered around the table and began to sing directly to me. In Mexico it would appear it is illegal to sing any song that does not make at least one reference to *mi corazón*, 'my heart'. This one, of course, did.

They got to the chorus: '*Volver, volver, volver.*' Judy leaned over. 'It means "return".' As I mouthed another bite of birria and thought about how much I had enjoyed my first few days in Mexico, I was pretty sure that was not going to be an issue.

From Guadalajara we made our way towards Cristina and Judy's home-town of Morelia. By the time we arrived it was early evening, and the five-hour drive had taken its toll on us all. I let my hosts head off to their house and checked into my hotel, which I was thrilled to see was described as the most romantic in Mexico. Unless I suddenly developed an unhealthy fetish for Big Red, that was also not going to be an issue for me.

When we met up again the next morning, the town was already awash with the vibrant blue and orange marigolds used to decorate the *ofrendas* for the Day of the Dead. People were beginning to dress in traditional costumes, and the shops had built their own shrines, on which they had placed loaves of the specially baked bread, pan de muerto. Cristina was the perfect guide. Her passion for the food of Mexico was obvious, and she was as excited about the opportunity to show it off to a guest as I was to eat it. At each turn she would point out something new and memorable, and for supper that evening she had a particularly unusual suggestion.

'We are going to church', she told me.

The construction of the church of the Immaculate Conception had been partly funded by a kermesse, a food court run by locals. It had become so successful that, even now the church was finished, the locals kept it going on a weekly basis, in the basement of the completed building as a way to bring the community together.

As we arrived, it was already packed with local families, whose members ranged in age from new-born babies to elderly men and women with walking frames. Around the edges of the basement makeshift kitchens had been set up, each serving food and refreshments. We had to shout to make ourselves heard through the happy din of chattering families, and the smells of fresh cooking were already thick in the air. We bought a book of vouchers to be used as payment and took a tour around to see what looked best and most popular, using the age-old theory that the stalls with the biggest queues must be the best. There was a vast choice, and we each took up a position in a queue regrouping ten minutes later carrying trays laden with fresh tamales, enchilada, quesadillas and pozole, which we washed down with large glasses of frescos. Mexican food is certainly not the prettiest I experienced on my trip, but it is never less than tasty and always made with great honesty and served with a generosity of spirit that makes eating in Mexico one of the great food experiences in the world. Here in the basement of a local church, as the locals milled about, pans clattered and fryers spattered, was one of my happiest meals of the trip.

Cristina was keen for me not just to taste the food but also to see other aspects of the Mexican way of life, to understand how families are so important to them and why family members come before anything else.

'Even if they are no longer alive', she said cryptically.

The next morning we drove out to pay our Day of the Dead respects at the cemetery of Tzintzuntzan, about 40 minutes' drive from Morelia. Half of the state of Michoacán had the same idea, and the roads were clogged with cars and pick-up trucks loaded with entire families.

Inside the graveyard all the headstones had been decorated, and some of the more recent graves were surrounded by large shrines with pictures of the deceased and a selection of their favourite things: records, books, foods and sporting equipment. As we walked through the graveyard, our respectful glances were greeted with genuine smiles of welcome. A crowd had gathered around an elderly priest who was blessing the shrines and, as he did so, the crowd began to sing a quiet, impromptu hymn. It was another of those moments on the journey when I had to pinch myself to remind myself where I was.

We returned to Morelia, and Judy and Cristina invited me to have lunch with them. It was my last day, and we had not yet had the chance to share a home-cooked meal. Their lovely home had a small but well-maintained garden, and we sat outside chatting while Cristina made chilaquiles, a dish made from eggs, day-old tortilla, onions and chilli. I was heading to Mexico City the next day, which was exciting, but I could not help but be a little disappointed that I would not be able to see it through the eyes of my new friends. They had shown me real Mexican food and introduced me to the people of this friendly and extraordinary country. A song was playing on the radio. It was the same one that the mariachi band had played at El Chololo. I sang along, '*Volver, volver, volver.*' I was definitely going to come back.

Mexico City has a reputation for pollution, corruption and for being one of the most dangerous cities in the world. It's all true: it is a dirty city, with some areas that make the Bronx look like the Upper East Side and a fug of car fumes so thick in the morning I could barely see past the end of my bulbous nose. I rather liked it. My opinion is, however, based only on a two-day stretch there, and I know I did not do it justice. I did not have time to leave the city and see the astonishing sights of the Aztec pyramids and I spent more time doing laundry than inside its many museums, art galleries or churches.

It will make people who know me from my past life laugh to know that I arrived from Morelia on a bus. I don't normally do buses. They remind me of my trips from Rotherham to London in the 1970s, when my parents would gleefully deposit me on a National Express coach, with an egg mayonnaise sandwich wrapped in foil, in the vague hope that my grandparents would be there to meet me at the other end. The coaches would often break down, leaving us stranded on the hard shoulder of the M1 for hours on end, and I can still recall the grim service stations with their perfume of old fat and urine.

Mexico's buses are another matter, however – smart, clean, efficient and comfortable. They have to be, because there is no train service in Mexico. Quite what that means Mexican nerds do on a Saturday when their mums make them a burrito and a flask of weak cactus drink, I don't know. But five hours after leaving Morelia, I was at my hotel in the heart of Mexico City.

Cristina had suggested I should visit the Mercado de la Merced. 'It's not like any market you will have seen before', she said when I suggested that I was already a little marketed out. So I took her at her word and almost as soon as I arrived, set out for the long walk from my hotel. I stopped for a short while in the Zocalo, Mexico City's main square, one of the largest in the world, built in the same spot as the centre of the Aztec city. It was already heaving with people. In one corner queues of people lined up in front of native Indians, who were cleansing them with ritual smoke. In another corner an early, open-air mass was being said, and in another, a rally supporting gay rights was being held by hundreds of men naked but for a picture of the Mexican president covering their crown jewels. I could have easily taken a seat in one of the surrounding coffee shops and spent a good few hours watching the spectacle, but I wanted to get to the market before it began to wind up for the day.

The Mercado de la Merced is in Avenida del Salvador, not the most salubrious part of town, and as I approached, I noticed that the surrounding streets were full of streetwalkers, their pimps and pushers. It was not in the slightest threatening, and I was more alarmed the closer I came to the market, seeing that every street stall was now prominently displaying pornographic DVDs, many of which were proudly announcing the involvement of animals you could also probably buy at the market.

I was pleased when I finally hit the market proper and ducked into the main hall. Cristina was right: it was an astounding sight. Everywhere I looked, mounds of fruits and vegetables towered from floor to ceiling, butchers were displaying hundreds – no, make that thousands – of carcasses swinging from metal hooks and the alleyways between the stalls had a constant flow of powerful-looking men pushing carts containing everything from churns of milk to cows' heads with their eyes still open and their tongues lolling from the sides of their mouths.

I walked around for two hours, taking well over a hundred pictures, always asking '*Puedo* – may I?' first. I was never refused. In one stall, where a man was busy feeding corn masa into a machine churning out hundreds of tortillas every minute, I was invited in to have a go myself. I found it harder than it looked to scoop the right amount from the dough and to keep the rhythm of feeding the machine. As I left, they presented me with a packet of the tortilla I had helped make. I had nowhere to keep them, so, as I left the market, I put them on a bus stop bench where I hoped someone might put them to good use. Pimps and pushers have to eat too.

Mexico City, as the capital, of course has representatives of the cuisine of all of the country's thirty-two states. I couldn't try them all, but Cristina had recommended one particular place, at the end of one of the lines on Mexico City's efficient metro system to the National University.

Ricardo Muñoz, the chef at Azul y Oro, is the author of *The Gastronomic Dictionary of Mexico* and considered as one of the finest chefs in the country. I can see why. Azul y Oro is a simple, canteen-like restaurant with a short menu. Everything about the place showed the benefits of good ingredients and attention to detail.

I wanted to sample a mole, one of the most famous of Mexican dishes, from the Pueblo region. Cristina told me that Ricardo made some of the best, and I ordered mole negro con pollo, asking for the version that came on the bone. Mole is made by slow-cooking a huge number of ingredients, including onions, chillies, peppers and, most famously of all, dark, bitter chocolate, which thickens the sauce and gives it depth. The version served at Azul y Oro was a revelation.

The chicken, while tasty enough, was just a vehicle for the sauce, glistening and black. It had layers of flavour I had never experienced before: heat, of course, but also smokiness, bitterness from the chocolate and sweetness from the onions. I scooped up every last bit with a wheat tortilla before, looking around to see no one was watching, picking the dish up and licking it clean – the perfect meal to end my time in Mexico.

20

Love Me Tender

They say it's an ill wind that blows no one any good, and, arriving in Buenos Aires, you understand what they mean. Just after the Millennium the Argentine economy collapsed and the currency plummeted to a fraction of its former worth; it has still not recovered. It's a horror for the locals, of course, but for the visitor it means that this elegant and sophisticated city can be enjoyed at a fraction of the former cost.

I discovered this soon after my arrival as I walked to the trendy district of San Telmo in search of the one thing that comes instantly to mind when one thinks of Argentina: big hunks of dead cow. The Argentines' obsession with beef mirrors my own. No country in the world eats as much beef per head as they do, and the quality of their steaks is rightly famous for its taste and texture.

I found my way to Desnivel, a local favourite, and at midday it was already buzzing with a mixed crowd of tourists and businessmen. The menu was short, and I chose a local morcilla, blood sausage, to begin with, followed by a bife de chorizo with batatas – sweet potato crisps. A half-bottle of the local wine came, as it always does in a *pingüino*, a small carafe shaped like a penguin. The blood sausage was interesting, with a softer texture than any I had tried before and with a hint of spice, but it was the steak that was an epiphany. I had tried Argentine steak before in London and New York, where great store is set by flying it in vacuum packs to maintain the freshness. Here it was the real deal, served juicy and rare, the beef prepared fresh from slaughter rather than being allowed to age.

The cut meant it was tougher than other steaks I had tried, but tenderness is a much overrated virtue. Too many people acclaim a steak for being 'so tender you could cut it with a spoon'. When was steak meant to be cut with a spoon? A good steak should not be as tough as old boots, but it needs you to put in as much work eating the flesh as the animal did building it. If you want soft food, go and eat an ice cream. This, suffice to say, was an excellent steak, the juices retained in the meat by the quick cooking on the searing grill. The bill, of about £4 for the whole meal, made it taste extra-sweet. As I said, it's an ill wind.

My only contact in Buenos Aires was a man by the name of Fernando Cwilich Gil, whom I had met at the London Bar Show. Unfortunately, he was flying out of town, but he had managed to arrange for me to have supper with his uncle and aunt the next evening.

I woke up late and spent the day clearing my head with one of my marathon walks through Puerto Madero, the new port development, with its expensive restaurants and bars. There was little to attract me to any of them, and instead I followed a group of workmen obviously taking a lunch break and found myself alongside the main canal feeding into the port. There I spotted a row of vans selling Buenos Aires's favourite street food, bondiola and choripan, which they were preparing on flaming grills. This was obviously where the men had been heading. I went for a bondiola and was presented with thick slices of beef in a crunchy roll, which I was invited to lace with chilli and chimichurri from small bowls on a table next to the van. The meat was even tougher than the previous day, but worth it, as each bite let out incredible flavour.

The effort required did rather exhaust me, and I needed little else to eat until that evening, when I joined Martin and Liljana Sánchez Gil at La Brigada, perhaps the most famous of the Buenos Aires parilladas, or steak restaurants, deep in the heart of San Telmo.

'I am sorry for the ridiculously early hour for supper', Martin said by way of introduction. 'I wouldn't normally even consider eating until 10 p.m.'

He explained that before my arrival they had already committed to attend a party and so had to fit in supper beforehand, even though, as Martin bemoaned, eating at an hour most Argentines would find shameful was going to play havoc with his digestion.

Martin took his meat incredibly seriously and, with very typical Latin American machismo, took control of the ordering without a glimpse of the menu. He summoned the waiter and began a long discussion about the cut of beef he wanted, exactly how long it should be cooked and what dishes were to proceed and accompany it. First, we were presented with a slab of melting provoleta cheese.

'You can tell how good a restaurant is going to be by the quality of its cheese', Martin said, wagging his finger at me to emphasize the point.

This was followed closely by some offal in the form of goat sweetbreads and chitterlings, fried to a beautiful crisp and sprinkled with salt. I was instructed to add five drops of lemon, no more and no less, to wake up the flavour before I was allowed to tuck in. Finally, the main event, the bife, a sizeable hunk, cut across the grain to give the most flavour. I tucked in, mentally marking it down as one of the great steaks I had tried. Martin chewed more slowly and with consideration, before looking up and saying, 'Passable'.

As I said, Martin takes these things very seriously indeed. In Buenos Aires, if meat is important, then wine is almost more so. Martin, determinedly in charge, ordered a spectacular Malbec from the Salta region, whose spicy damson notes served to bring out all the flavours from the meat.

Martin and Liljana insisted on picking up the bill and then invited me to join them at the party. As we arrived, a local singer was setting up to perform, and for the next hour she sang her heart out. Which is just as well, as every song, as in Mexico, contained the words '*mi corazón*' at least once. In sixty minutes the poor love had her heart stolen, stamped on, stabbed and broken in any number of painful ways. But she kept going back for more, so I guess it was her own fault.

Martin and Ljilana appeared at my side and asked me if I wanted a lift home. It was 2 a.m. How the hell did that happen? I had a taxi booked barely ninety minutes later to take me to the airport for my flight to Brazil.

I had been in the city only a couple of days and had barely scratched the surface. I had not even begun to think of trips to places outside the city, such as Mendoza or Salta, because of my tight schedule. Argentina was yet another country I would have to revisit. I was rapidly coming to the conclusion that *Eat My Globe* could become a full-time job.

21

A Painful Brazilian

My guesthouse in Salvador da Bahia was basic but beautiful, with blue tiled walls, spacious rooms and wide balconies. It was a welcome sight after a nightmare flight from Argentina, and, best of all, it was a few minutes' walk from the beach, the perfect choice for a few days of rest and relaxation, so necessary during a trip like this. I changed into my fetching three-quarter-length shorts and set out to explore, my backpack over my shoulder.

'You are not going out with that bag are you?' a voice from behind the reception admonished.

'Well, er, yes', I replied.

'I wouldn't advise it', he added. 'Just take enough cash for dinner and keep your camera hidden. There have been a lot of muggings recently.'

Once I went outside, I could see what he meant. Fear breeds paranoia, and I don't consider myself a particularly nervous tourist, but in Salvador I never really felt entirely safe. Not once in all my time there. I felt as though every eye was watching me and every person was viewing me as a potential mark or victim. It may have been unfair, but it was a feeling that never really left me.

It was great shame, as the beach area was indeed lovely: sands golden in the declining sun and the shorefront lined with men selling coconuts from which they swiped the tops off with worrying-looking machetes before inserting a straw for you to suck the chilled liquids inside. I dipped into a beach-front restaurant for supper, which consisted of deep-fried salt cod cakes, tough meat, rice and chips washed down with a Brahma beer and headed back to my hotel slightly dispirited about the thought of spending the next five nights looking like a walking dollar sign.

After a good night's sleep, however, I decided I was going to make a better fist of it, starting with a superb breakfast, one of the selling points of the guesthouse: fresh fruits, soft, warm semolina cakes, guava juice, hot bread and strong tea. I felt better already and began to strike up a conversation with a young Chilean woman called Macarena, sitting at the table next to me. She told me that there was going to be a big party in the Pelourinho, the old town, that evening with bands playing, drum orchestras and lots of dancing. She did not want to go on her own, so, despite my own aversion to matters dance-related, I agreed to join her.

After breakfast I set out to explore the city, without bag, of course. I must have walked about ten miles, from the beach area through the new town and down to the Pelourinho, which I had been chatting about at breakfast. I disliked it intensely. The buildings were in an appalling state of repair, and the Pelourinho itself was a depressingly ugly tourist trap with a hustle on every corner. I fought my way through the street pedlars and hustling cab drivers to the Elevador Lacerda, a huge elevator that linked the top of the city with the lower part. At the bottom was a market where you were able to sit and watch young men from the local projects performing capoeira, a distinctive form of martial arts developed by slaves under the guise of native dance. It is hypnotic and impressive – as, indeed, was the ability of the men performing to prise money out of the bystanders.

Around the edges of the market were stalls selling acaraje, small balls of black bean paste filled with peanuts or shrimp and deep-fried in dende, the local palm oil. I bought a small bag from one vendor, trying hard not to inhale the frankly noxious smells from the cooking oil. I took one bite and left the rest on the table next to where I was sitting for someone more desperate than me to eat.

It would be fair to say that up to this point Salvador had not impressed me, and I was beginning to regret my choice of both Salvador and Brazil as a stop on the journey. The evening proved to be more fun. Not that the town itself ever held any great allure for me, but that night, when I arrived to meet Macarena for the evening, I found that we had been joined by four others from the guesthouse. They were a good crowd and having far more fun in Brazil than I was. Being with them lifted my spirits, and it was an enjoyable evening as we headed up to the old town and joined in the party. It was a hell of an event, with live bands playing, drums sounding and deafening noise wherever you turned.

Soon after we arrived, our group was adopted by young local, Elton, who took us under his wing in the hope of getting a few dollars at the end of the evening for watching our backs. He was a good guy and led us to a large church in front of which a band was playing reggaeton, an irresistible combination of reggae and samba music. On the steps of the church a packed crowd was swaying rhythmically, and we fought our way through to a prime vantage point and joined them, even me, as we sucked down cans of cold beer we had bought from local vendors. As the clock struck midnight, Elton suggested that it was a good time to be heading back to the relatively safe enclave of the beach area and helped us all squeeze into a cab after we had gratefully pressed a few notes into his hand.

Having not had time to eat, all of us were starving and headed down to a seafront restaurant where we shared a moqueca, the large seafood stew made with chunks of fish, shrimp, coconut milk, peppers, tomatoes and lots of garlic. It came served in a traditional capixaba clay pot and bubbled away fiercely for minutes after it was placed in the table. We washed it down with far too many caipirinhas – lethal cocktails of cachaca, Brazilian rum, lime juice and sugar – before staggering back to the guesthouse at around three in the morning.

I wish I could say that this evening of fun changed my view of Salvador, but it didn't. It may have been the fact that I had no more than three hours sleep each night, because my room turned out to be Bed Bug Central, or it may have been that on one day I had at least three people try to pick my pocket as I walked along the seafront in broad daylight.

Or it may have been the fact that, on the whole, the food was grim. I may not have done it justice, but there appeared little to do justice to, and when it came time to leave Salvador, I did so willingly. I posted about my experiences on a food website and someone replied saying that, on their visit to Brazil, they felt like 'fish food in a shark tank'. I know exactly what they meant.

I had a layover in São Paulo before my flight to San Francisco. The airport was one of the ugliest I have had the misfortune to pass through, and as I slumped dejectedly on Big Red for the best part of twelve hours, I couldn't help but think there were other countries out there I should have visited instead. When my plane finally took off, I leaned over my neighbour and gave Brazil a very recognizable hand signal through the window.

22

Giving Thanks in Santa Cruz

The very first invitation I received when I posted about my planned trip on the internet was from a woman called Tana Butler, inviting me to join her and her extended family for Thanksgiving in Santa Cruz, California. I had no idea who she was, but reading her posts on the food websites, I smiled at what I saw. They were very funny, painfully honest, and she shared my innate ability to piss people off in cyberspace, though that is not difficult in these virtual worlds where there are people who are extraordinarily eager to find a reason to be pissed off at someone they have never met and probably never will meet.

I wrote back saying I would be delighted to join her, and over the next six months we swapped regular e-mails, so by the time I came to pick up my rental car and make the short drive from San Francisco, where I had spent a couple of days recovering after Brazil, I already knew I would like her.

I was wrong. I didn't just like Tana: I adored her. Sharp-witted, funny, vulnerable, open-hearted, generous and spirited, Tana is best described, in the nicest way possible, of course, as being mad as a bag of ferrets. From the moment she walked into the lobby of my anonymous hotel and greeted me with the words 'I hope you are feeling strong, honey, you have a 25 lb turkey to carry' I knew that she had not been kidding when she promised me an eventful Thanksgiving in Santa Cruz. But then, Santa Cruz is perfect for people like Tana.

The west of just about every country attracts the oddballs, kooks, crazies, waifs and strays and people who just don't fit in anywhere else. It is certainly true in San Francisco and Los Angeles, and here in Santa Cruz it was gloriously and shamelessly nuts and filled with the abundant energy that comes only from people who not only don't care what people think about them now but probably never did care in the first place.

The turkey was a big old bugger of a bird, putting to shame even the colossal ones that used to give their lives for the clan Majumdar's Christmas festivities. Tana informed me that we would be having two of them and then began to reel off all the other dishes that were being prepared by her and her friends for the meal. I made a mental note not to bother with the free breakfast of multi-coloured cereal in a polystyrene bowl at my hotel as I heaved the turkey into the boot of her car and then climbed into the passenger seat.

Tana turned to me. 'I am worried about taking you to my house. It's not at all fancy.' I made an exaggerated gesture of examining myself in the mirror, then turned to her and replied, 'I think it will be just fine. As far as I can tell, I have not suddenly turned into the Queen Mother.' Tana let out what I soon began to recognize as her trademark laugh, deep, rich and genuine. Any ice there may have been still to be broken was smashed to smithereens.

Her house was, as I suspected, warm and welcoming. More than that, it was a home, with a large garden, beautiful views towards the hills and littered with toys discarded by her irrepressible grandson Logan. For the next few days Tana made her home my home. As we pottered around the kitchen preparing food for Thanksgiving, with Louis Prima as our soundtrack, her husband, Bob, kept me topped up with wine and beer and Logan gave me regular updates on the fierce battles between the plastic figurines of knights and superheroes he was overseeing in the yard.

On my first night we enjoyed the simplest supper imaginable: roast chicken and mashed potatoes. Logan threw a tea towel over his small arm, bowed deeply in waiterly fashion and served up a dollop of potato to each of us as Bob carved the chicken into big slices. It tasted as good as anything I had eaten for a long time, and I said so, not caring how silly that might sound.

'It is because you are eating it with family', Bob said, and he was right.

I had eight hours of uninterrupted sleep that night for the first time since my return from Brazil. So by the time Bob came to collect me the next morning, I was up and busy tapping away at my computer. Tana too had been up since the early hours, fussing over her turkey, making her signature devilled eggs and getting up to her elbows in stuffing.

'I don't think the turkey is going to cook in time,' she wailed, 'the oven isn't working properly.'

The oven was, of course, working properly, and the bird looked like it was doing splendidly, turning to a glistening bronze colour as it cooked. I did what any self-respecting man would do in such a situation when there is so much to be done: I opened a bottle of wine, poured myself a large glass, despite the fact it was barely 11 a.m., and sat back in a comfortable chair to watch the fun. Of course, when called upon, I did a little bit of chopping here and a little bit of mixing there. But for the most part I just sat, drank, stole devilled eggs when no one was looking and enjoyed the spectacle.

When the turkey emerged from the oven, it did Tana credit: a gorgeous golden-coloured fowl with crispy skin, juices bubbling away merrily just under the surface. Tana had roasted the bird on top of its giblets to add extra flavour to the gravy and now went to toss them in the bin.

'What the hell are you doing?' I squealed in a high-pitched voice that would have troubled the neighbourhood dogs. 'They're the best bits.' She did not look convinced but reprieved the innards from their garbage bin dungeon and put them on a plate for Bob and me to nibble on while she got everything ready to transport over to the location of our supper.

We loaded up the car, and we headed over to her friend's home to find about thirty other people were there ahead of us, already sipping champagne and laying out plates on a long table. The amount of food was staggering: our bird was soon joined on the table by another. They sat next to mounds of salads, pristine white mashed potatoes, creamy dips, cheeses, smoked hams, sauces, cakes and pies. It was what my father calls 'a three-Zantac meal' and I was ready to dive straight in.

Before the meal, however, our host, Laura, took the opportunity to propose a toast, giving thanks for all the people who were there: friends, family and even the bald, half-Welsh, half-Bengali in the corner trying to pull a bit of skin off the turkey without anyone noticing. It would have been easy, being a stranger among such obviously close friends, to feel intimidated and uncomfortable, but that was never going to be allowed to happen and I was immediately part of this extended family.

It was a uniquely Santa Cruz occasion. Everybody seemed to be related to everybody else in some labyrinthine way that I never quite got to the bottom of. The women all referred to each other as 'goddesses', without any hint of irony that I could detect, and at the end of the meal guitars appeared and people began to sing songs that I suspect were about butterflies or saving whales.

Tana was entirely in her element, making sure that everyone had enough to eat and drink, taking photographs, punctuating conversations with that laugh of hers and, at the end of the evening, gathering a group to sing a gentle lullaby that sent Logan to sleep before Bob carried him out to the car for the trip home. In the middle of it all I sucked on the bone of a turkey wing and made a promise to myself that, if at all possible, I would return to Santa Cruz for Thanksgiving every year, even if they didn't want me.

Some things in this life are, as I said, a matter of trust. I had had no idea what to expect before I arrived, but I had loved my first Thanksgiving. I had eaten delicious home-cooked food and made a host of new friends. Best of all, I had met an extraordinary woman called Tana Butler, whose strengths and weaknesses, passions and prejudices, successes and failings are dealt with more honestly than just about anyone else's I have ever met. A truly human being and my new friend – that was definitely worth giving thanks for.

I spent my last couple of days in Berkeley, a short drive north from Santa Cruz. Thanks to the efforts of local resident and my good friend Alexandra Eisler, I had been able to secure a reservation at one of the USA's most famous restaurants, Chez Panisse, and also the company of two dining companions for the evening.

In the late 1980s, when I first began to eat out regularly, a reservation at a well-known restaurant would fill me with nerves and excitement. My very first visit to London's legendary restaurant Le Gavroche was preceded by three nights of sleepless tossing and turning as I thought about the meal to come, a state of unrest I had last experienced when I got tickets to see The Clash in 1979. My mother was less sanguine about me going to see Joe Strummer and the boys, primarily because I had sent her to buy tickets and she had spent over four hours dressed in a thick fur coat standing among a Mohican-wearing mob.

Inevitably, as I dined out more often, levels of anticipation died down, dampened by as many bad meals as good. By 2007 it would have taken something pretty special on the dining front to give me the shivers of my youth. A reservation at Chez Panisse did, however, give me a genuine thrill. It is an iconic restaurant and, since Alice Waters opened its doors in 1971, it has become one of the must-visit restaurants on any food traveller's itinerary in California.

I had something else to look forward to first, however, as Alexandra invited me for a pre-supper supper with her and her family at their house, not far from the restaurant. There had been an oil slick in the Bay area not long before my visit and, because of that, crab-fishing in the area had been suspended. So Tom, Alexandra's uncle, had driven down from the upper reaches of Northern California with an icebox stuffed to capacity with freshly boiled beauties, which were soon piled on the table ready for us to attack. With a sprinkle of Meyer lemon juice, some warm bread and mayonnaise to dip the flesh into, they did not last long. Just as I was sucking the sweet meat from a claw, which I am not proud to admit I may have stolen from the plate of Alexandra's seven-year-old daughter, she told me it was probably time for her to give me a lift to the restaurant.

My companions for the evening were already waiting for me and looking forward to the meal as much as I was. I had been fortunate enough to be given a tour of the kitchen that morning by one of the pastry chefs and saw the ingredients for our supper. This served only to raise the level of expectation again.

After all that anticipation, it is a shame to have to say that the meal was not just a disappointment but shamefully bad. Chez Panisse bases its meals on a set menu. You get what you are given, which means the success of your meal depends on two things: the quality of ingredients and the quality of the execution. The ingredients had looked good enough when I saw them being delivered earlier in the day, so heaven can only guess what they did to them in the kitchen. My heart went out to a plate of leeks, beets and pancetta that looked as though Jackson Pollock had puked on the plate.

It was followed by lamb smothered in a sauce so salty I could feel my blood pressure rise as I took my first bite and vegetables so mushy I wanted to look in the kitchen and see if my old school dinner lady had been flown in especially for the occasion. With a desultory cheese course and a bland dessert, our meal at Chez Panisse came to an end as we each handed over $110 with almost as little enthusiasm as had been shown in the service.

It was a disappointing end to the trip, but after one of my companions dropped me off at the motel, I began to make my notes. Berkeley may not have come up with the goods on this trip, the memorable crab dinner aside, but I had definitely had an unforgettable two months on the road with more food than it should have been possible and was probably sensible to eat.

I had been to four countries, over twenty cities. I had met old friends and made many new ones. I had experienced the down home charms of Texas and New Orleans and the urban glitz of Manhattan. I had experienced the outstanding hospitality of the West Coast and the frightening indifference of Brazil.

I was heading back to the UK now, to spend Christmas with my family and to have a much-needed break. I had another fourteen or more countries to visit, but they would have to go some to match the tastes and memories I had experienced so far.

God bless the Americas.

23

Three Men and a Still

'Of course I am not bloody all right, I am throwing up blood. In which universe is that considered being all right?'

Admittedly I was not at my best as I was driven in the early hours of the morning, across the island of Islay to its tiny Accident & Emergency department but, looking back, I was being more than a little harsh on my new friend, John Glaser. Even if the fact that I had spent the last few hours emptying my guts should have given him an inkling that all was not tickety-boo with me tummy-wise.

I am getting ahead of myself.

It was the half-way point of my journey, and I was knackered. I had gained about 10 lb in weight, and my bones had started to give a rather alarming 'crack' when I heaved Big Red onto my shoulders each morning. I had expected to be tired, but not to be quite so weary-to-my-bones exhausted.

As soon as I got back from California, my body rebelled. Before the journey I was always an early riser, up by six o'clock. Now I found it hard to get out of bed before midday. My body needed rest, and I allowed myself the luxury of slobbing out, waking up whenever I wanted, walking around my apartment unshaven, dressed only in a pair of sweatpants I found at the bottom of the laundry basket and flopping on the sofa to watch daytime TV, almost inevitably left tuned to the cookery channel.

I was shaken from my torpor a week or so later by the arrival of flight tickets for the next stage of the journey, to South-East Asia and India. I had to get back to work. There was accommodation to be booked and people to contact. I had another fourteen countries to visit, and all that gorging was not going to organize itself. Before I headed out on the next four-month leg of the trip, however, I had planned a few short trips closer to home.

Of all the people with whom I came into contact on the *Eat My Globe* trip, it seems strange that one of my favourites should have been not only one of the first people I met after announcing my resignation at work but also one who lives across town from me rather than across the world. A quietly spoken but intensely passionate American, John Glaser is, with his company Compass Box, by stealth turning the arcane world of Scotch whisky on its head. I first met him when I wandered into my favourite bar in search of a Martini and found him in the middle of a tasting with my friend the cocktail guru Nick Strangeway.

I was invited to join in and soon found myself sticking my nose into John's business as we sampled a range of his whiskies with names like 'Oak Cross' and 'The Peat Monster'. These, John explained, were pure malts – blends of whiskies made from combining only single-malt whisky, as opposed to the malt and grain mixes of what are known as 'blended whiskies'. It can be confusing stuff, but John's enthusiasm to debunk the mythic nature of Scotch is catching, and we were going to get on when he announced 'Making whisky is like making pornography. Both need good wood.'

John invited me to visit him at his offices so he could explain more about his company and what he was doing. It turned out to be a hugely enjoyable day, and at the end of my time with him, as we sat over a meal in the leafy courtyard of a local restaurant, John suggested that I should add Scotland to my itinerary, so I could see the sauce at source, as it were.

A couple of days later an e-mail popped up in my inbox, filled with lots of useful information and lots of useful contacts. Half-way through the e-mail was a line that said, 'Kilchoman – brand new distillery on Islay. Running a weekly whisky-making academy.'

This was perfect. Islay was home to my favourite whiskies, renowned for the dense taste of peat cutting through an almost soapy smell after it has been cut with a little water. It is unmistakable, and countless Majumdar meals have come to their natural conclusion with the gentle sigh of a stopper being pulled from a bottle of Laphroaig or Lagavulin.

I was soon booked on the Kilchoman course in December, days after I returned from the USA, and was thrilled to find out that both John and Nick had sculpted time from their hectic schedules to join me for the week. Thus it was that the three of us were to be found standing in the still room of Kilchoman on a cold December morning, the day after a rather frightening short hop from London via Glasgow to Islay's tiny airport.

Before we started work, there was obviously the important matter of a cup of tea to be had as we sat with the owner, Anthony Wills, and master distiller Malcolm Rennie. Anthony created the distillery in 2005 to sit alongside the other seven world-famous names on the island. Given that the spirit needs to age in barrels for at least three years before it can be called whisky, and given that it needs even more than that to take on the distinctive hue from its oak barrel containers, their first release would not be available until at least 2010. We would be helping to make the 'new spirit', a sort of 'proto-scotch' that is the result of the second part of the distillation process just before barrelling.

The process itself sounds simple but is a painstaking combination of short bursts of action coupled with long hours of watching and waiting for the end-result – a bit like having a baby, I imagine. Being a man of little patience, the watching and waiting would drive me around the bend, but it appeared not to bother Malcolm and his colleague Gavin in the slightest as they filled their time with endless cups of tea, slices of cake and amiable bickering. Once called into action, though, it was a different matter, and they soon had us hard at work.

Putting it simply (now listen carefully, this is an expert talking, I have a certificate to prove it and everything), whisky is made when barley is malted (heated to create extra starches), steeped in water three times (to create moisture and start germination), dried (to stop germination), in the case of Islay whisky over peat, mashed to produce a week beer-like liquid, and then distilled twice, the second time to produce the fine, pure liquid that is then barrelled to age into Scotch whisky. Simple in theory but allowing for endless variations, which give every distillery its own unique characteristics.

Malcolm and Gavin took great delight in giving us all the choice, back-breaking tasks to do. Prime among these was shovelling the grain from the malting floor to the mash tun, a job that took the three of us the best part of a morning and resulted in frayed tempers, aching backs and the creation of some very imaginative swear words as we got in each other's way and generally created havoc. At the end of our morning's labour, the two professionals came in to see if our efforts passed muster.

'Aye, you've no done bad', said Gavin casting an appraising glance at a floor cleaned of even the smallest grain.

I looked at them with new-found respect for having to do three times a week a task that had resulted in blistered hands, clothes wringing with sweat, and which had pushed John, Nick and myself as close to blows as we were ever likely to come. 'That's why', Gavin began with a gleam in his eye, 'we use yon machine over there. It makes it a lot easier.' He pointed to a shiny-looking mechanical beast in the corner. It was only the intervention of John and Nick that prevented me from re-creating Bannockburn on the malting floor with a large malting shovel and Gavin's head as props.

Over the period of the week we turned up diligently every morning to be given our tasks, but we were pleased to find out that the afternoons were going to be free, giving us time to explore the rest of Islay. One afternoon Nick suggested we visit the Islay Oyster Company, a farm whose bivalves are sought after throughout Europe as being some of the very best on offer. Which brings me back to the opening of the chapter.

Oysters and I have had a troubled relationship. We used to be madly in love, and I could and would devour dozens of the things at a sitting. Then we had a falling out, a major row caused by a dodgy one at a meal with a client during a trade fair. I did not heed the lesson and have occasionally tried to sneak oysters back into my diet, with the inevitable results. On one occasion, dining with TGS at J. Sheekey, London's most famous seafood restaurant, I gave in to a request to share the Assiette de Fruits de Mer and ate oysters primarily because he made loud chicken noises. A barb that no brother can leave unchallenged, even if you are both well into your forties. The result was inevitable, and I had two days off work to reconsider my position *vis à vis* the oyster. Nick used an altogether more subtle approach: yummy noises, and lots of them. As he downed half a dozen in less than five minutes, he made noises that suggested he was close to either death or orgasm.

'Go on,' he cajoled, 'you are never going to find one as fresh as this. Ever.'

He was right. These were as good as oysters are going to get. Just looking at them made me forget all that had gone before. Lady Oyster sucked me back in one more time, and it was lovely: a beautifully plump specimen that was taken from the water in front of me, cut open and sliced free from its shell. It was meaty and delicious, tasting slightly of the sea. It went down with a single pleasing gulp. Damn me, I had forgotten how good they were and, to top it off, I felt fine. Hallelujah, I was cured. A new, oyster-filled world opened up in front of me. Raw oysters, deep-fried oysters, oyster po-boys, oysters Rockerfeller. It was a miracle.

Cue mad rush, in the wee small hours of the next morning, to the little building the Islay folk like to call their local hospital and my less than friendly response to John's genuine expression of concern. After listening to the doctor tell me to drink lots of liquid and follow that up with the redundant suggestion that 'I probably would keep away from oysters from now on', I was driven home and sheepishly headed back to bed to spend the day sleeping fitfully and dreaming of salty vomit.

While I slept, John and Nick had spent the afternoon visiting some of the other famous distilleries on the island: Laphroaig, Lagavulin and Ardbeg. Because of John's reputation in the industry, they were treated royally and sampled tastes from some exceptional barrels, which they drank in as heartily as they did the astonishing scenery amid which the distilleries sit.

Being good sorts, however, the next day, our last, when I was feeling a little better and had managed to have a light breakfast of cereal, eggs (two), bacon, sausages, black pudding, tomatoes, mushrooms and toast, they suggested we go and revisit them so I could see them too. First, we had to head back and say our farewells to the good people of Kilchoman and to take a small multiple-choice test to see if we had taken in any of the information we had been given during the week. It ill behoves me to say who came out with top marks, particularly as John, in an act of incredible but unsurprising generosity, picked up the tab for the whole trip. So, all I will say is that the industry professionals did not fare well and I, well, I rock.

We moved from the still-room to the warehouse and tasted the new spirit. It is an odd experience, like looking at the photograph of someone you know well when a child. All the elements that make up their character are there, but in undeveloped form. The new spirit is clear for a start, the colour coming from time spent in the barrel and, in many cases, from the legal addition of spirit caramel. The hint of flavours to come are present too, but overpowered by the alcohol, which will reduce over the period of ageing.

After saying our 'goodbyes', we headed back out to visit the other distilleries. They were solid white structures stunningly situated between the rolling hills and the edges of the roaring sea. That night we sat in front of the flickering fire in our guesthouse and cracked open a few bottles from the distilleries we visited. As I sipped, Nick and John talked shop about the subtle differences between the distilleries we had visited and the scotches we were trying. For once, instead of being desperate to hear my own voice, I took the rare opportunity to listen to two of the most respected men in the industry sharing their knowledge. I learned a lot.

In fact, I learned a lot that whole week. I learned how my favourite whisky is made, and, because of that, it will never taste the same again. But, most of all, I learned I should probably keep away from oysters.

24

Immer Essen in München

Over the last few years TGS and I had begun a new tradition of January road trips to Germany, a country I had come to know very well over the years and had grown to love – both for the people and, perhaps more surprisingly, for the food. This time we chose Munich, and the first week of the new year we arrived at the city's impressive airport ready to hit a few beer halls.

Going on a short break is never an easy task for TGS. He is the organizer supreme and extreme. Even the shortest trip takes months of planning, and it was no great surprise, one day, to return to the apartment and to see him seated at the dining-room table surrounded by maps and guidebooks. His computer was already buzzing, and it was clear that he had begun serious investigation into the best München had to offer. That didn't alarm me; nor did the fact that that he had already begun to fashion his own rudimentary guidebook by slicing appropriate pages from all the others and sticking them together with pages he had printed from the internet.

I was used to that level of dedication and, to be honest, quite grateful. I had plenty to organize of my own, so to leave Munich in the hands of an expert was more than a pleasure. What did alarm me this time was the fact that he was also gleefully look-ing at a clip on YouTube, which showed the plane in which we would be flying to Germany. At this point I had to leave the room.

There is a method to his madness, however, and the moment we arrived at Munich airport TGS's notes pointed us straight in the direction of its own dedicated beer hall and our first impressive-sized brew, served with a local speciality of Grammelschmalz, a delicious dish of fat laced with chunks of ham and fried onions. Cardiologist-unfriendly it may have been, but it worked incredibly well with our first beer of the day.

The people of Munich – Bavarians, not Germans, as they are keen to remind you – do things with considerable gusto, and it is not hard to see why. Munich has the highest standard of living in the whole of Germany, and there are opportunities to enjoy one-self everywhere, from the cafés, bars and restaurants to the galleries, museums and parks. It is a truly lovely city, thanks mainly to its forefathers, who had the good sense to preserve the original plans for every building, which meant it could be rebuilt exactly as before after the destruction of the Second World War.

We were not there just to sightsee, however. TGS had drawn up a schedule and a map with, in big letters 'BEER' and 'MEAT' written at the top. He had drawn lines from these words to various places on a map of the city. I began to shiver, and not just from the cold. In Bavaria they take meat very seriously. The sausage is a religion, from the Weißwurst, on which the light of the noon-day sun must never be allowed to shine, to the Schweinswurst, which slips down all to well with a dark Dunkelbier.

They take their beer just as seriously. It is strong stuff, but because of the Reinheitsgebot, a series of ancient purity laws governing the brewing of beer, it is not as prone to give you a hangover. That is, of course, not unless you drink a tin bathtub full of it, as we planned to do.

In Munich the joys of beer and meat come together in perfect harmony in that greatest of all Bavarian institutions, the beer hall. Perhaps the most famous is the Hofbräuhaus, where drinkers from many nations flock to be served tall glasses of dark brew alongside frightening portions of food served by women dressed in dirndls, all the while being serenaded by scary-looking men in leather shorts pumping out oompah music on battered brass instruments.

As ever when we arrive in a new town on our travels, we became a bit over-excited and managed to work our way around about five of the best halls before early evening and found ourselves walking through the streets of Munich swaying ever so slightly in the rapidly chilling evening air. But our evening had not ended. If the daytime had been about beer, the evening was about spirits as a local friend, Stefan Berg, took us to bar after bar until everything became a blur. Being a good German boy, Stefan made sure that we stopped off at the Ratskeller for some food to soak it all up and deftly ordered plates of bread topped with thick spicy pâtés, mounds of mashed potatoes and, of course, lots more wurst. Despite that very necessary break between drinks, by two in the morning both TGS and I were reeling, and we said our goodbyes, heading off on uncertain feet towards our hotel.

I woke up five or so hours later to the sound of TGS drinking a bottle of water and having a quiet moan to himself. It took me a good fifteen minutes before I could persuade myself to open my eyes and, when I did, I regretted it immediately as shards of sunlight pierced my brain like needles. I squealed like a small child and dived back under the covers, making my all too regular pledge never to drink again.

And we didn't – well, not that day anyway. Instead we spent our time walking around one of the most beautiful cities in Europe and watching the people of Munich enjoy their weekend. Like so much the Bavarians do, the weekend's activities centre around food, and much of that activity involves the bustling Viktualienmarkt, where the locals come to buy their weekly groceries and to enjoy a plate of Weißwurst.

The Weißwurst is sacred to the people of Munich and only meant as a snack between breakfast and lunchtime because, as a fresh rather than a smoked sausage, it should not be kept more than a day. It is a glorious thing, made from veal, bacon and seasonings of lemon, mace and parsley in a clear porkskin casing. The locals like to eat their special sausage in a special way, deftly splitting the skin and sucking out the insides, which they eat with another of their other passions, Breze, a pretzel-like bread. It is not as easy as it sounds, and our attempts to prise the flesh delicately from the skins, accompanied by loud slurping noises, received cold looks from the neighbouring tables in one of the small market cafés.

We hurried through our meal and headed out to explore some more. TGS had a route figured out which took us around half the city and back to the hotel in time for a short, restorative nap to be fully rested for that evening's meal. He had also selected another beer hall, the legendary Altes Hackerhaus. Here, as in all beer houses, the menu is predicated on one thing, pork. There are other items on the menu, but you come here for pig in many forms: in my case, a plate of Spanferkel, suckling pig with creamy, slow-cooked flesh hiding its light under a bushel of crackly skin. For TGS it was perhaps the most challenging dish of all, the Schweinshaxen, pork knuckle with the same crackly skin but tougher meat, coming, as it does, from an older animal.

As though hunks of meat the size of a basketball were not alarming enough, alongside them sat both potatoes, which Germans eat by the sackload, and, more worryingly, a baseball-sized dumpling made – oh, what a surprise! – from potatoes as well. It was an impossible task. We both polished off our meat down to the bones, but the dumplings remained untouched, sitting there wobbling and viewing us with contempt for having such paltry appetites. They were right: we didn't even have room for strudel, when every other man, woman and child in the place was tucking into pudding and ladling extra cream on top. What kind of girly men were we? Shamefacedly, we paid our bill and slunk back to the hotel, where we spent the night comparing stomach gurgles and mainlining Zantac until the early hours.

For at least ten years my friend Isabelle Fuchs had had the considerable misfortune to sit opposite me at trade fairs as I tried to sell her gift books. She was surprisingly affable about the whole thing and over the years even bought a few from me. When she heard about *Eat My Globe* and about my trip to Munich, she offered to spend an afternoon showing us her home town.

Although originally from across the border in Austria, Isabelle loved Munich, and it showed as she strolled with us through the Englischer Garten, the beautiful green lung of the city and one of the biggest parks in Europe. It showed as she took us to her favourite beer hall and introduced us to a Schnitt, a double-strength shot of beer served in small measures with an enormous head of foam. It showed as she sat across from us at supper and ladled spoonfuls of Saures Lüngerl, a stew made from calf's lung, onto our plates and smiled as we nodded in delicious agreement that the addition of vinegar to the sauce cut through the fatty meat perfectly. And it showed when she looked at us with an equal measure of disappointment as we pushed our plates away at the end of the meal and said, 'But you have not touched your bread dumplings'.

25

Rotten Shark, Rotten Weather

If possible, Iceland has an even worse reputation for food than Britain, and it would not have been in my plans but for an intervention by my friend Magaret 'Magga' Kristiansdottir. Magga managed of one of my favourite bars, which she ran with ruthless Nordic efficiency. At the end of an evening I often found myself chatting to her over a well-made cocktail. The day I handed in my notice, I dropped in to tell her my news. She turned and gave me one of her ice-blue stares and said, 'Come to Iceland. You can eat sheep's head.'

Now, if anyone else had made that suggestion, I would have made it very clear that I would rather put my John Thomas in a vice. But as it came from Magga and after a Martini, I found myself thinking it might just be a good idea. Which is how I found myself at Reykjavik airport in January wondering whether my testicles would descend from my torso ever again.

The cold obviously did not bother Magga; nor indeed did it bother her best friend, Erla Guðrún, who was busy rummaging around for cigarettes in the glove compartment of her battered old Nissan as I sat there hoping my nose would be the first thing to fall off. When we finally got going, they pointed the car not towards Reykjavik but in the opposite direction, towards a supper that I was told was going to be in the tiny town of Stokkseyri. Magga promised me the restaurant there was one of her favourites in Iceland.

The ride proved to be a hair-raising slalom up hills and down slopes in increasingly thick snow until we finally pulled up in front of a picturebook-pretty restaurant called Pjorubordid. Magga explained that it was famous for serving one thing: bowls of crayfish called 'village lobster', dressed only in melted butter and served with sweet new potatoes.

If the cold had nearly caused me to have a heart attack, then the prices of the drinks almost finished me off. I realized the small beer I had ordered was going to cost £10 and a bottle of wine that I would turn my nose up at the local supermarket was going to come in at £40. I would have snorted beer through my nose in disgust, but it was too expensive to waste.

Magga explained to me that the high prices of alcohol in Iceland came about for two reasons. The first is obvious. It is a tiny country, with a population of only about 300,000, so just about everything has to be imported. The other reason was the prohibitive policies of successive Icelandic governments, who had only allowed the overturn of prohibition laws within the last twenty years. Whatever the reasons, I stopped chugging and carefully nursed the remaining precious liquid until our food arrived. When it came, the smell on its own was enough to make us fall on our plates, and we were soon ripping the shells of small, incredibly sweet seafood and giggling happily as the butter from the dressing ran down our chins. When Erla declared that she could not possibly finish her bowl, I dived in before anyone could say 'locals hold back'.

Erla had decided to decamp for three days to her boyfriend's place and leave her entire flat back in Reykjavik to me. On arrival, I fell asleep almost immediately, and I awoke the next morning to find a thick layer of snow across the city. Pleased that I had brought a thick hat to cover my wing-nut ears and my non-slip walking shoes with me, I ducked out to meet Magga.

Reykjavik is a small but buzzing town. Prosperous and neat as hospital corners, the people too seemed very smart and content with their lot as they wandered around designer shops and the myriad coffee bars on a Saturday morning. Magga, however, wanted to take me for 'a taste of real Iceland', which, she suggested intriguingly, could be found at the bus station. I followed along behind her, trudging through the ever thicker snow drifts until we came, as promised, to the local bus stop, where at the corner was a brightly lit café with a larger than life-size picture on the outside wall of the owner proudly holding a plate of food. Inside, as we shook the snow from our boots, I was instructed to sit down as Magga went off to order.

She came back beaming broadly, as she placed a tray on the table containing a bottle of lurid orange drink, a can of malt tonic and half a sheep's head on a plate. 'It's called a swidd', she announced matter-of-factly, blissfully unaware that I was engaged in a staring contest with the one remaining eye in the sheep's head and that I was losing.

'You drink Christmas ale with it', she added as she opened the bottle of orange pop, mixed it with half of the can of malt drink and handed me a glass of the murky result.

I took one sip and pushed it to one side, turning my attention to the sheep's head in front of me. With an encouraging nod from Magga, I tore a chunk off from the jowl. It was nowhere near as bad as I expected: fatty and with a slightly charred taste from where, I was told, the fur is singed off before boiling. I didn't even balk when Magga suggested that I eat the eye, which popped pleasingly in my mouth like meaty Space Dust. Magga was in her element. After we had removed most of the flesh from the skull, she picked the whole thing up, prised open the jaw-bone and began to chomp on the tongue.

'It's the best bit', she mumbled, globs of fatty lamb splattering her face. All this and she could mix a Martini too. She munched happily for half an hour until the bones were picked clean and then wiped her chin on a napkin, before telling me she had something more important to do and heading off into the snow, leaving me alone with the fleshless grinning skull of our lunch.

Even with one of the highest standards of living in the world, the weather makes Iceland a hard place to be in the twenty-first century. God only knows what it was like in times past, when, for huge chunks of the year, it was isolated from the rest of humanity. It is for this reason that Icelanders developed a food culture that is considered to be one of the most challenging anywhere.

I learned all about this on my last evening as Erla took over the reins, showing me around on a short driving tour around the city – including a visit to the presidential residence. Erla announced proudly that in Iceland everyone has the constitutional right to make an appointment to see the president if they have something they wish to discuss. I was delighted to see that the only security was a small sign saying 'Please Don't Pass This Point If You Don't Have An Appointment'. Just try that at Downing Street.

Erla's main task, however, was to explain to me all about the Thorrablot, which she translated as 'Thor's Feast'. She explained that, during the harsh winters, fresh food was almost impossible to find and people lived off the fish and meat they had caught during the warmer months and preserved by smoking and pickling. At the end of January, in the depths of midwinter, a sacrificial feast was held in honour of Thor, and people came together to eat, drink and sing. When the Vikings were converted to Christianity, the festival was banned, but it had experienced a revival during the last couple of centuries as Iceland struggled for independence and clung to emblems of its past.

Now it is a regular part of the calendar, and shops are filled with traditional foods for the feast. I wanted to take some back for TGS, so Erla pulled into the lot of a large market and took me inside, where a section had been set aside for Thorrablot goodies. It's challenging stuff all right. Sour ram's testicles, roast puffin and seal flipper obviously caught my attention, as did blodmor, the local version of blood sausage. But there was one item in particular I was looking for: hákarl, rotten shark meat.

With its strong ammonia stench I can understand now why many tourists, including me, believed the folk tale that the curing process involved people peeing over it. Quite how the Icelanders came up with the notion of burying shark meat for three months to extract from the flesh the poisonous uremic acid, used for flotation, I am not sure. But the end-result is chunks of dried, horribly pungent white flesh, to be downed in one go with a shot of brenivin, the local sesame-based hooch.

It was undoubtedly the single most unpleasant thing I have ever put in my mouth, worse than rat or dog and much worse than cod sperm sushi. I bought a small tub to take home, along with a bottle of the brenivin and some blood sausage, and presented them proudly to TGS. Six months later they all remain untouched and unopened, sitting threateningly at the back of the fridge. Come back in a few years time, and they will still be there.

26

Sawadee Ka

Three days after my return from Iceland I was off again, this time on one of the longest legs of the journey: three months in South-East Asia and India on a trip that would take in six countries and nearly twenty cities. But after a few weeks back in Europe, I was itching to be off again and ready to discover more amazing food.

My first meal in Thailand could not have been more simple and delicious: a plate of fried rice and vegetables cooked in front of me at a stall in a small street market in Bangkok and served for less than the price of a daily paper back in London. I knew immediately that I was going to fall under the spell of this beautiful country. My favourable impression stayed with me until I left a short few days later. It was a feeling that is hard to explain unless you have been to Thailand and experienced the genuine warmth of its biggest resource, the Thai people. Energetic and passionate, they were also one of the most genuine and gentle nationalities I met on the whole trip. I never lost the impression that they were being utterly sincere when they greeted me in the traditional way: 'Sawadee ka.'

Thailand has its difficulties too, of course, particularly in the capital, with similar problems to every developing nation: pollution to rival that being spewed into the air by China; a chaotic transport system, even with the relatively new Sky Train; and worst of all, the huge level of poverty and with it the attendant vices of drugs and prostitution. Despite this, you can't help thinking that many of Thailand's problems are caused by foreigners, the expats who still treat the country, and particularly the capital, as a playground where just about anything goes, and the visitors who flood in to take advantage of loopholes in the laws against sexual tourism.

My guesthouse was in Sukhumvit, close to smart shops, bars and restaurants. The opportunities for eating were endless. Unfortunately, Sukhumvit was also the area where Bangkok's dark side reared its ugly head, as I found out the night of my arrival.

I had made a reservation for an introduction to royal Thai cuisine at Ban Kanitha, a well-recommended restaurant close to my guesthouse. I sat outside in their small garden and was presented with a fiery salad of bean sprouts and basil in which raw shrimp had been 'cooked' in a mixture of lime juice, chillies and fish sauce. As I gulped on a cold beer to take the sting from my mouth, my next dish arrived – a plate of small soft-shell crab, each of which had been deep-fried in a light batter so that it could be eaten in one pleasing, crunchy bite. Next to it, the waiter placed a pad thai, perhaps the most famous of all Thai dishes, comprising rice noodles stir-fried with eggs, chilli, vegetables and chicken. Every taste of each dish was a revelation to me and reminded me why I was on this journey.

On the walk home I took a detour through one on Bangkok's more infamous streets. Soi Cowboy was lined with girly bars, apparently all filled with fat, ugly European men draping girls young enough to be their daughters on their knees as they negotiated the cost of their evening's entertainment. A few of the girls called out to me, 'Come, buy me lady drink' or 'You want massage?'

Their lips formed thin smiles, but their eyes were blank behind the bars of this most vile profession. It was my first experience of Thailand's seedier side, and it made me as angry as it did nauseous. I went to sleep with the sounds of Sukhumvit filtering through my window and those small, sad smiles of the small, sad girls filtering through my jet-lagged dreams.

I had marked a number of Bangkok landmarks on my map as places with good eating potential. Chatachuk market was already heaving when I arrived at 8.30 a.m., after a ride on Bangkok's efficient Sky Train. After exploring for an hour or so, I quelled my hunger pangs by following my nose, which led me to a small stand selling chicken, which was being dusted and deep-fried. I am a sucker for fried chicken, and this was fabulous stuff with crunchy skin and sweet, moist flesh and a powerful dip of soy sauce laced with chilli.

Crunchy food is a bit of an obsession for the male members of the clan Majumdar. As a child, when my mother roasted a chicken, she and my sister would help themselves to the plump breasts while the four men would fight over the bones and the crispy skin, which we would reduce to nothing but a pile of saw-dust. My mother would have been proud of my efforts on this day, as was the owner of the stall, who nodded approvingly as I left nothing but a few shards of bone at the end of my meal.

The humidity by now was almost unbearable, and I made my way to the air-conditioned comfort of one of Bangkok's extraordinary shopping malls, Siam Paragon – one of the largest I had ever seen, with luxury car dealerships on the third floor. Even better, it had an excellent food court. Quite unlike the grim versions back in the UK, this housed a selection of bars and self-service restaurants that would satisfy the needs of a small town. An army of chefs was preparing food freshly to order, and after pre-paying I was able to return time and again to fill my tray with bowls of tom yam soup, crab cakes and belly pork with glass noodles.

Before I left Bangkok, I wanted to fit in some sightseeing. The next morning I used Bangkok's efficient boat service to criss-cross the Bangkok river from Wat Pho to Wat Arun and back to the Golden Temple, before ending up at the Royal Palace. It was thronged with people dressed in black, and much of the palace was cordoned off.

I had not really kept up with news, so I made my way to

an information booth to find out what was going on. Princess Galyani Vadhani, the sister of the king of Thailand, had died a few days earlier, and the whole country was in mourning. The Thais treat their monarchy with great reverence. There are severe penalties for showing disrespect to the King, and simple customs such as standing for the national anthem in a cinema are universally adhered to. The dignified displays of mourning and affection for the deceased princess were genuinely moving. It did mean, however, that my plan to spend the afternoon in the Royal Palace had to be abandoned. I dug out my map and realized that I was only a short ride in a tuk-tuk, one of Bangkok's frightening, but cheap auto rickshaws, from my chosen spot for lunch.

Chote Chitr is a small restaurant with a big reputation. Its walls were covered with reviews both national and international raving about the simplicity and freshness of the food. When I arrived, a handful of tables were already occupied by local office workers, but I was able to slot in to a table near the kitchen, where I could watch the food being prepared. After ordering a cold Tsinga beer, I asked the owner to make my choices for me, as I do often if, quite frankly, I don't know what the hell I am doing.

I was presented with three beautiful-looking dishes: a salad of banana blossom served with seafood and chicken and spiked with the sharpness of tamarind; mee krop, a dish of fried, crispy vermicelli mixed again with chicken and soured with Thai citrus fruit; and finally a fiery red curry made with slices of duck, Thai basil and lime leaves.

That evening, my last, I wanted to try another of Thailand's classic dishes, the green curry. The versions I had tried in the UK had always left me thinking that there had to be more to this popular dish than a lurid green sauce and chunks of chicken. With the help of the receptionist at my guesthouse I found my way to another small street market and sat in front of an elderly woman as she prepared my supper. Behind her another woman was grinding the ingredients for the sauce, the scent of chillies, shallots, garlic and galangal filling the air as she pounded them in a mortar and pestle. The cook tossed chicken in a wok with a little oil before adding the sauce to spit away its rawness for a few moments. She poured in two ladles of coconut milk and allowed it to sit bubbling away for a few seconds before spooning it into a large bowl, which she placed in front of me with a plate of rice and some limes. The tastes were incredible. Sparky with lime, fiery with chilli and savoury with garlic and shrimp paste. I cleaned the bowl to the last drop of sauce.

It was exactly the kind of meal I had hoped to eat in Thailand, exactly the sort of meal I had hoped for when I first set out on the journey. I had been looking for the chance to find out what these famous dishes, so often served in the West but neutered by bad ingredients and lack of soul, taste like when they are made properly and with care. I could not have asked for a more perfect end to my short visit to this remarkable country.

27

Call Me Ismail

'Darling. It's too spicy, too spicy.'

Chef Ismail Ahmad picked up the plate of fish heads from the table and handed it back to one of the chefs with a shake of his head.

'You see, darling,' he said, turning back to me, 'if it is too spicy, all you get is heat and none of the flavour.'

I was standing in the kitchen of Restaurant Rebung in Kuala Lumpur, Malaysia. I had been invited to spend a day with Chef Ismail as he and his team prepared a buffet of over forty dishes taken from the nearly four hundred items in the chef's traditional Malay repertoire. Standing next to me as we watched this force of nature at work was Lex Ster, an irrepressible nineteen-year-old blogger who had offered to show me around her home city.

She told me about Rebung and about Chef Ismail, one of Malaysia's best-loved chefs and TV personalities. It took a while to figure out what she was on about, not because her English was bad – it was impeccable – but because, being nineteen, she spoke mainly in text-speak and had not yet developed the ability to breathe between words. We had already been on an eating tour through Jalan Petaling, Kuala Lumpur's impressive Chinatown, and now we were in PJ State, at one of her favourite places for chicken rice. I was eating on my own that night and had asked her for some suggestions.

'Rebungisawesome thechefisreallyfamoushere anditserves thebest traditionalMalayfood inthecity. LOL☺'

Or something like that. She also decided at this point that she should start calling me 'Uncle'.

'AnotherMalaytradition   foranolderman. LOL☺', she smiled knowing that she had turned my self-image from vibrant independent traveller to withered old man in one easy sentence.

I took her at her word about Rebung, however, and used Kuala Lumpur's shambolic public transport to find my way up to Bangsar for supper on my first evening in the city. I had arrived just as they were opening and was shown to a table inside and given a menu. I ordered a plate of kway teo bandung, a soupy noodle dish, which, although pleasant, gave little reason to think the journey from my hotel had been worthwhile.

'Darling, what are you eating?' a friendly voice boomed out.

I looked up to see Chef Ismail smiling at me, his eyes shining merrily through thick spectacles.

'Didn't you want to try the buffet? It's famous darling. It's famous.'

He beckoned me to follow him to the outside terrace, where by now a vast array of dishes had been laid just out of my view. My heart sank. It all looked and smelled wonderful, but I was already full.

'Don't worry, darling,' he said, pouring me a bowl of clear chicken broth, 'have this and come and talk to me.'

As we chatted, I told him about my trip.

'Well, you must come back on Saturday and you can spend the day with us in the kitchen', he waved his hand as though there was simply no other solution. It was too good an offer to turn down: the chance to watch a star chef in action and to learn more about the traditional Malay food of which he was so proud. After giving me a bear hug, he returned to the kitchen and I finished my broth to the last nutritious drop and set off back to the hotel.

I was only staying one night in Kuala Lumpur before flying directly to Penang to visit some of the famous hawkers' markets there before they closed for Chinese new year. I would be back in Kuala Lumpur on Friday night, perfect for returning to take up my invitation at Rebung.

Malaysian food is a magnificent combination of its immigrant history. Authentic Chinese sits happily alongside a fusion with Malay cuisine and the same is true for Indian food, where excellent north Indian tandoor cooking can be found alongside a uniquely Malay take called nasi kandar, which I went searching for as soon as I arrived in Penang.

The name originates from the Malay word for 'balance'. Hawkers used to carry pots of curries balanced on poles on their shoulders, but now street stalls have taken their place, with trays of rice, curries, fried chicken and seafood in front of them, from which you choose, having them spooned over the rice, so the sauces combine to a rich amalgam – all to be mopped up, of course, with a freshly cooked roti. It is gloriously messy but deliciously good fun as you eat with the right hand, clearing the plate and licking your fingers as clean as possible.

That evening I headed to one of Penang's famous food courts to make sure I sampled some of the local Chinese specialities before everything closed down. Already they were gearing up for the big day, with red banners everywhere and men in dragon suits frightening the kids. I selected a handful of stalls and came back to my seat with a mixture of Malay, Chinese and local nyonya dishes.

I had chosen Chinese char kway teo – flat fried noodles stir-fried with vegetables and seafood, which were traditionally cooked in pork fat but now increasingly, because of an increasing Muslim population, cooked in oil; a bowl of asam laksa, noodle soup, topped with chunks of fish and soured with tamarind; and finally popiah, a fresh spring roll, spread with hoisin sauce and filled with egg and been sprouts. All very different and representing some of the many cultures of Malaysia, but they sat together as happily in my stomach as they did on the plate.

I was shattered and anticipated a good night's sleep. Instead, I spent the night being bitten by bed bugs and had to change my room twice until I found a mattress that was not infested. In the morning I counted the bites: there were over 150 of them, and one, on the side of my head, had swelled up until I looked like a lollipop on a stick. To make matters worse, when I headed out covered in cream to stop the incessant itching of my spots, I realized that I had my dates wrong and most of the shops and restaurants were already shut for the new year. Things began to look bleak.

I found a Malay Indian *mamak*, which was open and had a breakfast of roti canai, a Malaysian staple brought over by immigrant workers from India: flat bread made with egg, flour and ghee (clarified butter), it is eaten only in the morning, with a bowl full of delicious thin lentil dahl, and is incredibly addictive. I ordered four of them before I had to push myself away from the table.

Although many of the shops and restaurants were shut, there were plenty of things to distract me during the next two days. During the evening, however, it was more difficult to pass the time and, after I had eaten in one of the few open places, I would head back to my hotel to write, hoping that I would not get eaten myself. I was pleased when the time came to fly back to Kuala Lumpur.

I had invited Lex to join me on my visit to Rebung. When we arrived on Saturday morning, things were already getting under way and Chef Ismail's restaurant manager, Alfred, was busy organizing the kitchen, which was laid out in traditional Malay home style, with sides open to the air and large steel woks placed on ferocious burners. There is relatively little stir-frying in traditional Malay food; slow cooking is used instead, to bring out the flavours of foods preserved by drying and salting.

There's plenty of fresh stuff too, and soon the buffet was being stocked with large bowls of raw vegetables to crunch on, salads made of banana flower hearts, aubergines covered in fiery sambal, fresh fish grilled on banana leaf or rubbed with turmeric and fried in palm oil and beef and chicken cooked in fiery sauces – more than forty dishes in all chosen from Chef Ismail's repertoire.

People had begun to arrive, and Chef Ismail, happy with what was happening in the kitchen, moved to front of house to greet the guests. Seemingly everywhere at once, Ismail was greeting guests as they arrived, making sure to flirt shamelessly with all the elderly ladies, ladling out bowls of soup to take to each table and bringing plates of new dishes hot from the kitchen.

'Try this, darlings. Do you like it? OK, let's put some on the buffet.'

It was more like attending a large family dinner party than going to a restaurant. Ismail beamed at the noisy chatter and sounds of appreciation from every table.

'That's the way I want it, darling', he told us. 'This is food my grandmother used to cook. It's family food.'

After hours of watching the food being prepared, I was starving – all the more so as I had missed out before. We joined the queue and loaded our plates with fresh popiah, curries and salads – all to be eaten, of course, with our right hands.

'Ihadbreakfastalready butthisissogood Icouldjustkeepeating. LOL☺', Lex mumbled through her umpteenth spring roll. I did not understand a damn word she was saying, but I knew exactly what she meant.

'Thanksfor askingmealong☺', she smiled.

'No problem, love. What are uncles for?'

28

Crouching Down for Pho with Uncle Ho

I am happy to share with you a very successful technique for staying alive in Hanoi, Vietnam, when confronted by the thousands of motor cycles that fill the streets and shoot down the alleyways at an alarming speed twenty-four hours a day. You can thank me when you go there.

Never be ashamed to use a local as a human shield.

The locals have in-built instincts about when to cross a busy road and at what speed. If you cross when they do, you have a chance. If they get it wrong, at least it is them who will be hit first. I am not proud, but I will admit that if it is between me and a doddery old woman in the road survival stakes, granny's going down.

My quirky guesthouse in the Old Quarter of Hanoi appeared to be the Vietnamese equivalent of Boys Town, with half the male teenage population of the city asleep on blankets laid on the floor of the reception. I left Big Red and went straight out for something to eat, immediately bringing into play the survival technique above, while scooters shot either side of me as I walked along the alleyways towards Hoan Kiem Lake in search of breakfast.

Vietnamese food has become increasingly popular in the West in the last twenty years. In part this is due to massive emigration during and after the Vietnam War, which brought sizeable expat communities to America, France, the UK and particularly Australia, and with them came their cuisine. But more than this, the light, clear flavours of Vietnamese food, combined with its use of fresh ingredients, small amounts of protein and little fat fits well with the current Western obsession with healthy eating.

The most famous dish of all is pho, a noodle soup, which is good any time of the day but a must for breakfast. Pre-cooked noodles are placed in a bowl with slivers of meat or seafood, sprinkled with spring onions and fresh red chilli and then topped off with ladles of hot beef or chicken broth. As I walked down through the Old Quarter, the air was already filled with the smell of pho being prepared and, using the trusted adage that the best and safest street food is to be found at the busiest places, I selected a crowded spot, pulled up a small plastic stool and pointed to a bowl of beef soup, indicating that I wanted the same. Less than a minute later, I was presented with a steaming bowl filled to the brim and topped off with a freshly cracked egg softly poaching in the hot broth. Every spoonful had layer on layer of flavour and texture. I spiked the broth with chilli paste and added a dash of fish sauce for salt. It was as good a dish as I had tried in a long time, and I knew that for my few days here breakfast would be taken care of.

No one would ever call Hanoi an attractive city. It suffers the attendant problems I had seen in so many countries on the trip: pollution, dirt, poverty and decaying infrastructure, in this case made worse by the strict Communist regime, which has neither the finances nor the inclination to do anything about them. But it still has plenty to offer and is made enjoyable by the sheer energy of its locals, who appeared cold at first but over time were very welcoming.

I spent the day in search of Vietnam's most famous son, Ho Chi Minh, to this day revered in the country as the greatest hero and liberator, known to everyone as 'Uncle Ho'. His body was mummified, against his dying wishes, and in true Communist leader style housed in a mausoleum in Ba Dinh Square. I made my way around the square to the entrance, guarded by young soldiers who barely looked old enough to carry toy guns, let alone real ones. Surprisingly, there was hardly any queue at all, and I joined the small line, handed my camera and bag over and filtered respectfully along in front of the body of Vietnam's great leader. He was in better shape than I imagined – owing to the fact that he apparently goes on a two-month holiday to China every year for a bit of a wash and brush-up. The quiet tears of the older people in the line made for an unexpectedly moving experience.

On my journey from the airport to the city I had shared a cab with a young man from England called Darran, and we had agreed to meet up later for a drink. By his own admission he was not that experienced when it came to food, but he was willing to try anything, and over the next couple of days before he had to join his own travel party, he became my wingman as we went in search of things to eat.

All over the Old Quarter signs were posted offering 'bia hoi' for sale. The three main Hanoi breweries, as well as making their bottled beers, also produce barrels of fresh beer made with no preservatives. The beer won't last more than a day, so it is sold for a few pennies a glass at shops all over the city, where you hunker down on small plastic stools to sip the refreshing brew. After a few glasses Darran and I felt as though we could conquer the world, and we agreed that the next day we would find our way to La Mat, also known as 'Snake Village', the place in Hanoi to eat our slithering friends. Viewed through the bleary goggles of 'bia hoi', the idea had sounded good to us. The next morning, when Darran arrived at my hotel bleary-eyed, he looked a lot less certain, as indeed did I.

We found a cab for the short journey out of the city only to find, when we turned down a small side-street, that we were suddenly surrounded by a posse of men on scooters, each employed by a different snake restaurant and screaming at the driver to bring us to their establishment. When the driver finally disgorged us, we were almost immediately surrounded by people trying to per-suade us to eat in their restaurants. I was not ashamed to admit that I was having second thoughts.

'I don't fancy this much, mate.' I looked across at Darran, who looked back with a grateful look in his eye.

'Me neither.'

We walked around the neighbourhood for a while, trying to convince ourselves that we had done the right thing as we saw the shops filled with snake medicine and wines until we found another cab to take us back to the city. That night we shared a last beer, but inside I felt lousy. I had turned down this unique eating opportunity because some nasty men on bikes shouted a bit. As I said my goodbyes to Darran, I went back to my guesthouse feeling like a fraud.

The next day I had booked myself onto a cookery course at the ultra-smart Metropole Hotel, another remnant of French colonial times, where Graham Greene had lived when writing *The Quiet American*. It was a fabulous day. The young woman chef who led the course was a delight and, after a visit to the famous Cho 19 market, we spent the rest of the morning watching and taking part as Thuong Thuong, our teacher, showed us how to make everything from fresh salads using the hearts of banana flowers to whole fried fish and, of course, the small, delicate spring rolls for which Vietnamese cuisine is famous. Afterwards we decamped to the hotel restaurant and helped ourselves to the buffet, a collection of nearly a hundred dishes, made in small portions to maintain freshness. I sat with my fellow students and enjoyed the meal, but I kept thinking back to my failures at La Mat and that somewhere there was a snake with my name on it.

I had arranged to go on a tour on my last day in the city, but when I awoke, I still had snake on my mind and decided that Halong Bay could wait. I had to go and right my wrong. I girded my considerable loins and caught another cab, this time making sure he dropped me off about ten minutes walk from La Mat so that I could pick out a likely candidate without hassle, and found myself entering a restaurant called Quoc Tien. It was more sedate than I imagined, and far from the gloomy den of iniquity I had anticipated, being light and airy with a smart terrace.

As for the meal, well, after selecting a snake from the tank as one would a lobster, I watched as it was killed and its heart was placed in a glass with some spirit laced with a little blood. I drank it down in one gulp of burning alcohol, but the heart reminded me of an oyster and I remained convinced throughout the meal that I could feel it beating. I drank the bile that had been milked from the small glands of the snake, which was bitter, and I ate the rest of the snake, which was, thankfully, served in rather more ordinary preparations – soups, stir-fried with vegetables and in dainty spring rolls.

What did it taste like? I hate to say it, but it tasted like ... well, you can finish the rest of that off yourself.

29

A Filler in Manila

Few places on my trip surprised me as much as the Philippines. My expectations were low, and my impressions of the country had been gleaned from Western media horror stories of crime, corruption and crippling poverty. It was only the intervention of my Filipino aunt Evelyn in New York that changed my mind and my itinerary, as I decided to bypass Cambodia and Laos and head to Manila instead.

The Philippines are hardly on the tourist radar of South-East Asia. Its government has been seriously lacking when it comes to promoting just how beautiful and varied this archipelago of over 7,000 islands is. They have also failed to promote the range and quality of the cuisine, leaving people to assume it consists entirely of adobo, the famed dish of pork and vinegar, lumpia, the local versions of spring rolls, and lechon, barbecued suckling pig. Add to this the fact that it is not considered a cheap or a safe option for travellers, and it is easy to see why the security-wary and budget-conscious often give it a miss.

Evelyn reassured me that Manila was a worthwhile city to visit, that the food had great variety and, most important of all, that she would be in the country at the same time.

'You have lots of cousins there. I will make sure they look after you.' I was sure they would. Few people ever say no to 'Auntie Evelyn'.

I had also been contacted by a terrific food writer called Robyn Eckhart, who runs a website called Eating Asia. She got in touch to give me some helpful hints about Malaysia but, in passing, had mentioned that she thought Filipino food was one of the 'undiscovered treasures of Asia'. That was enough for me.

There is no doubting that Manila has many problems. The traffic is chaotic, and going even the shortest distance takes much planning; and, of course, with the traffic come the problems of noise and pollution, made worse by the stifling humidity. Poverty and the uneven distribution of wealth are readily apparent too, as the shanty towns clustered by the runways of the airports give way to the luxury hotels and private houses, all in secure compounds. With poverty come its unhappy bedfellows drugs and prostitution: the area around my business hotel in Makati was surrounded by girly bars and massage parlours, all catering for the grim recreational desires of fat middle-aged men. However, as I knew from my travels, these were the problems of any developing nation, not just the Philippines, and despite them there was much to recommend the place to the potential visitor.

You have to begin with the country's greatest asset, its people, who swamp you with their hospitality and goodwill. The cheery greetings of the staff at my hotel were genuine and followed up with hand-drawn notes showing me where to find the best food. The drivers of Manila's plentiful and cheap taxis were, after a gentle bout of haggling, trustworthy and another useful source of information, and stallholders, restaurant staff and shopworkers could not have been more helpful.

Then there is the beauty of the country – not Manila, which is as ugly as a rejected set for *Blade Runner*, but head a few hours outside or to the far reaches of one of the islands, and the scenery is breathtaking. Most of all, for me, however, it was the food. I had not been prepared for the bewildering variety on offer or the enthusiasm, bordering on psychotic obsession, with which food was treated by just about everyone I met, including my relatives. It was an obsession I had not encountered since I had been in Mexico, which, given the fact that the two countries were both ruled by the Spanish and the fact that many governors of the Philippines came from Mexico, should not have come as a surprise.

There appears to be no such thing as a quick meal or a small meal, and when the Filipinos eat, they like to indulge in their other great obsession, talking. They talk about anything and everything and have an opinion on everything and any subject, even if they know nothing about it. It is more important to have an opinion and to express it than for that opinion to have any basis in knowledge. We had a lot in common.

They are most opinionated about food, as I found out during my first meal with my cousin Carlo Tadiar at a restaurant called Abe. Laconic and with a dry wit, Carlo, like many Filipinos, had a slight American twang to his English, which he explained was a legacy of the era of American 'protection' after the Spanish left the country. So indeed was the shopping mall in which the restaurant was situated. The Filipinos love malls, and at times you would think you were in Kansas rather than Manila.

Carlo was the editor of a popular men's lifestyle magazine in the Philippines, and, as he talked to me, he was also ordering food and shouting in Tagalog, the local language, into his mobile phone at the same time. Between conversations he managed to take me through the plates of food that kept appearing on the table. Delicious and deeply savoury, each dish was packed with astonishing new combinations of flavours.

A slow-cooked kare kare stew of oxtail was cooked so that the bones released their gelatin and thickened the sauce. Then there were chunks of bangus fish 'cooked' in lemon juice and palm vinegar and topped with chilli; roast chickens stuffed with Filipino rice and dried fruit; lechon, the legendary suckling pig, served with a sauce made from the pig's liver; camaru, a bowl of crunchy, deep-fried crickets served with sharp raw onions; and finally a bicol express, an arse-threateningly hot dish of pork, coconut milk and fiery green chillies. It was wonderful, the sort of food that raises taste buds from a jaded torpor – sharp, clean flavours, savoury, delicious stews and the crunch factor that Filipinos demand from at least one dish every meal. I adored it.

As I dived headlong into bowl after bowl of food, Carlo explained what was planned for me during my visit. I grunted in understanding as he listed where I would be going and who I would be meeting, but in truth I wasn't really listening. I was too busy focusing on the plates of food in front of me, to make sure that he and our two dining companions did not take my fair share of anything. He might just as easily have told me that I was about to have a hydrochloric acid enema on live TV the next day and I would have given him the same nod of enthusiastic agreement, as I pierced another piece of suckling pig with my fork. If this was how good it was going to be, I could hardly wait for the next few days.

On the Thursday Carlo collected me in a car and announced that we were heading out of Manila on a two-hour drive to the city of Angeles, in the Pampanga region. He had decided to include an article about my trip in his magazine and to combine it with a 'meeting of minds' between me and a famous local artist and gourmand, Claude Tayag.

Claude, Carlo told me, was one of the most noted gourmands in the country and had agreed to prepare a meal for us at his home, a *bale dutung* or 'house of wood', worth seeing in its own right, he told me, as it had been constructed entirely by Claude himself from remnants of local churches and farmhouses.

A true polymath, Claude Tayag was a painter, sculptor, writer, musician and cook, who had not only laid every wooden plank in the house but also made every piece of furniture, all in a traditional Filipino style, with the living quarters elevated and the side panels removable so that air could flow through on humid summer days. He led us out on to a large deck overlooking a garden in which half a dozen of his sculptures, made from old ploughshares, were standing, and seated us around a table (which he had made, of course) to begin the meal.

It is hard to describe just how good this meal was. I sat in rapt attention as Claude and his wife brought out dish after dish, explaining how each was prepared. A salad of crunchy paco ferns served with pickled quail's eggs came with a dressing made of duck egg yolks. It was followed by bulanglang, a seafood stew with guava and fresh prawns, with heads so large that Claude instructed us to rip them off and allow the fat to dribble into the soup as a thickener. Fried hito fish came next, served wrapped in mustard leaves with balo balo, a condiment of fermented rice, which of course Claude makes himself and sells under his own label. And there was yet another version of the kare kare stew I had tried before, but this time made with fish.

Most simple and most delicious of all, adding the necessary crunch, was a bowl of bagnet, deep-fried belly pork. There was rice too, of course: no meal in the Philippines happens without rice. I was staggered by it all, the generosity and the food. This was one of the best meals I had eaten, ever.

After the meal Claude shepherded us towards his car for the short drive into the city. He wanted me to taste perhaps the quintessential Filipino dish – sisig. Created in his home town of Angeles, this is the dish that every Filipino loves to have with a cold beer. It is made up of left-over bits of pig – cheek, nose and ear – chopped up finely with chilli and cooked on a hot plate to form a crunchy layer on the bottom. It is served communally so that people can fight over the crispy bits as they talk. It was deliciously savoury, and I am sure I could still taste it as we headed back into Manila.

Over the next few days of my stay I set out to explore what else was on offer, sometimes alone and sometimes in the company of yet another cousin, Ethan. He was a huge teddy bear of a man, with a deep laugh that peppered his conversation. I liked him immediately.

'Man, I hear you have been doing some good eating? Heh, heh', he boomed at me in his baritone voice. 'Let's see if we can't do even better. Heh, heh.'

And we certainly tried. We ate lechon at Salcedo, the weekend market for middle-class Manilans. 'It's from Cebu', he told me knowingly. 'They don't serve it with the liver sauce. They say if you need sauce, there is something wrong with your lechon.'

We tried sinigang, the Filipino equivalent of Jewish chicken soup, soured with tamarind and flavoured with pork, beef or seafood – in this case with a huge hunk of corned beef simmering in the broth.

'It has to be sour, man or its not sinigang,' Ethan advised as he slurped up another mouthful.

We tried crispy pata – yet more pork, but this time braised, hung up to dry for up to twenty-four hours and then cut into chunks and, you've guessed it, deep-fried. And we tried pork skewers. 'My favourite', Ethan said, joining a long line for them at the market. He emerged from the queue brandishing four meaty examples.

'One's never enough', he said, without any argument from me.

He really was a man after my own heart attack, and thanks to him, Carlo and my aunt Evelyn, I enjoyed my time in Manila more than I could have possibly imagined. I was delighted when she joined us for a last meal at the enormous family home. Prepared by Carlo, the main course was perhaps the best-known dish of all, adobo – pork and chicken marinated in chillies and vinegar. For many Filipinos it is the ultimate comfort food.

Ten of us sat around the table and ate, drank and, of course, talked for over five hours until the small hours of the morning. We talked mainly about food, about how things should be done 'properly' and about how so many young people now took short cuts. Everyone shook their heads mournfully. I felt totally at home, and I could not have been happier. I had 'discovered' a new cuisine, and one that could not have been more suited to my taste for hot, sour and crunchy. And best of all, I had discovered a new family, a family who shared my own obsession for food. My next stop was to discover my old family.

I was off to India.

30

India: Crazy, Beautiful

Nothing you have ever experienced prepares you for India.

First, the negatives: the assault on every sense, the noise, the smell, the pollution, the poverty, the filth-strewn streets, the bewildering number of people and the shattering of every value and belief you hold as normal.

And the positives? India seems unstoppable, not just tapping at the glass ceiling placed above developing nations by developed ones, but head-butting it with increasing ferocity. It could soon be the most populous nation on earth. It could soon overtake many countries in the West in terms of its GNP, and it is already at the forefront of medical and technological development.

The capacity for inspiring awe and irritation in equal measures is the hallmark of a country where you can be stunned by the vast landscapes and the remnants of ancient history but still queue for two hours at immigration because they have not printed enough landing cards, and you can see a large neon sign outside a bank that reads: '24 hour ATM (except between the hours of midnight and 6 a.m.)'.

Perhaps I should just concentrate on the food, which cannot be bettered anywhere in the world in terms of variety, range and quality. There are seven union territories and twenty-eight states in the Republic of India, from Kashmir in the north to Tamil Nadu in the south, from Maharashtra in the west to Bengal in the east. Each has its own distinct cuisine, born out of the geography and political history of the region, from the north, where Mogul invaders brought grilling and the subtlety of cream and almonds, to the south-west, where the cooking of Goa shows the Portuguese influences of garlic, chillies, tomatoes and vinegar.

It is no easy matter knowing where to start with India. But then it is no easy place for me to know where to start with being Indian. If indeed, that's what I am. So instead, let me start with my father, Pratip Majumdar, or Baba.

Baba first moved to Britain in the mid-1950s, primarily to complete his medical training as an orthopaedic surgeon but also to escape the expectations of his father that he would join the family homeopathic practice back in Calcutta. My grandfather was, by all accounts, a brilliant and well-respected man, a member of the Indian Communist Party and part of the intelligentsia that pushed for independence from Great Britain after the Second World War. But his relationship with my father was an uneasy one, punctuated by long periods of non-communication, which resulted in my father's all too infrequent returns to India and the fact that I never met him.

My father is an extraordinary man, and I am very much his son. He has never suffered fools – a trait I share – and while we are both intensely loyal to those we consider friends, we cut those who cross us out of our lives like a malignant tumour. I have many reasons to be grateful for his strength, generosity and support over the years, but the unwelcome side-effect of his fall-out with my grandfather has been a profound lack of identity.

I joke that I am half-Welsh, half-Bengali, but in reality I have always felt half-non-Welsh, half-non-Bengali, not particularly comfortable or welcome in either camp. I speak neither language and while my glistening olive skin may be a surefire hit with the ladies (not a word), it has led to me being called 'Paki' in Rotherham (the double whammy being both racist and geographically incorrect) and a 'half-caste' in India. I wasn't expecting an epiphany, but India promised to be interesting, and not just for the food.

New Delhi is to India what Washington D.C. is to the USA. It's not the most exciting city, but as the administrative heart it makes a decent starting-point and reasonably sane place to begin an introduction to the most insane country in the world. I use the word 'reasonably' with caution, however, because this is still India we are talking about.

On my first morning in the city after arriving from Manila, I flagged down one of Delhi's infamous auto-rickshaws. Yellow and black, thousands buzz around the streets of the capital like angry hornets. They are fun, if extraordinarily dangerous. Above all, they are cheap: as you haggle with the driver over a fare, you have to keep reminding yourself that the amount you are arguing about is loose change that you would not stop to pick up if you dropped it on the streets back home.

I asked the driver to drop me at the Red Fort, the centre of the Mogul ruler Shah Jahan's new capital, which takes its name from the miles of red brick that formed its outer wall. On previous visits nearly every tourist I had seen had been a foreigner. Now most of them seemed to be from India itself, a sign of the country's burgeoning middle class. It is an impressive place, but I was more moved by my next stop, the home of a woman many still consider the mother of modern India: Indira Gandhi. Since her assassination in 1984, the simple but dignified bungalow she called home has become a museum to her life and a shrine to her legacy. At the rear of the house in a neat garden is the path along which she walked to meet the man who turned out to be her assassin. It has been covered in glass to protect her last steps in the gravel, and the point at which she fell is now marked.

By now I was starving and had my auto-rickshaw buzz me to the heart of Old Delhi. There is a romantic notion that street food always tastes better than equivalent food in restaurants. This is, of course, complete and utter rubbish. The mere fact that you eat food while standing at a street corner does not give it any more intrinsic quality and, of course, you add to it the Russian roulette element of not knowing whether you will make it back to your accommodation before your arse explodes. I often meet travellers along the way who wear their encounters with dysentery as a badge of honour.

'Oh yah, I only eat on the streets. It is where the real people eat', they would proffer. 'That's why they all die at fifty', is an obvious reply.

I had, of course, already eaten food from roadside stalls in China, Malaysia, Vietnam and Thailand, but I had taken great care to head to places crowded with locals, with the view that a rapid turnover would mean fresher food and less chance of me spending the night heaving into the porcelain. So far I had been lucky, but I was less inclined to take the risk in India, for two reasons. The first was that the locals here seem to have stomachs that can cope with anything at all, from the fieriest chillies to germs that would have biological terrorists shaking their head in disbelief. The second is that, of all of the Asian countries I visited, India has easily the lowest standard of hygiene. Old ingredients covered in flies can be cooked in old oil served on plates washed in the same murky water for days on end. I just knew there was a dodgy meal there with my name on it, so instead I based my research around local restaurants.

Karim's in Old Delhi was highly recommended and, as I sat down at one of the communal tables in one of four rooms surrounding a courtyard, the smells coming from the kitchen reminded me of why it would be impossible do a world tour and leave India off the list. There was the unmistakeable whiff of grilling meat, ghee, onions and spices to set the heart racing. As I looked at the menu, a young man sitting opposite began chatting to me, introducing himself as Sunit. He turned to the menu board on the wall, saying, 'They are famous for their mutton dishes here, but try the butter chicken. It's excellent.'

Butter and chicken together – I liked the sound of those odds. When the waiter arrived, we both ordered it and my new friend, Sunit, added a side-dish of mutton kebabs, which he insisted I should share. We were both presented with large bowls of chicken in a gravy made with tomatoes. On the top was a slick of melted ghee and to the side a sliver of green chilli. It was every bit as good as Sunit claimed and, like him, I ate with my hands gnawing the chicken bones and mopping up the sauce with fresh paratha bread, occasionally turning my attention to take big bites from our side-dish of kebabs.

It is at moments like this, when food this good is put in front of you, that you can forgive India all its craziness. At the end of the meal Sunit insisted on paying the bill. By local standards it was not expensive, but it was still an incredibly generous gesture and one that made me feel all fuzzy inside. I only hoped that the butter chicken would not do the same.

On my final day in Delhi I decided that it was time to have one of my occasional blow-outs and to spend my entire daily allowance in one high-class restaurant as a counterpoint to the cheap and homely places that were my normal destination.

After a morning visit to the moving memorial to Mahatma Gandhi, I had my auto-rickshaw drop me off in front of the Sheraton Hotel, where my chosen restaurant was Bukhara, regularly featured in lists of the best restaurants in the world. It is no surprise to find that Bill Clinton was a fan, but more of one to discover that he is joined by Vladimir Putin of Russia, who insisted on eating here every time he was in Delhi. Their dishes come from India's Northwest Frontier, where intense flavours from tandoor-grilled meats and creamy, slow-cooked dahls combine to produce an intensely robust effect.

A waiter appeared and wrapped a bib around my neck, explaining that since I had ordered the house speciality of tandoor chicken, I would need it to protect my clothing. When a platter containing the whole bird was brought out of the kitchen, the smells preceded it and I was slobbering before it hit the table. Tandoor chicken appears on the menu of every Indian restaurant in the world, and in principle it is one of the more simple dishes to make. Marinate the chicken in yoghurt and spices and grill it. But getting it right is so much harder than it seems. Too much marinating makes the meat spongy, too little and it dries out.

Here it was as perfect as I have had anywhere. This is not a dish to nibble at politely – you vacuum it up, chomping loudly with no thought for the mess you are making on the table, your hands or your clothes. Thank God they gave me the bib.

The chicken was so good that I almost forgot to turn my attention to their other signature dish, the Bukhara dahl, a version traditionally made by allowing urud lentils to cook in milk and spices overnight in the embers of the cooling tandoor. To it are added onions and garlic, spices and so much butter that each serving should come with its own defibrillator. It is so good that the handful of fluffy paratha breads with it scarcely seemed enough, and I found myself looking around and then picking up the bowl before licking it clean. I would have got away with it too, if it had not been for those pesky waiters.

Returning to collect the plate, one of them said, 'You have a stain on your face sir'. I turned to the mirror by my seat to see my reflection with a tell-tale ring of sauce around my face from the lip of the bowl.

'Don't worry, sir', he said calmly as he handed me a hot towel. 'It happens a lot.'

I am sure it does. I wondered if it had ever happened to Billy Jeff or Vladimir before. I was pretty sure it would happen to me if I went there again.

31

Mumbai the Unstoppable

Delhi may be the capital, but it is to Mumbai that everyone looks to lead the way in India. With well over 16 million people and seemingly as many cars, the sights, sounds, noise and smells of Mumbai make it India to the power of ten.

Mumbai crackles with a raw energy that seeps out of every open sewer and explodes with every 'parping' horn from the black and yellow taxis that churn out enough pollution to make your eyes weep the moment you set foot out into the decaying streets. No trip to India would be complete without a visit to a city where you feel as though you are riding on the world's fastest roller-coaster without a harness.

There is, of course, much to deplore about India's cities in general, and this one in particular. The gut-wrenching poverty is heart-breaking, and the decay of the crumbling buildings and roads seems to suggest that, when the British left, they took all their tools with them. The stench that fills the air from the filth-strewn streets and clogged gutters makes even the most seasoned traveller cover his mouth and nose. It is a challenge to every Western value and an assault to every sense. At once exciting, vibrant, challenging and appalling, Mumbai is truly one of the world's great cities, and it doesn't really care whether you approve or not. You get the feeling that, if you were to mess with Mumbai, Mumbai would just turn around and kick your ass.

Nowhere is this more apparent that when it comes to food. Mumbai has a reputation as the best city in which to eat in India and perhaps in the whole of Asia. Its staggering variety is made possible by the influx of people from every corner of the subcontinent. Its coastal location made Mumbai 'the gateway to India', and here you will find Muslim sitting down with Parsi, Bengali sitting down with Jain and Tamil sitting down with native Maharashtran for meals ranging from local favourites of phav bhaji or bhel puri to parsi dhansaks, Bengali sweets, tandoored rolls and kebabs, konkani seafood cookery from the south-west coast or creamy korma from the north, all washed down with juices from fresh fruits and sugar-cane or a long, cold beer, as taste and religion dictate.

Mumbai is not, however, one of India's great sightseeing destinations. Once you have looked at the deeply unimpressive Gateway to India and sailed out on a rickety old ferry to the Elephanta Islands, you have more or less 'done' Mumbai. But that leaves plenty of time to explore what Mumbai is really about, with visits to Crawford Market or Chor Bazar producing eye-popping sights both to astonish and to disgust and trips to Chowpatty Beach to watch Mumbaikars at play and doing what they do best: eat.

I had just a few days there and knew that I was not going to able to try everything, but with my own research and e-mails I had received from locals I had already made a plan. My hotel was just around the corner from a true local institution, Vithal Belwala, where for generations they have been serving one of Mumbai's signature snacks, bhel puri, consisting of puffed rice mixed with a combination of sev (sticks of fried flour), onions, potatoes, tomatoes and chilli, dressed with chutneys of tamarind or coriander. It's a great introduction to the area, and after two large platefuls of their 'special dry bhel' I was ready to walk it off on the way to the location I had in mind for supper.

Mumbai is well known for its konkani seafood cuisine originating in the south-west of India, and one of the best restaurants is the small and recommended Apoorva. Like so many neighbourhood places in Mumbai, it doesn't appear desperately welcoming at first, being mainly a place for working men to come for a drink and some food after work. The lighting was dim and the only air-conditioning a rattling fan above each table. But the food was fantastic, with a classic dish of prawn gassi – small, sweet shrimps cooked in a spicy sauce of coconut milk soured with the juice from the kokum, a native fruit renowned for its medicinal properties.

They place a knife and a spoon on the table for you, but in India people seldom use them. Here it is all about the hands. Eating with your hands has many benefits. You are able to combine the ubiquitous mound of rice with the sauce of the dish you are eating so that each grain gets a proper coating. It also just tastes better. Don't ask me why, it just does. So, as I scooped fingers full of spicy rice to my lips and spooned up the sauce with a crispy appam – a bowl-shaped pancake made of fermented rice flour – my cutlery remained untouched.

I asked the waiter what was in the sauce. In the USA, if you are silly enough to ask such a question, they can easily spend more time describing a dish than the chef did cooking it. 'It's an infusion of milk from a cow called Doris from Johnson State Farm, with Meyer lemons from the second branch from the top, mixed with cilantro picked at midnight while we all sang "76 Trombones" from *The Music Man*. The chef used his right hand while preparing the dish and laced the final emulsion with two tears shed while thinking of his mother.'

'It's a gravy', my waiter responded.

'Yes, but what's in it?' I pressed, and he headed off to ask someone who might know. Returning, he announced proudly 'It's a red gravy' and went off to serve other tables.

The next day I set out to visit two of Mumbai's most famous shopping districts, Crawford Market and Chor Bazar. I returned to my hotel about thirty seconds later, the scurry of a rat over my open-toed sandals having persuaded me that a good pair of solid walking boots might be a better option.

By this time in the trip I was beginning to be a bit marketed out, but India's markets are something else. The stench makes

Chinese markets seem like a basket of roses, and when I saw a cage truck laden with white-feathered chickens – most of them dead but some still struggling as they were dragged out and quickly dispatched with a rusty knife by a bored-looking worker – I decided that I would probably do something of a vegetarian nature for breakfast.

Phav bahji is traditionally a lunchtime dish or an evening snack, but a nearby stall was already serving this classic Maharashtran dish to market workers who had been at it for hours. It is curry in a bun: a mixture of potatoes, chilli, tomatoes and peppers mashed together on a large metal hot plate and then served on a bun. It is laden with fat, and the soft, white bun is the stuff of Atkins nightmares, but it is entirely delicious.

By mid-morning the city was in full flow. I dodged the traffic to head to the Maidan, the much-needed parkland lungs of the city. It was already filled with crowds of men playing cricket. So much more than just a sport in India, cricket truly is India's one unifying religion, with star players being worshipped like deities or reviled like demons, depending on their performances, and with cricket matches attracting crowds that would make Billy Graham jealous. Every spare inch of newsprint or minute or airtime is dedicated to discussion shows about the successes or, more often, the failures of India's national side. Even away from the parks any spare stretch of street can be turned into a pitch with makeshift stumps and bats. As you walk, you need to be constantly vigilant as the words 'ball, ball, ball' are shrieked to warn of a missile coming your way.

On my last night I had plans to head to one of Mumbai's many excellent smart restaurants after a visit to watch the Mumbaikers in relaxation mode. During the day Chowpatty Beach, a stretch of sand at the top of Marine Drive, is deserted, but as I arrived in the early evening, it was already kicking into action. Itinerant astrologers fought for my attention with ear cleaners and hawkers while crowds descended on the snack stalls selling bhel puri, which they were busy scooping into their mouths with the help of more of the flat, fried bread. There was plenty of action, but my sightseeing there was done, and I took a cab for the short journey down Colaba Causeway to what I was reliably informed is the only legally sanctioned street stall in Mumbai, Bade Miyan, considered one of the best in the whole of Mumbai. Even if I had not known the directions, I would have found my way there because of the incredible smells and the crowds of eager diners. At an early hour the streets around the stall were packed with customers, and cars were double-parked as people came to eat or to get food to take away.

A young man with an official badge around his neck handed me a short menu, and I ordered a mutton roll. He dived again into the throng and reappeared a few moments later with a small parcel containing my pre-supper snack. I turned in the direction of my dinner destination, unwrapping my kebab as a nice little pre-appetizer appetizer. I took a bite and stopped dead in my tracks. It wasn't just good, it was sensational. So good in fact, that I stood rooted to the spot until I had finished every last shred of the spicy meat wrapped with onions. All thoughts of my planned supper were gone. I turned on my heels back to Bade Miyan and spent the next two hours there working my way through the menu until I realized it was past midnight.

The taste of those kebabs stayed with me until I arrived back at the hotel. In fact, if I close my eyes, the taste stays with me still. But that is true of so much about Mumbai. It stays with you and, despite its savagely unforgiving elements, you leave thinking that you have barely scratched the surface of this unstoppable city.

After leaving Mumbai, I carved a space in my schedule to recharge my batteries and to catch up on some much-needed sleep. I wanted to eat well, of course, but I didn't have any plans.

I chose Goa, the former Portuguese colony on the south-west coast of the subcontinent, which only became part of India in 1962. The north of the state is highly developed with resorts and now overcrowded with tourists from all over the world, but primarily the UK and, increasingly Russia. It was not for me. The south, however, remains relatively unspoilt, and I chose a basic but pleasant-looking resort in Cavelossim and arrived there on an early morning flight.

The difference from Mumbai was striking the moment I left the airport. It was quieter, obviously – anywhere would seem quiet after Mumbai – but more than that, the whole pace of life was much more gentle. The Portuguese legacy still remains in the faces of the people and the names on the shops and buildings we passed *en route* to the hotel. It is also in the architecture, with as many church steeples on show as there are temples.

The hotel was basic but would suit my needs down to the ground. It was moments' walk from the beach, so I quickly changed into flip-flops and pottered out along the rice fields to see what was on offer. The beach was the stuff of a holiday brochure photographer's dreams. Stretching on for miles in either direction, the sweeping sands, waving palms and blue seas were broken up only by the occasional beach shack serving food to the few people around at that time. I flipped off my flops and spent the next hour walking on the hot sands before choosing one of them at random and sitting down for my first meal.

The food too takes its lead from the legacy of the Portuguese, who introduced, among other things, chilli, tomatoes and garlic to the cuisine. They also ate pork, untouched by Muslims and Hindus in the rest of India but popular with the primarily Roman Catholic population of Goa. All of these ingredients come together in the signature dish of the region, pork vindaloo, which takes its name from its two key ingredients, vinegar and garlic.

Few dishes are more misunderstood than the vindaloo. It has become synonymous with the Friday-night 'curry house' meal, sopping up the binging of weekend warriors in shiny suits who have spent the hours since they left work swilling cheap lager in the local pub. This beautiful dish has become debased. It has become all about the heat and all about making the experience as close as possible to eating broken glass.

A 'proper' vindaloo is certainly fiery, with the pork being marinated for a long time in chillies. But there is so much more to it than that. The best examples involve chunks of pork shoulder marinated overnight in a mix of palm vinegar, ground spices (including cloves, chillies and lots of garlic) and then slow-cooked without added water until the meat is tender and the sauce a thick gravy with immense depth and layers of flavour. When well done, as it was at my chosen beach shack, it is one of the best Indian dishes of all, and I sat with the sound of the waves lapping in front of me, spooning hunks of flesh into my mouth with a large paratha.

My time in Goa was exactly what I needed. Each day I would head out for a breakfast of fresh fruits and curds from the market stalls in Cavelossim before taking a long, luxurious, barefoot walk along the beach until I felt it was time to have something else to eat. As I walked, I would watch the local fishermen beach their small boats, haul out their catch of local fish and seafood and take them straight to the shacks to be prepared immediately for waiting diners. I can't recall too many times when I have had seafood this fresh, and for relatively little money my lunch each day consisted of large lobster simply grilled and doused with limes picked from the trees behind the shacks or stir-fried and served in a sauce made of coconut milk and fresh green chillies. The afternoon was spent by the pool sleeping or chatting to the other guests, mostly couples who had been returning to the same resort for years.

To my delight I was soon included in their group as we congregated by the bar every evening to drink rather too much of the locally made spirits with names like Blue Ship Gin and Honeybee Whisky before having supper at a local restaurant, which made the best chicken tikka I have ever eaten in my life – alive with spices and sparkling with drops of lemon juice sprinkled on it just before serving.

Towards the end of my stay Serrafino, the owner of the hotel, invited me to join him at a meeting of local businessmen and guesthouse owners who had created a forum for responsible tourism. Although the area around Cavelossim seemed like a paradise, under the surface many problems were becoming increasingly apparent – particularly, he explained, with the influx of new tourists from Russia.

'They see Goa as a brothel', he explained, sharing with me the horrific figures for sexual tourism, drug-related crime and sexual abuse of children. And the all-inclusive resorts, he told me, were owned by major international companies, which meant that little of the money generated found its way into the local community.

At the end of the meeting an owner of one of the local guesthouses provided supper for us all in the shape of a seafood thali, served in the traditional manner, on banana leaves, with a mound of rice surrounded by ten or so small portions of different dishes, including fried clams, shark cooked with kokum juice and squid cooked simply with spinach. It was a simple meal shared with local people, and the talking went on until nearly midnight as we ate under the stars in the garden of the local church where we had gathered. As we drove back with Serrafino, I told him I hoped that tourism would not ruin what I considered one of the most beautiful places I had visited.

'The trouble is,' he sighed, 'we want people to come and see how beautiful Goa is. We want them to meet our people, eat our food and, of course, spend money in our community. But the very action of them coming changes for ever what we want them to see.'

It is the great dichotomy of tourism, of course, but with people like Serrafino, perhaps Goa may be able to strike that balance. I hope so.

After a welcome few days of peace and quiet, I was ready to get back in harness again. I was excited and nervous in equal parts, I was truly heading back to the land of my fathers. Next stop Kolkata.

32

Kolkata: Land of My Fathers

I always compare Kolkata to an ex-lover, one who you know is bad for you, but about whom you cannot stop thinking. They have let you down over and again, treated you badly, and you have promised yourself hundreds of times that you are not going to spend any more time in their company. But then, just as you think you are finally over them, they do something so utterly alluring, so impossibly irresistible, that you find yourself falling in love again. That is my Kolkata, the land of my fathers.

Kolkata is not easy-access India. It is not like Rajasthan – India 'with training wheels', as I call it. It is not as easy to navigate as Mumbai, and it does not have the beauty of the south, with beaches and palms; nor does it have the mountains ranges of the north. Everything about it is a challenge to what you think you know to be right and proper: the sheer volume of people, some 15 million and rising, all of whom seem to be on the streets all the time; the stultifying humidity, which even in spring can have you and your clothes dripping in sweat within thirty seconds; and the pollution, which can have you and your clothes turning a lovely shade of grey in the same amount of time.

It is impossible to understate the scale of the deprivation and degradation under which large sections of the population in Kolkata live, clinging by a thread to life by any means available, foraging through piles of festering garbage in search of scraps to eat, hustling for work on the streets, selling anything they have to offer (including themselves) and, of course begging, always persistently and often aggressively. It is little wonder that few foreigners, if any, mark the city as a tourist destination. Yet Kolkata is also a magical place, a city filled with unexpected beauty, immense intelligence and passion, astonishing sights – and some of the best food in India.

This is the Kolkata in which my father grew up and where my mother spent the first year of her marriage learning how to cook. This is the Kolkata spoken of in the stories they regaled us with as children – stories of flying fighting kites from the roof of the family home, of playing cricket in the compound housing all the different branches of the family, of servants climbing trees to fetch the juiciest lemons to make cooling drinks and of Brahmin cooks producing meals of great simplicity but stunning flavour using few ingredients and even fewer spices. It is a city to which I still have strong emotional ties because of this family history and a city that never fails to astonish, whether it is your first visit or, as in my case, the latest of many.

I thought about all of this as my companion grabbed hold of my arm for support as we fought our way through downtown Kolkata, avoiding cracked paving stones, pools of stagnant water, mounds of festering rubbish and the inquisitive attentions of everyone to my very white, very red-haired friend. Vanessa Sly's eyes were popping out of her head, and she had a look on her face that said 'What the f**k is a nice middle-class girl like me from Michigan doing here?' She looked like she wanted to be almost anywhere else in the world. Even Michigan.

Vanessa was responsible for the purchasing of tea at the famous Zingerman's deli in Ann Arbor. During my brief visit there I had mentioned my upcoming trip to India and that it would include visits to Kolkata and a Darjeeling tea garden. Vanessa asked whether I would mind having a companion. I was only too pleased to agree, but I was sure that, as she began to see Kolkata in all its glory, she was regretting her decision.

'Loooook', she grabbed at my shirt sleeve and pointed. There was a woman washing both her clothes and her small, naked child in the same puddle of dirty water.

'You are going to see a lot more of that, I am afraid', I said, concerned that she might find it all a bit hard to take in.

'No, that', she pointed again, this time more firmly.

Behind the woman on the pavement were two small monkeys who were going at it like, well, monkeys. I made a note to myself to remember the sight – not that the image of two monkeys shagging on the streets of the downtown area of one of the largest cities in Asia is one you forget in a hurry.

Finally we found the address we were searching for and were ushered into the quiet, air-conditioned rooms of Ashok Gandotra, one of the most prominent tea traders in Kolkata. As we arrived, a range of teas was being allowed to brew in boiling water and then laid out in a line with spoons for us to taste. Ashok explained what was in front of us: first- and second-flush single-estate leaf teas from some of the finest gardens in Darjeeling through to leaf teas from other countries so we could make comparisons, followed by blended teas, using whole-leaf, broken-leaf, fanning (basically left-overs after sorting) and dust. Each blend, he explained, was designed for the taste of a different region or country: thick, strong teas for the Middle East, for example, and consistent but mediocre blends for the UK, where, he explained we drink a huge volume of tea, but not of great quality. He was most disparaging about the tea drunk in the USA, where my own unscientific research shows it would be easier find Lord Lucan than a decent cup of tea.

'They basically just want a neutral liquid they can drink cold with ice. It could be anything, it just has to be brown and wet', he said slurping from a bowl marked 'US Blend'.

This was Vanessa's show, and I stood back as the two experts tasted together, sucking up tablespoons full from each bowl and rolling them around their mouths to release the flavour before spitting out.

'It is not just the taste that makes a good tea', Ashok explained, holding up a bowl to the light. 'There is colour and brightness.'

First-flush tea, harvested at the end of March, is a greener, astringent tea with a pale colour. Generally considered to be weaker than the second flush, picked in May, which has more depth of both flavour and colour, first-flush has, however, developed a large following for its ability to refresh. By comparison, the teas produced from broken leaves or fannings were duller to the eye and to the palate.

Once the tasting was over and we had left the office, I wanted Vanessa to get her first real taste of Bengali food. Before Independence from Britain, Bengal was one of the largest states in India. It still is, even though is now split into two: West Bengal, where Kolkata is found, and East Bengal, which became East Pakistan and then the beautiful but blighted nation of Bangladesh. Bengal in general and Kolkata in particular are known as the literary and political heart of India. Kolkata was the capital before Delhi, and in India there is a saying 'What Kolkata thinks today, India will think tomorrow.'

It remains one of the safest places in India, and Bengalis are among the friendliest people you will find in the world. The food too is unique. Unlike in much of India, where the food can be characterized by strong tastes and pungent spicing, Bengali food, or more accurately Kolkatan food, is subtle and understated, using few spices to complement their cooking of ingredients. Turmeric, mustard oil and powder, ginger and fresh chillies are commonly used alongside the bony river fish with which Kolkatans have an obsession. It is from these roots that my own obsession comes. With respect, I never thought it came from Wales.

The people of Kolkata spend most of their waking lives talking about food, from the simple breakfast of luchi, the local version of puri, which are stuffed with potatoes or chickpeas before being dipped in sour tamarind water, to pre-lunch snacks of shingra, the local version of a samosa, stuffed with cauliflower, to lunch, taken on the hoof or in a restaurant, to supper with their family, to a late-night snack of spicy fish rolls. When they are not eating, they are arguing about eating or talking about past meals. It all sounded very familiar.

Kewpie's Kitchen was the real deal, like sitting in the front room of a traditional Bengali home. We chose a thali, a selection of dishes served together on a silver tray, and while we waited we sipped on an aampora shorbat made from mangoes, black salt and cumin seeds to give the sour-sweet taste Bengalis love.

When the meal came, I used the fresh puri to help the varying plates of vegetarian dishes from plate to lips. Lao, a marrow-like gourd, was slow-cooked simply with nigella seeds and melted creamily in the mouth. Bowls of shukta, a mixture of hard and soft vegetables, were again cooked with the Bengali version of five spice: panch phoron, a mixture of fennel seeds, black mustard seed, fenugreek seed, cumin seeds and nigella seeds. There was aubergine dipped in chickpea flour and deep-fried until crispy and little balls of steamed aubergine in a sauce made with doi, Bengali yoghurt. Best of all there was LSD, Life Saving Dahl – the Bengali equivalent of Jewish chicken soup, made with red lentils and, compared with many versions of this Indian staple, very thin.

When my father returned to India for a short while in the late 1950s, he took with him his young Welsh bride. The family were wary of a marriage outside the caste but took to my mother primarily because she developed an immediate and deep passion for Bengali food which allowed them to rationalize that 'she must be a reincarnated Brahmin'. As I watched Vanessa scoop up her lunch with perfect hand technique, I could not help thinking my family would have approved.

When it comes to sweets, the passion of the Bengali goes beyond obsession and becomes almost feral. Never, ever try and come between a Bengali and their rightful ration of sweets. These can be challenging to the uninitiated, however, and the textures of these delicacies, made mainly from milk, can be unpleasant on the tongue. The amount of sugar in them probably explains why the levels of diabetes in Kolkata are higher than those anywhere else in the country.

But Bengali sweets are incredibly addictive, and those at

Kolkata institution K.C. Das are produced to a quality that you will struggle to find anywhere else. Pre-eminent in the pantheon of sweets is mishti doi, a simple combination of yoghurt and cream. (It may be simple, but it is mother's milk to most Bengalis, and grown men in the Indian diaspora will become teary-eyed at the very mention of it.) It can come in many flavours but is best plain and eaten from a small, unfired earthenware bowl, which can be discarded after it has been wiped clean, of course.

Alongside it are two more favourites: gulab jamun, popular all over India and made of milk solids mixed with cream and then served in a rosewater-flavoured syrup, and my mother's own personal favourite, rasgulla, made from cheese rolled with semolina and then poached in syrup. They originated in the neighbouring state of Orissa but were brought to Bengal by Brahmins employed as cooks by wealthy families such as my father's. K.C. Das was one of the first places to sell them commercially, and even now, some 130 years after it first opened, they remain as popular as ever.

We would be heading back to Kolkata for a few days at the end of our time in India, and I hoped then to have chance to connect with some of my father's family. But after a long, wearying day it was time to head back to the guesthouse and pack our bags for the journey up to Darjeeling and the Goomtee estate tea gardens.

33

The Darjeeling Express

Darjeeling produces the finest black teas in the world and has done so since the British first experimented with the growing of bushes there in the middle of the nineteenth century. Now there are more than eighty different gardens helping slake the world's thirst for this most refreshing of brews.

I am a self-confessed tea nut. I drink several cups a day, from the first one, to help prise my eyes open in the morning, to the mid-afternoon cup with a digestive biscuit to my post-supper quencher. I can't do coffee. It will empty my stomach quicker than a porno film starring Andrew Lloyd Webber. It has to be tea. However, like many Brits, my knowledge of tea was limited to the strong, dark brews beloved of construction workers all over the country. Give me a large mug, preferably with a humorous motto on the side, filled with a threateningly dark brown liquid, and I am as happy as Larry.

It was nearly four hours to our destination from the nearest airport, Bhagdogra, which meant a long and perilous drive from the plains up towards the mountains before we reached our accommodation. There was rubble on the roads, we were told, caused by recent riots in favour of the separation of the region from West Bengal to become its own state of Ghorkaland. On every spare wall, graffiti had been daubed supporting their claims: 'Ghorkaland Is Our Demand.'

By the time we pulled into the Goomtee estate and settled into the guesthouse it was already dark, and because the air was much thinner at the altitude of 4,000 feet, it was cold enough to catch us out and have us running to put on sweaters and jackets.

Goomtee comes from the Nepalese word for 'turning point', and the garden, set in a fork in the road, has been owned by the same family since the 1950s, when it was bought from the British by Mahbir Prasad. Its reputation for producing some of the finest teas in Darjeeling made it the perfect place to watch the process of production from picking to packing.

Our stay at the guesthouse included all our meals and, of course, innumerable cups of tea made from the leaves harvested in the gardens. As we sat down to enjoy our first pot, served in the British way, with milk and a tray of biscuits, Vanessa became slightly alarmed when I took the tea cosy from the pot and placed it over my head. I don't see it as particularly peculiar behaviour. Most men have done it. I have always done it: it seems a perfectly sensible way to recycle the luxurious warmth from the pot. I do, however, sometimes forget to take it off and on more than one occasion have opened the door to my apartment and treated the postman to the sight of me wearing a tea cosy shaped like a kitten.

In the Goomtee Guesthouse there was a permanent staff of five people, all of whom, given that we were the only guests, were dedicated to our care. If we wanted tea, we asked for tea. If wanted a snack, we only had to ask. After our hikes around the gardens and the factory, there was precious little else left to do but read, eat and sleep – a welcome relief after the last hectic couple of months. The cook at Goomtee had a great reputation, and the food he prepared for us was simple but memorable. He used few ingredients to stunning effect to produce dishes from all parts of India, Nepal and Tibet, close neighbours to this part of India.

Breakfasts were small steamed rice cakes called idli, served with a fiery sambar. Lunch, the biggest meal of the day, would be Tibetan steamed dumplings called momo, served with fresh salads, Bengali dahl, rice of course, and vegetables deep-fried in chickpea flour batter. Best of all, for supper the staff would bring out plates laden down with shingra, the Bengali samosa stuffed with spicy cauliflower. Food was brought in a never-ending succession to the table until we held our hands up in submission and went to walk it off in the manicured grounds or flop on the sofa with a book.

Fortunately, we also got lots of exercise. Vanessa had timed our trip to coincide with the first harvest of the first flush from the Goomtee estate, and very early the morning after our arrival we were summoned into the impressive and slightly frightening presence of the estate manager, Mahesh Maharshi, who had run the garden with an iron fist for over thirty-five years.

'You see', he began, as we cowered slightly in our chairs on the other side of the desk. Every sentence that came from his mouth began with this booming introduction.

'You see. I have instructed the section supervisors that we should begin harvesting today. But', he warned, 'it is looking like rain and we may have to cancel until tomorrow.'

We headed out with him to the gardens armed with the knob-bly walking sticks he had insisted we would need to help us on the uneven roads. Already the supervisors were gathering to be given their instructions, and the pickers were arriving from the homes the estate provided on the grounds. As Mr Maharshi began issuing his instructions, the grey clouds in the sky began to shed their loads, at first in a gentle drizzle but then with increasing ferocity as the winds grew in strength.

'You see,' he boomed, pointing upwards, 'we can't pick in this. It will damage the leaves and make a bad end-result.' With that, he sent the workers back to their houses with strict instructions to be ready if the weather changed and sent us off with Michael, one of the managers, for a tour of the factory.

The processing of tea is complicated. First the collected leaves are withered to remove as much moisture as possible and rolled to break up the buds into the recognizable strands we know as tea. These are then fermented or oxidized both to change the colour to black and to increase the release of flavour. Finally, before being packed, the tea is dried once more over blowers of hot air. As in so many factories I visited, levels of hygiene here and throughout the garden were high, and I found myself, for the lord knows how many times on the trip, donning a pair of boots and a set of overalls before entering. Interesting though it may have been, I had seen enough factories on this tour to last me a lifetime, and I was pleased when we were finally able to head back to the guesthouse and catch up on some much-needed sleep.

Fortunately, the next morning dawned bright and clear. At 6.45 a.m., as we arrived at the meeting point, groups of pickers, mostly immigrants from neighbouring Nepal, were already being sent to designated gardens with a yield target to harvest during the day. I asked why all the pickers were women.

'You see,' Mr Maharshi explained, 'women have smaller hands and are better able to pick the stems with two buds we need to make good tea, without damaging them.'

We were sent with Michael to walk through the gardens to watch the picking in action. Set against the snow-topped hills, with the sun already breaking through the thin cloud cover, the women were already hard at work filling the baskets attached to their backs by a cloth draped over their heads. They stopped picking as we approached, intrigued by Vanessa's fiery red hair and pale skin but even more by her smooth hands. We watched them deftly snap buds from the waist-high bushes and toss them over their shoulders into the baskets, which can hold nearly a kilogram of tea each. Every picker is given a target not just for the amount they harvest but also for the quality of the buds they collect, and the details are filled into huge, handwritten ledgers.

The work is tough, that was obvious, but by comparison with many in a region with crippling poverty and much unemployment, the workers in tea gardens consider theirs a lucky lot, with schools, hospitals, meals and houses provided.

'We work very hard,' Michael explained, 'but workers are treated well and stay here for a long time', he added, explaining that he too had been with Goomtee for over thirty-five years. Our time with them, however, was up, and after our tour we headed back for a taxi to Darjeeling itself.

The journey, a further couple of hours upwards, was even more terrifying than the journey from the airport to Goomtee. I was only pleased that we did not take up the option of using the 'Toy Train', Darjeeling's famous narrow-gauge railway, which chugs over several bone-shaking hours from the top to the bottom of the mountains every day.

Darjeeling is a pleasant town, but after the tranquillity of Goomtee, coming to a place predicated on serving tourists, who use it as a base before heading to Nepal, it was an unpleasant return to the real world. I was not sorry when, two days later, it was time to head back down to the airport and to Kolkata.

When I checked my e-mails, I was thrilled to see that I had received a note from two of my relatives. Baba's middle and older sisters had invited us to visit them on our last day in Kolkata. Baba had not been back to India for thirty years. As with so many in the Indian diaspora, he had always meant to return, but with the passing of each year and then the passing of my mother, it became increasingly unlikely. Now, as he had said to me in a phone conversation before I left on this stage of the journey, 'Britain is my country. India hasn't been my country for fifty years.'

Inevitably he had lost touch with his siblings, and I still wondered what reception we would receive. I need not have worried: they were, after all, Majumdars by blood even if by marriage rather than name. I warned Vanessa that food would be involved, but she wouldn't listen as she shovelled the delicious breakfast of channa masala and luchi down her throat in the guesthouse that morning.

'Sure, sure', she said as I dodged a volley of bread from her mouth.

At the first port of call my father's elder sister hugged us both and then led us into their apartment, where my uncle was already seated at a table heaving with food. 'We thought you would have taken breakfast already, so we just did some snacks', she said, pointing apologetically at plates of spiced potatoes, mutton cutlets and a pile of balloon-like puri breads. Rather relishing Vanessa's obvious discomfort at the sight of more food, I added 'Vanessa loves Bengali sweets too'.

'I'll send someone out to get some', my aunt added, hollering into the kitchen for the maid to run out and buy some. We somehow managed to work our way through most of the spread, including the desserts, with some effort, before my aunt announced, 'We have a taxi coming to take you to your middle aunt. She just phoned. I told her Vanessa likes sweets, so she has just sent someone out to get some.'

Vanessa gave me a withering look, but it was worth it to see her face turn almost as green as the top she was wearing. True to form, when we arrived at our next port of call, bowls of mishti doi and rasgulla had been laid out and my aunt stood over us as we force-fed ourselves spoons of creamy yoghurt from the store below my aunt's house.

'Much better than K.C. Das', she nodded approvingly.

By the time we left, we were both feeling decidedly peaky and headed back to the guesthouse to sleep it off before it was time to take Vanessa back to the airport for the start of her long journey home. I was not leaving until the next morning, which gave me time on my own to reflect on my visit to the land of my fathers. Had I actually discovered anything? Not really. I felt no more Indian than I had before I arrived. I was pretty certain, however, that it would be a long time before I headed back to India again. It's just too crazy for a half-Welsh half-Bengali to cope with.

34

It's My Party and I'll Braai if I Want To

'Steaks should be juicy. They should be thick, and they should be saucy.'

I certainly wasn't going to disagree with Emil Den Dulk. For one thing he was well over six foot tall and built like a prop forward, and for another thing he was wielding a wicked-looking cleaver. He was using the knife to carve two-inch-thick steaks from a 10 kg strip of sirloin, ordered for the occasion of my first South African braai.

Outside, Emil senior, his father, was busy stoking the flames of the barbecue and adding more wood to the fire, while back inside the kitchen his mother, Sonette, was fussing about preparing the traditional accompaniments. Neal McCleave, a friend of mine for over twenty years, turned to me, glass of wine in hand.

'It doesn't get too much better than this', he said, sipping on his drink and pointing to where the sun was dipping behind the mountains on the horizon.

I had been delighted to get an e-mail from Neal asking me if he could join me on my trip to South Africa and Mozambique. The appeal of solo travel was rapidly beginning to lose its shine. Neal likes his food but doesn't share my obsession with it and often deflates my long-winded descriptions of elaborate meals with a curt 'Just start wearing a dress and get over it'. His own favourite food story involves coming home from school one day and finding his father munching happily on a cheese sandwich that Neal knew for a fact had been in the bin twenty-four hours earlier.

I was on the road again. After a three-day stopover in London to visit my flat, I flew across the equator to South Africa, where Neal would join me two days later in Cape Town. If there is a more beautifully situated city in the world, I would love to see it. With Table Mountain towering over one side and the waters of the ocean lapping on the other, it is little wonder that South Africans go teary when it is mentioned, and before Neal arrived, I spent two enjoyable days wandering around the shops of Long Street and the marinas of the impressively restored waterfront.

I was less impressed with the food, however, most of the options being ersatz versions of European and American restaurants supplemented by cheap and cheerful food for the huge number of backpackers who use Cape Town as an easy access point for their exploration of southern Africa. It says a lot that the best thing I ate was a boerwors, a spicy South African sausage, served from a night-time stall on Long Street. It was tasty enough, but hardly the basis of an entire cuisine.

Cape Town, like all of South Africa, has its problems. Apartheid may have gone, but huge divisions still remain between the races. The white, black and coloured South Africans are still separated by huge levels of mistrust and the even more powerful forces of economics, which means that the black population still fills the majority of menial roles and live in the townships, while the white population still controls the majority of the wealth. Despite this, the South Africans have an almost insatiable passion for life and for enjoying themselves, and few people I met on the trip displayed that more than Emil Den Dulk.

I had been given Emil's contact details by my friend John Glaser of Compass Box Whisky and first met up with him the previous night, when he had collected me and Neal, who had arrived by now, at the end of a boat trip to the infamous island prison Robben Island. We had both been silent and deep in thought on the return journey, after a tour of the sombre buildings of the jail and a glimpse at the tiny cell in which Nelson Mandela had been held for so many years.

Emil announced that he had tickets for the Taste of Cape Town food festival and drove us to one of the most beautiful parts of the city, where local restaurants had set up stalls to serve two or three of their signature dishes each. We spent two or three hours wandering from stall to stall with Emil and his friends eating everything on offer and sampling South African wines before heading back to the city and the more genteel environment of Bascule, a bar with the biggest selection of whisky in the southern hemisphere. Some of the food had been good and some had been ordinary, but I couldn't help thinking that it was still a pale reflection of what I might be getting back in London or any other major city. I wanted to find something truly South African and, as Emil poured me a couple of fingers of peaty malt whisky, I told him so.

'Well,' he smiled back at me, 'you're certainly going to get that tomorrow. We're going to have a braai for you out at the farm.'

That was just what I wanted to hear. The braai is at the very heart of South African cuisine. It is not just a meal: it's a way of life and a celebration of South African culture.

We were waiting, ravenous and ready when he came to collect us late the following afternoon. We even tried to add in some pre-emptive exercise by attempting to climb Table Mountain, a feat that I singularly failed to achieve, in no small part thanks to the rather stupid combination of a huge hangover, malaria medication and a large fried breakfast, much of which ended up in a puddle on South Africa's beloved rock.

Emil's parents run one of the most prestigious wineries in South Africa, De Toren, in the heart of the Stellenbosch wine region, set in 26 hectares of the most beautiful land imaginable, with mountain ranges in the distance on one side of their house and the ocean in the distance on the other. Their wines from the estate are well respected, particularly one named Fusion V, made from the same five grapes as Bordeaux, and it wasn't long after we arrived that Emil senior had already begun to open two or three bottles from different years for us to try and Emil junior began to build the barbecue using wood from pruned vineyards.

Soon he had a roaring fire going and had started to prepare the meat. The strip of sirloin was carved up into steaks, which he rubbed with a dry marinade. A large boerwors was formed into a spiral and skewered so it would hold together. Emil produced a dish of small round bundles called skilpadjies, made of minced lamb's liver mixed with coriander leaf and then wrapped in fat before being roasted.

There are a lot of rules and rituals when it comes to braai. The preparation of the grill and the cooking of the meat are men's work. In fact, it is one man's work and, while the designated griller, the 'tongmaster', takes charge, the other men stand around drinking, offering sage words of advice about the size of the flames and the position of the meat on the grill. The women's task is to provide the traditional accompaniments to the meat: cheese sandwiches, grilled on the fire to be eaten as an appetizer, and meili pap, a porridge made of ground maize and served with a sauce made from tomatoes, onions and chilli.

Sonette introduced me to an Afrikaans word. 'Lekker,' she said, sniffing the air filled with the smells of cooking, 'it's going to be lekker. It means lovely.'

When it all came together, we gathered around the family dining table and joined hands to say grace before sitting down to one of the biggest meals I can remember. The steaks were every bit as good as I had anticipated, with a spicy crust formed by the rub giving way to a flood of juices once I cut through the flesh. The meat was fresh, not aged, reminding me of the steaks in Argentina rather than the ones in the USA, and the meili pap proved to be the perfect starch to soak up not only the juices but also the innumerable glasses of wine Emil senior kept pouring for us.

Above all, it was the hospitality of the Den Dulks that I shall remember. Neal leaned over to me as he was ripping apart his dessert of koeksister, a dense, syrup-coated doughnut: 'It's hard to believe we had not even met these people twenty-four hours ago and now we are sitting in their winery eating their food and drinking their wines.'

Emil senior topped up my glass with more of that excellent Fusion V, and I looked at Neal: 'Welcome to my world, mate. Welcome to my world.'

Neal's world, however, is the internet, and he is good at it, having risen to a high level with a service provider in London. In a booze-addled moment of generosity he had offered to organize and pay for the two of us to spend a few days of rest and relaxation at one of Mozambique's secluded beach lodges, and after two more days touring the stunning wine country around Cape Town, we caught an early morning flight to Maputo, the capital.

Cape Town had not felt like Africa. It was developed and prosperous. Maputo felt like Africa from the moment we landed: the strong military presence at the airport, the chaos of clearing immigration and the inevitable battle for a taxi to our hotel. There too things were a shambles, and we entered our room to find that it had only one bed and that it was occupied by a large naked man watching football and scratching his gonads.

'Welcome to Africa', Neal gave me a thin smile and stomped off back down to the reception. He had that look of the consumer crusader about him which I had seen many times over the years, so I waited with the bags while he went to give the staff what for. Eventually, after two more changes, we found ourselves in a room with air-conditioning, two beds and a working television.

The staff obviously planned their revenge, because the next morning Neal looked as though he might not live until lunchtime. We had eaten in the hotel the previous night, supplementing a few local beers with a plate of mystery meat, which was now happily making its way out of both ends of Neal.

He was determined to battle on, and we hired a taxi for a guided tour of the city. It's a hideously ugly place and reminded me of Salvador, Brazil – no surprise really, as both are former Portuguese colonies. Like Salvador, Maputo does not feel particularly safe for the visitor and, as our driver deposited us at each point of interest to walk around, he watched carefully to see that we were not separated from our wallets or worse. There's not a lot to see: a crumbling old fort, a train station and a tin house built by Mr Eiffel, of Parisian tower fame. That's your lot.

More than anything, I wanted to sample the huge and succulent prawns for which Mozambique is famous, so I asked the driver to take us along the coast road to Costa do Sol, a remnant of colonial days and still considered the best fish restaurant in the city. Neal was still looking a bit green, so I chose a young Portuguese wine to match the colour of his face and a plate of fried squid to begin with.

Then the main course arrived: twenty-four of those astounding shellfish, grilled simply and doused in butter. I ripped the shells from the flesh and bit into one. It was beautifully sweet and meaty, and I did not care that the butter was dribbling down my chin onto my shirt. The ones on Neal's plate looked just as good and tasted even better when he finally declared he could eat no more without risk of vomiting. Of course, I helped him finish them, all the time making exaggerated yummy noises to emphasize just how good they were. He may never forgive me, and I don't care.

Neal had decided we were going to spend a few days at Guludo Lodge, a five-hour jeep ride from Pemba, in the north of the country. It was a small resort predicated on responsible tourism, which employed most of its staff from local villages and which was built from local materials. Our accommodation consisted of bandas, which opened up almost directly onto the powdery white sands of the beach and with no electricity: light came only from oil lamps. For the three nights we were there we drifted to sleep and were woken up by the sounds of the aqua-blue sea lapping gently near by.

The food was good, although limited by what could be

collected from Pemba and what was brought up to the kitchen from the beach by local fishermen. Meals were served under the stars at tables set back from the beach, and Neal, who was obviously travelling light and could not pack more than one joke, came out with the same line every night, 'Shall we go to our special table, darling?' Oh, how we laughed.

It was good to have a few days where food was not at the centre of my every waking thought, and I took the opportunity to do as little as possible, swaying gently in a hammock for hours on end while catching up with some reading. My only exercise came when I visited the local village with Neal, and we found ourselves being followed everywhere we went by a gaggle of beautiful, inquisitive children keen to see the videos and pictures of them we would take on our cameras. I could not resist it and was soon playing Pied Piper, hurtling around the narrow dusty streets of the town with half the childhood population in tow squealing and giggling with delight.

When it was time to leave the lodge and head back to Maputo and from there to Johannesburg, we were both slightly deflated. The pace of life at the lodge, or rather the lack of it, was just what we had both needed, for different reasons. I was heading on to the next stage of the journey and Neal back to work. I was sorry to see him go. There are few things better than a holiday with good mates, particularly when they are kind enough to pay for it. But it was time to head our separate ways, and I was off to Senegal.

35

Teranga

In the local language of Senegal, Wolof, *teranga* means 'welcome' and is not just a greeting but a state of mind, the expression of the hospitality of the nation towards visitors. It obviously doesn't apply to weary travellers on round-the-world trips, because the welcome I received on my arrival in Dakar was not one that the Senegalese tourist board would ever wish to put in a brochure.

My friend Isabelle Fuchs, in Munich, had previously been married to a man from Senegal. When she heard about *Eat My Globe*, she promised me that the food in Senegal was good and that her ex-husband, Keba, and his family would look after me. So, knowing better than to doubt a German, I added Dakar to the itinerary.

It started well enough. The plane from Johannesburg was on time, and immigration was a breeze: they even had swish new landing forms emblazoned with that word 'TERANGA'. With only a handful of bags to come through, I collected Big Red in ten minutes. So far, so good. Then, to use the technical term, it all went pear-shaped.

As I stepped out of the grim arrivals hall, the people who were meeting me were nowhere to be seen. I had a phone number, which I punched into my mobile. After a few rings it was answered in French. Had they wanted to know the way to the Sacré Coeur from the Eiffel Tower or 'les choses nécessaires pour préparer le petit déjeuner', I would very much have been their man. Unfortunately, my schoolboy French was little use in Dakar airport at midnight looking for someone I didn't know.

If my expected hosts were not there to greet me, plenty of other people were, and suddenly, in a scene straight from a zombie movie, I was surrounded by about thirty heaving bodies, all with arms outstretched. Touts I could deal with. I could 'Non, merci' with the best of them to the would-be taxi drivers and the people selling phone cards and chewing gum, although I really did want to ask the man who proffered an edition of French Scrabble 'Classique' to a weary passenger at midnight, what the bloody hell he was thinking. But others had less professional matters in mind. One person grabbed my arm while another tried to prise my mobile phone from my hand. Another had already laid 'dibs' to Big Red, on which I was sitting, and was trying to push me off using a short run-up and a shoulder charge he must have learned from watching wrestling.

I heard someone barking loudly, again in French, and looked up to see a man beaming at me through a ring of gold-capped teeth. This was obviously Keba, and all was saved. 'Hurrah' for him and 'yah boo sucks' to all my assailants, who were drifting back into the shadows from whence they had come. My saviour gave me another beaming smile and then said, in a tone I found slightly less friendly than one would hope for from a welcoming party, 'Give me $50 and I will make sure no one hurts you.'

Oh, just great. Now I was the bitch of the local mobster. He began to push my luggage trolley over to the side of the car park and turned, beckoning me to follow with a wicked grin before flicking open a mobile phone and hollering down the mouthpiece. A good-looking boy like me could fetch top dollar on today's market, and I fully expected to be packed off by noon to serve as a love slave to a blubbery woman in an Arab state with a name that sounds like phlegm.

Just as I had nearly given up all hope of ever seeing my beloved Big Red again, I felt another, altogether more gentle, hand on my shoulder and turned to see the wide, engaging grin of a tall man in a black bomber jacket.

'You must be Simon', he said. 'I'm Bath. We've had a lot of

trouble getting through security. I hope you haven't had any trouble.'

'Trouble?' I wanted to scream at him. 'Trouble? I've practically been gang-raped. That man over there, walking away with my bag, by the way, is on the phone right now trying to sell me into slavery, and to top it all off, someone tried to make me buy the French edition of Scrabble.'

But before I could say a word, he had spoken quietly with my self-appointed bodyguard, who gave in without a fight, and was lifting Big Red onto his shoulders gesturing for me to follow him to a waiting taxi.

The way I felt that night, I would have cut my stay in Senegal down to as short a time as physically possible, a feeling added to when Keba, standing nonchalantly by the taxi, told me that I was not going to stay with him after all, as he was leaving for Germany the next day, and we needed to find a hotel. The fact that it was well past midnight did not seem to faze him at all. He instructed the taxi driver to take us to a procession of hotels of diminishing quality until we found one that had space and met the requirements of my meagre and hastily calculated budget. I finally got to crash in a hotel room that was as tired and worn out as I was by about 3.30 a.m.

It tells you all your need to know about Senegal that, despite the unpromising start, it turned out to be one of the most enjoyable stops of the trip, thanks to my new friend. Sakhary Sy, or Bath (pronounced 'Batch') as he was known to everyone, spoke perfect English littered with Americanisms picked up while acting as a translator for the US military. It was not just his English, however. It was his manner.

Tall and constantly smiling, Bath was one of the kindest, most gentle people I have ever encountered. He was about my own age and lived with his family, including a 97-year-old father, in a town some twenty miles outside Dakar, and seemed to know everyone in the city. He knew every beggar and pan-handler in Dakar by name, and often gave them a few coins.

'Charity is one of the pillars of Islam', he explained.

He sent hawkers away not with a shout but with a smiling 'Benenyon Inchallah' ('Next time, if God wills it') and used his loose change to purchase small songbirds, kept in cramped wooden cages, so he could release them into the skies, saying, 'Perhaps as they fly away, they will pray for me'.

He loved his city and announced to me, slightly incongruously, that it was his 'hood'. I liked him immediately, and on our first morning, as he took me on a walking tour, I explained to Bath why I was there.

'Food?' he replied. 'Well, I love food and we have great things to eat here.'

With that, he turned and headed in the direction of Sadaga, the central market of the city. The market was interesting, but, the real reason we were there was to try mafé, one of the staples of West African cooking. Bath led me to Chez Khady. It bore a name that reflected the city's French colonial past, but the restaurant itself was pure Africa. Communal tables were already heaving as we arrived, pre-paid for our meal and carved out a place for ourselves amid the bustle of men in flowing robes and women in explosions of colourful material. When the food arrived, it was simple, delivered without airs and graces on a plate of rice served next to a bowl of mafé with a pleasing slick of oil on the top.

Beef or goat was slow-cooked with chilli, onions, tomatoes and local vegetables, including cassava, until it thickened to form a rich, satisfying stew with a real kick. Not enough of a kick for Bath, however, who showed me how to mash up the scotch bonnet pepper so it slowly released its powerful juices into the gravy as you ate. The end-result was a dish so deeply savoury I could taste it for hours afterwards.

Dakar turned out, against all expectations, to be a pleasingly laid-back city with one or two sights of interest. But I began to realize that it was only going to take a couple of days to see everything, and I would still be killing time that could be better spent elsewhere.

In between sight-seeing, however, Bath was determined to fill my time with good food and wanted to introduce me to another Senegalese staple, yassa, a dish of chicken marinated with chillies, oil, lime juice and garlic before being roasted and then served in a sauce soured with palm vinegar and olives. The restaurant he chose was packed with locals, and plump servers in flowing robes were shimmying between tables fussing over the customers. Our lunch was placed before us, and we tucked into the communal pot. It was another great taste, simply prepared and served but with layers of flavour, from the sourness of the vinegar to the heat of the chillies. The accompanying local Gazelle beer, which Bath insisted we drink, was a perfect match.

Senegalese food was a very pleasant surprise to me. As in many developing nations, where food is fuel before it is fun, it's simple stuff: expensive proteins in the shape of beef, chicken, fish or goat being padded out with filling carbohydrates of rice, millet or potatoes. But the Senegalese make sure it is never dull, both by the preparation, which involves fresh ingredients, slow cooking and challenging heat, and the way it is served, with added doses of hospitality and tables often sharing from one large communal plate.

Bath's dream was for every visitor to love Senegal as much as he did, and he suggested we travel to his home town of Rufisque, where I would see real life away from the capital. He suggested we go by local taxi – one of the private cars that congregate by Independence Square ready to be hired for the hour-long journey. I was slightly alarmed that our chosen carriage appeared to have no doors, but Bath was not fazed and, joined by three others, we squeezed into the car, which sank until it was just clearing the ground. Two of the driver's friends appeared, carrying the missing doors, and began attaching them to the car with the aid of packing tape, going over and under the car until, satisfied, the driver set off on the journey with us trapped inside a Christmas present on wheels.

An hour later we waited patiently for the driver to cut the package open, Bath took me to his home to introduce me to his family. His two sisters had been busy preparing lunch: one of them gutting and cleaning fish, the other pulverizing spices in a pestle to create 'soul', used to flavour perhaps the most famous dish of Senegalese cooking, thiebou djene. It means simply 'fish with rice', but that does not do justice to a fabulous dish in which sweet, bony fish are cooked with vegetables and served on spiced rice that has been allowed to cook until the bottom layer develops an addictive, crunchy crust.

When mealtime came around, Bath took me into his room, where we ate together from one large plate placed on a small table. The rest of his family sat outside in the courtyard enjoying their own communal meal. The pleasure he took in serving and then eating the meal was obvious.

'Have some sauce,' he said, ladling a spoonful over a portion of rice for me, 'the flavour is the best.'

'Mix some hot sauce with the fish. It brings the sweetness out.'

We cleaned the plate down to the last grain of rice, and he pushed back his chair with the same huge grin on his face that had been such a welcome sight at the airport.

'Man, my sisters can cook', he said with a satisfied sigh.

If *Eat My Globe* was about anything worthwhile, it was about moments like this. Here I was, in a house in Senegal with a man I had only met a day or so before, sharing a meal prepared by his family.

At the end of my stay he insisted on seeing me to the airport, even though I had to check in at 4 a.m. 'I don't want you to have the same experience leaving Senegal as you had arriving', he explained over my protests. As we said goodbye, I fumbled in my pocket and found a handful of loose change that I would not be able to use. I handed it to him, thinking he could at least use it to buy some of that Gazelle beer he liked so much.

'Thanks. I'll use it to buy some more birds to set free', he said with another broad smile. 'I'll ask them to pray for you.' With that, he extended his hand to touch knuckles and headed off back towards the city. That was Senegal. That was my new friend Bath, and that, in the end, was the true meaning of *teranga*.

36

Off on the Road to Morocco

Casablanca, Morocco's capital, gets a horrendous press. One guidebook described it as 'unloved and unlovely', and another one calls it 'actively rank'. I can see why. It is not a pretty city and has few of the attractions tourists look for in Morocco. There is an industrial port and a rather tatty-looking Medina, and that is about it. Except for, of course, the Hassan II Mosque, which was completed recently and is second in size only to Mecca in the Islamic world. It's impressive, with a capacity of over 100,000, and the calls to prayer blasted out by its sizeable speakers can be heard all over the city.

I rather liked it. It had all the hallmarks of a city that really appeal to me – a city not based on visitors but full of normal working stiffs getting on with the task of earning their daily crust and then spending the rest of their time figuring out where to have that daily crust. Casablanca has its own bustling charm and enough food options for even someone with my jaded palate to perk up and take notice and certainly enough to fill the two days I had to kill before catching the train to Marrakech.

Morocco, because of its mainly Muslim population, is a predominantly dry country. The few places that sell beer are as dark and unwelcoming as a Soho sex shop. I decided that a few dry days would do me no harm at all and instead found my way to one of the many cafés that litter the streets and alleyways of Casablanca. Serving little else except strong coffee and thick, sweet mint tea, the coffee shop is at the centre of Moroccan culture. It is where men – always men – come to meet and argue over anything and everything. Chairs are always set so they are facing the street to allow people-watching, making for a perfect point to relax, jot down some notes and decide what to do with my limited time there.

Of course, this mainly revolved around eating. I caught a cab up to the Quartier Habous, the new city built by the French in the early twentieth century, and found my way to a strip of butchers specializing in camel meat. The heads of the meat's previous owners were swinging from hooks outside the shops, just in case you had any doubts, and at the end of the strip a man behind a large grill was charring large steaks and kebabs. I bought a kebab and doused it in chilli sauce. It was the toughest meat I had ever encountered, like old beef, and after chewing furiously on the same piece for over twenty minutes I discarded the rest and went to look for something a bit softer.

Benis, in the same district, is one of the most famous patisseries in Morocco. I bought a box full of sublime pastries – some light and crumbly, others filled with pistachios and cream and some drowned in honey, all incredibly addictive – and I polished off a box of fifteen as I walked back towards my hotel. But the best treat was the most simple. On Mohammed V, one of the main roads through the city, was a small market selling fruits, vegetables, fresh fish and meat. In the surrounding streets were shopfront cafés preparing food from the market. At one end men were running across the street with freshly killed chickens to thread on to rotisserie skewers, and at the other end there was the constant whirr of machinery as fresh juices were pumped into small glasses. I chose a shop at random and sat on a small bench. Using my schoolboy French, I was able to order half a roast chicken with bread. You would think such a simple meal hardly worth remarking on, but it is if it is a freshly killed chicken, grilled slowly on a spit until the flesh remains moist and falls from the bones while the skin is crispy and delicious. It is if it is served with a bowl of olives warmed through with juices from the chicken mixed with olive oil, lemon juice and lemon zest. And it is if the whole lot, including a fresh pomegranate juice, costs under £1. Honest food prepared by working people for working people with immense friendliness and hospitality.

As much as I liked Casablanca, I found it hard to warm to Marrakech. It's certainly beautiful. With the twisting alleys of the Medina, the explosions of colour in the labyrinthine souks and the well-preserved remnants of its royal past, it should be the perfect place to experience Morocco and Moroccan cuisine at its very best.

There are vast numbers of tourists, mainly French, but also Spanish, Germans, a smattering of Brits and huge numbers of fearful-looking Americans with their unerring ability to blend in seamlessly with the locals. I was adding to the tourist numbers by one, obviously, so I shouldn't complain, but I will anyway. Like all cities that predicate themselves on the arrival of visitors from many nations, everything in Marrakech seemed neutered and false.

The mayhem of the Jemma El Fna, the main square of the Medina, with its snake charmers, acrobats, dancers and fortune tellers, felt more like a ride in a theme park than a real expression of the character of the city. The bustling streets had all the edge of a well-polished pool ball. As with the city itself, so with the food, much of which seemed aimed at extracting cash from the gullible rather than providing quality and a taste of genuine Moroccan hospitality.

Obviously it is possible to eat well. In my case it took the help of the owner of my charming and well-placed guesthouse, nestled away in the alleys of the Medina, to point me in the right direction, particularly in my search for some of the royal Moroccan food for which Marrakech is famous.

Riad Dar Mimoun came highly recommended and, like most riads, worked on the basis of a set menu, giving the opportunity to try a superb example of a pastilla. It's a classic of Moroccan cuisine. The dense pastry filled with an unusual combination of savoury meat from pigeons or duck with sweet fruits is not to everybody's taste, but I cleared my plate to the last crumb. I followed it with a classic tagine of lamb with prunes and almonds slow-cooked in a style developed to preserve water. The meat fell from the bones, from where I was able to suck the precious cargo of blubbery warm marrow before using bread to mop up the thin juices.

Despite this memorable meal, I was not sad when it was time to leave Marrakech and take the train back to Casablanca. Moroccan trains are wonderfully efficient, and a first-class ticket confirmed a seat in an air-conditioned carriage. As I boarded, I realized I would have travelling companions for the journey; and, being one of the most hospitable peoples on earth, when the Moroccans travel, they bring food and when the Moroccans bring food, they share it.

My carriage was full as we pulled out of the station, and within half an hour everyone was chatting in a mixture of Arabic and French. Soon the food began to appear. Lots of it: loaves of soft bread, cheese, dried fruits, hunks of chicken someone had in a cold bag, and flasks of coffee and sweet tea. My contribution of half a pack of Pringles was shameful, but no one seemed to care and I was invited to join the party as we all happily stuffed our faces until the train pulled into Casablanca's Voyageur railway station.

I said my farewells, swapping hugs and business cards with my new friends, but I did not have time to linger. I needed to go straight to the station. It was time for a reunion. Together again with TGS, and where better to do that than Spain?

37

A Horeseman Riding By

Whenever I sent TGS a mail raving about whatever dish I happened to be enjoying in whatever country, the reply would come with the annoying but inevitable qualification 'Sounds good, but is it Spain?' He knew that, wherever I was and whatever I was eating, I would always be making comparisons with my favourite country of all, Spain. It's his favourite too, and we have both been obsessive about Spain since our parents bought a place on the Costa del Sol in the early 1980s.

They chose Fuengirola, a small fishing village turned Sodom and Gomorrah, where charter planes of people were disgorged every summer to spend all day getting as burned as possible on the beach and all night getting as drunk as possible in bars before ending their day's activities with a fight and a much-needed vomit. Despite this, we fell in love with the town, the country and the food.

To someone who has not visited Spain it is hard to explain why it captures the imagination so readily. For TGS and me the food, the wine and the people are a combination we have found hard to resist for nearly thirty years, and we make a point of going at least twice a year to Madrid, our favourite city, and other regions of this vast and remarkable country.

During my brief Christmas stopover I was invited to join the owner of a Spanish restaurant in London for supper. Next to me at the same event sat Andrew Sinclair, who worked for González Byass and whose job it was to persuade the UK that sherry is not just a drink you give your granny or a wandering cleric if they happen upon your doorstep. Sherry has a real image problem. Most people have never tried it and think it is something that tastes like melted Christmas cake, which it can do, but that is like saying that all opera involves big, fat women in armour shouting at you in German.

He was preaching to the converted. Sherry has always been one of my favourite drinks. When I was a student, for reasons I can never quite fathom, I decided that I needed to study theology. Each evening I would sit in the darkened room of my student accommodation, puffing on a pipe (no sniggering at the back) having important discussions about God with my fellow students, all the while sipping on a small glass of Harvey's Bristol Cream. Obviously, I was totally insufferable as I sat there pontificating – I still am when given half a chance – but at the very least it was my first introduction to this most under-rated of drinks.

As the Majumdar children grew older, our Christmas morning traditions expanded to include the opening of a bottle of crisp, cold fino sherry as we waited for a stupidly large turkey to brown in the oven. Even now, when I taste this delicate, slightly acidic wine, I half-expect to turn around and see my mother wrapping sausages in bacon or happily rolling balls of stuffing.

Over supper I told Andrew about *Eat My Globe*. 'You should come down to the Feria de Caballos in Jerez next April', he said. 'It is a fair for the local horsemen, but really it's an excuse to drink vast amounts of sherry.'

The words 'with knobs on' sprang rapidly into my head, particularly when he said I could invite TGS and that the company he worked for, Gonzalez Byass, one of the great sherry families, would be able to find some hotel space for us. By the time the trip came around at the end of April 2008, I was exhausted but excited. I connected with TGS in Madrid, and by late afternoon we were in our hotel in Jerez de la Frontera, ready to indulge in sherry and sherry-related products.

Jerez, however, did not seem quite so ready. Not one bar

was open. This wasn't the Spain we knew and adored. As we walked, we began to get a little desperate: it was, after all, nearly six hours since we had had beer and Ibérico ham at Madrid's Atocha station, and TGS was beginning to go cold jamón on me. Then TGS spotted gaggles of well-dressed pensioners walking in the opposite direction. We followed them, realizing what was happening. When the feria comes to town, the town itself closes, and all the bars move to the fairground to ply their trade there.

As we approached, we could already see the sky lit up by the lights from the fair, but nothing prepared us for the incredible sight as we walked through the main entrance. To call this simply a fair would not do it justice. It covered an enormous area, and was packed with *casetas*, lavish stands representing the bars, clubs and sherry bodegas of Jerez. Music mixed with happy chattering was deafening, as tens of thousands of people milled from stand to stand with glasses of sherry in their hand.

We were struck immediately by the good nature of it all and could not help but think that, if the same event was held in the UK, with all the booze consumed, the local police and casualty departments would be working overtime. Here the locals, young and old, were just determined to have a good time. If someone bumped into you, they apologized; if you were queuing at the bar for a drink, they would make way for you. For two boys from South Yorkshire, where touching someone's pint leads to a friendly kicking, it was all a bit disconcerting. Not disconcerting enough for us to leave, however, and we stayed until way past midnight sampling as we walked before calling it quits and returning to the hotel for a reasonably early night.

Jerez, however, had no such intentions. As we left, people a good deal older than us were just arriving for their night's entertainment, and the young folk looked as though they wouldn't stop drinking and dancing until the small hours of the morning. Us folk in the middle, however, were keen to indulge in a comfortable hotel and wanted to be on top form for the next day, when we had been promised a tour of the vineyards and bodegas of González Byass.

Founded in 1885, González Byass was a joint venture by the wonderfully named Manuel Maria González Angel and his English agent, Mr Byass. Nearly 130 years later it remains in family hands and is one of the most famous names in sherry, particularly for its Tio Pepe brand, named after Manuel's uncle, who was the first to create the fortified wine we now know as fino.

We had been promised a special treat by Andrew and met up with him and others from the group mid-morning to head out to the vineyards. From the look on their faces it was pretty obvious that they had been at the fair for a few more days than we had. Dark glasses were in evidence, and there was the slightest air of loin girdage about facing the final couple of days after what I gathered were one too many late nights and early mornings. TGS and I, however, were now in fine fettle, bouncing around in excitement as we were chauffeured to the enormous vineyards of Palomino and Pedro Ximénez grapes just outside the city. Well over 900 hectares, it is an impressive sight, but pales in comparison with the González Byass bodegas back in Jerez itself.

Each beautiful bodega, or warehouse, has its own aroma, taken from the type of sherry being produced inside. The lofty warehouses of fino barrels had that sharp, clean smell of fresh, young sherry. Those housing the Pedro Ximénez are filled with a sweet, almost musty hue. It would be as easy to get as drunk on the aroma as it would be on the wine itself. Martin Skelton, the M. D. gave us a short history lesson as we walked through, explaining that sherry really began with the transport of wine to Britain in the 1800s, when it was first fortified to keep it from spoiling on the long journey. Fino was created almost by accident as a failure to fortify the wine sufficiently allowed a must to develop on the surface of the wine, which stopped it colouring. Sherry is produced by the solera system which, sounds like a Mike Oldfield album but in fact refers to the way that barrels are stored: the oldest barrel is partly emptied and then refilled by the next oldest and so on, so that the final result is a blend of many ages of sherry.

Obviously the proof is in the tasting, and after the tour Martin led us to a tasting room, where a complete range of sherry had been laid out for us. This is where I wish all those people who claim not to like sherry could have joined me as we tasted all the way from sharp, crisp fino, perfect with the local speciality of fried fish, through to the darker oloroso, finishing with a range of staggering thirty-year-old wines, which would make the perfect accompaniment to chocolate or figs. These are magical wines and deserve a wider audience.

Martin then suggested that we head back to the feria for lunch, served, of course, with Tio Pepe bottled freshly for the event only days before. Now, in the early afternoon, it was already in full swing again, and every *caseta* was buzzing with the sounds of sherry-fuelled chattering. The air was filled with the haunting sounds of *sevillanas*, the local offshoot of flamenco, which summarizes the courtship between a man and a woman in twelve prescribed steps that everyone from small children to grandparents seemed to know and everyone seemed to be taking every opportunity to dance.

No one in their right mind wanted to see me get down with my bad self, so I settled down at a table in the lavish González Byass *caseta* for the more important matter at hand: lunch, consisting of huge plates of jamón, local Manchego cheese and mounds of freshly made *fritura* of fish and seafood – all washed down, of course, with more bottles of the zesty fino than anyone cares to remember.

We were joined by one of the descendants of the original Señor González. He wanted to share with us the fact that the previous day over 25,000 bottles of Tio Pepe had been sold at the fair. A record. As though in celebration, before he left the table, he waved at one of the servers and the table was suddenly covered again in platefuls of food and bottles of sherry. TGS picked up a crisp, freshly fried anchovy, plopped it in his mouth and swooshed it down to his gullet with a good slug of chilled fino. He turned to me and mumbled through a mouthful of food and booze, 'Every now and then, just for a moment, life stops kicking you in the ass'.

We don't always see eye to eye, but in this case The Great Salami was bang on the money.

38

Istanbul: Eating Eytan's Way

The Angel Mangal Turkish restaurant sat at the less glamorous end of Upper Street in London's Islington and was a regular standby in the Majumdar brothers' dining calendar. The grilled meats were among the best in London, and we could regularly be seen chomping at our standard order of 'special mixed grill with quail and a side-order of sweetbreads' washed down with pungent Turkish wine, which worked perfectly in context but tasted like camel urine whenever we were silly enough to open a bottle at home.

These being meals with TGS, however, things were never quite that easy, and we would have to take turns calling out what piece of meat we were to select next so that there could be no possibility the other brother could steal more than his fair share.

'We just did chicken wings. How about a lamb rib?'

'Have you just had a sweetbread?'

'That's a big piece. It counts as two.'

It simply became habit and remains so in every meal we share. So much so that Jay Rayner, the restaurant critic of *The Observer* newspaper, wrote, 'The Majumdar brothers have so many rituals they could job-share as the Pope', adding that the reason for our 'your turn/my turn' approach to meals was that we came from a large Bengali family, and if such methods were not enforced, there was a strong likelihood that the runts of the litter might starve.

As you can imagine, the notion that there might ever be less than enough food on the table to feed her brood went down like a cup of cold vomit with Gwen Majumdar, and we both received phone calls of the 'I am more disappointed than angry' variety the moment the paper hit the stands. I can still hear her voice now as she announced with Welsh defiance 'Well, neither of you look like you ever went hungry'.

Our routine, however, did have some roots in our childhood – more specifically, Sunday lunchtimes, when TGS was allowed into the kitchen as the roast joint was being divvied up. It was, as is the case for so many in Britain, the only time we all got to sit down together as a family, and Mum went to town with whatever large chunk of dead protein she was preparing, supplementing it with large Yorkshire puddings and as many vegetables as would fit on the table without it collapsing.

While Auriel, Jeremy and I would stand watching, noses pressed to the glass panes of the kitchen door, Robin would pull all the choice bits off the roast chicken, fat off the beef or crackling off the pork and eat them noisily in front of us and often giving us the finger, before finally allowing us to come to the table. He termed these his 'treats' and declared them his birthright as the eldest son. This scarred me deeply, and we now have an unspoken understanding that no one of us gets more than the rest, and an accusation of such a crime is a very, very serious matter in the Majumdar household.

While there may have been an underpinning of fairness about our way of eating, there is another, marginally more sane, reason we chose to eat our mixed grill this way, which was that it allowed us to compare the tastes as we ate the same morsel at the same time. Was the plump chicken wing, piping hot off the charcoal grill, as good as before? Was the thin lamb cutlet with a ribbon of crispy fat properly seasoned? Were the nuggets of thymus gland cooked so they still retained a little bite? Such things were and are important to us, and a good hour or so after the meal would be taken up with an in-depth discussion of the performance of the grillmeister and his steady hand with the seasoning.

The Angel Mangal is long gone now, but as I flew to Istanbul from Madrid, I hoped that it would live up to the expectations aroused in me by one of my favourite restaurants. The room in my small guesthouse overlooked the Blue Mosque, glowing in the light of a crescent moon. This seemed impossibly romantic until I was tossed out of bed a few short hours later by the first Islamic call to prayer. Unable to get back to sleep, I showered and headed down to breakfast, which in Turkey is a delight. Warm bread, eggs, cheese dribbled with honey and sprinkled with thyme, olives, cucumbers and tomatoes, all to be eaten with çay, or tea, which seems to come at a ratio of three large lumps of sugar to one thimble full of liquid.

With one foot in Asia and the other in Europe, Istanbul is one of the world's most vibrant cities. The population estimates I found seem to vary, but one thing is for certain: when Turkey joins the European Union, Istanbul will by far surpass London as its most populous city. Every one seems to be on the streets at the same time, selling stuff, making stuff or fixing stuff. The noise and smells are a heady combination and can easily bewilder. As, of course, can the incredible sights.

Istanbul is a sightseer's dream. Enough to fill a week of any-body's time, even if their unhealthy obsession is food rather than antiquities. There is the Blue Mosque, so lavish a testament to faith, with its six minarets, that the Sultan had to pay for an extra tower for Mecca so that this would not be seen as a challenge. There is Hagia Sophia, the greatest church in Christendom when built, and then, after the conquest of Constantinople by the Ottomans, another imposing mosque and still one of the largest enclosed spaces on earth. The Topkapi Palace, the home of gen-erations of ruling families with its elaborate warren of rooms and courtyards and, of course, the treasures, including the bejewelled Topkapi dagger. The Spice Markets and the Grand Bazaar, where just about everything you can imagine is offered for sale from stalls many of which are hundreds of years old.

I intended to take the opportunity to see all of it. But, of course, I was here for the food, and my expectations were high. I knew enough to get away from the touristy Sultanahmet region of the city, where all the restaurants seemed set up as methods of extracting money from visitors, and headed off into the back streets and towards the river – areas that in most cities offer up choice little hole-in-the-wall joints and eateries packed full of locals.

For whatever reason, it wasn't happening. I went into cafés filled with locals but still found myself presented with dried-out kebabs and miserable-looking vegetables, all served with the double-carb combo of rice and chips. A favourite pair of shoes was worn out as I traipsed from the Old City to the New City in search of something decent to eat. I found places with promising-looking displays of meat in the window, which, when they cooked them up for me, turned to inedible meaty bullets, and when I did stumble into a local café, I was either ignored or handed a tourist menu offering fish and chips.

In my first few days in the city the best thing I ate was a fish sandwich. To be fair, it was a spectacular fish sandwich. The balik ekmek is a local speciality, prepared at restaurants underneath the Galata Bridge, which spans the Bosphorus between Europe and Asia. It combines freshly grilled mackerel fillet on a soft roll with a good helping of sharp, raw onions. When doused with lemon juice and sprinkled with salt, it is incredibly delicious, but it hardly formed the basis for a seven-day visit.

I was slightly desperate and depressed and composed a post about my plight on the Dos Hermanos blog. I resigned myself to spending the rest of my time in Istanbul sightseeing and eating dire food.

Fortunately for me, Eytan Behmoaras decided to respond. A thirty-year-old Turkish man living in London, he was dismayed by my post and had taken the time to compose a list of possible suggestions proving to me that Istanbul was a worthy place for a food visit and not, as I had rather peevishly suggested, 'a place where the ingredients are mediocre and the techniques not good enough to cover that fact up'. Eytan's list was long and had obviously taken a considerable amount of effort, so it was only fair to put in at least as much effort to find the places he suggested.

Kadiköy, a short ferry ride away, is a bustling neighbourhood in its own right with shops and a busy market. Nestling among it was the first restaurant that Eytan had suggested. It looked promising, and I chose the largest room and claimed a table. With the waiter's help I picked out four items to sample from a wide selection on the counter and at once understood why Eytan had made the suggestion. Each dish placed in front of me was better than anything I had tried so far. A bowl of lamb stew was soured with local plums and came with whole, braised cloves of garlic. A dish of aubergine had smoky flavours that come only with from long, slow cooking. And best of all was a plate of lamb's intestines stuffed with a mixture of ground lamb mince and bulgur wheat. It may have been only a sampling, but already, as I mopped up the juices with a slice of warm bread, my perception of the food of Istanbul was changing for the better.

There was a lot more to sample in the immediate vicinity: fish restaurants offering meals of Black Sea turbot or snacks of fried mussels on sticks; cafés serving lahmacun, flat bread topped with spiced minced beef to be rolled up and eaten on the hoof; and tubs of fresh yoghurt, onto which honey was dribbled straight from the comb. My biggest regret, however, is that I have but one stomach to give and this particular internal organ was attached to a body that was close to shutdown with a sudden cold. I bought myself one last treat of baklava, the frighteningly rich pastry traditionally plumped out with lamb fat, and headed back to bed and shivered through the next few calls to prayer.

The next day was my last, so, despite the fact that I still felt miserable, I was determined to try more of Eytan's other suggestions. Taksim Square is at the heart of the New City, and jostling around its edges are innumerable stalls selling doner kebabs, freshly squeezed orange juice and, best of all, Turkey's own unique take on the hamburger. Pre-made, they sit steaming in glass cabinets. They are greasy, nasty and devoid of merit, and I loved them. I devoured two in about three minutes and sat there licking my fingers, wondering if I could fit in another two before I threw up. I did. I regretted it immediately, and it added to my secret fear that, in fact, when it comes to food, I have no standards: I am just a very greedy person.

Lunch called, and I worked off the grease as I walked back to the European side of the city, taking one last opportunity to watch the bristle of fishing rods on the Galata Bridge, and settled myself at a table on the terrace of Restaurant Hamdi, overlooking the Bosphorus. Theirs are known as the *ne plus ultra* of kebabs in Istanbul, and I can see why. Hand-minced with a frightening-looking knife, the lamb used is moist with fat and rich in flavour. The service was suitably miserable, and the wine I was drinking suitably rough. I raised my glass and made a silent toast to the Angel Mangal. I also made a toast to Eytan, whose advice saved me from getting an entire city wrong. Thanks to him, Istanbul and I were getting along just fine.

I am sure Istanbul will be just thrilled to hear it.

39

Palermo: An Offer I Can't Refuse in Sicily

'She is a cheek,' Claudio leaned over to me in a conspiratorial manner, hand covering his mouth, 'but she has a deek.'

It was one of the more unusual introductions I had experienced on the trip, but there was no doubting the veracity of Claudio's grappa-fuelled statement. The person sitting opposite me taking a deep drag on a cigarette may have been going for the feminine look, but the tight jeans 'she' was wearing sported a package that suggested there was still plenty of work to be done.

I am getting ahead of myself again.

Claudio was the owner of my small B&B in Palermo, Sicily. I arrived well past midnight after my delayed flight from Istanbul. My back ached, and I had a pain in my foot which I found out later was the beginnings of a stress fracture. I was in a sorry state. When I saw the six flights of stairs, I was glad of the help he offered in lugging Big Red up to the apartment.

I told him the reason for my visit to Palermo over breakfast the next morning, and he began scribbling down the names of local specialities. 'Ah', he sighed, twisting his finger against his cheek, a gesture meaning 'delicious'.

'Sicily has the best food in Italy, the best meat, the best cheese, the best pasta and the best wine. You are going to eat well.'

He explained that, because of Sicily's history and its proximity to Africa, it had 'nine denominations in one island' and consequently a wider range of food than anywhere else in Italy. Well, he would say that, wouldn't he? But I have watched enough films to know not to argue with a Sicilian, so I took the notes he offered, folding them into my back pocket as I went to explore the city.

I liked Palermo immediately, although it struck me as a city that had not quite made up its mind about its past, as massive restoration of historical monuments in one place sat uncomfortably next to gaping holes in the ground and derelict buildings in another. But you can forgive the occasional ugliness in a city with this much passion and raw, fizzing energy.

I spent the morning in the old town and the market districts of Capo and Ballaro, filled with stalls selling meats, cheeses, fruits and vegetables and fishmongers advertised by signs pierced by the fearsome spike of the head of a swordfish. From each stall the owners barked out a list of their wares in a cacophony of sound that soon had me dipping into a local café to escape the din.

By this stage of the journey I felt like I was running on fumes. I felt bloated and unfit, not helped by my worsening foot. My palate was jaded, and I felt lonely and depressed. I was ready to go home. It would have taken a very special place to reawaken my taste buds. Palermo was it. I had met many nationalities obsessed with food along the way, but few would be able to stand their ground with the Sicilians, for whom food is obviously an offer you can't refuse. From the morning coffee, which comes, inevitably, with a rich, buttery pastry to a mid-morning sandwich snack to long, leisurely lunches, afternoon cakes and mammoth-sized suppers, there seldom seems to be a moment in the day when Sicilians are not putting food into their mouths.

I ordered a thick, dark hot chocolate and a cannoli, the uniquely Sicilian pastry tube filled to bursting with sweetened ricotta cheese. One was enough for me, but others in the bar were working their way through mounds of them as though they might never eat again. Feeling more energetic after a huge intake of sugar, I took out Claudio's notes and began to think about a mid-morning snack. One thing in particular caught my attention.

A pani ca meusa is the favourite snack of every self-respecting

Palermo man and involves slices of calf spleen simmered in lard and then served on a soft roll with a good sprinkle of salt and lemon juice. You can have it 'single', which is just spleen, or you can have it 'married', to a few slices of additional calf's lung.

The best is served at a small storefront facing the harbour. As I approached, a queue of middle-aged Sicilian men was already forming, but service was rapid and minutes later I stood at the counter with a large sandwich in my hand containing the 'married' version. The meat was soft and melting from the long simmering in lard, the salt cut through the offal taste and the lemon juice lifted the whole thing up a level. The juices had soaked through the roll, and the final combination was entirely fabulous.

I could have eaten another there and then, but I had lunch to think of and wanted to turn my mind to matters pasta. Like everything else when it comes to matters food, the Sicilians are very specific about their pasta and about their sauces, and as I walked away from the harbour back towards the town centre, I took out Claudio's list again, reading it as I decided which one of the seemingly dozens of trattorie to visit. He had written 'spaghetti con la sarde' in large letters and underlined the word 'spaghetti' three times to make it clear that this was the only acceptable pasta to have with this sauce, made of sardines. I chose a place at random and ordered as instructed along with a flask of the local Nero d'Avola wine. It was a challenging plateful, given my breakfast, cannoli and spleen sandwich, but I managed to polish off a pile of pasta spiked through with garlic and meaty chunks of sardine in a tomato sauce flavoured with local wild fennel. The wine worked perfectly, and after my meal I sloshed a little of it into the almost empty bowl and wiped the resulting *mélange* up with a hunk of warm bread.

I had been tempted to give supper a miss, but Claudio was having none of it and invited me to share supper with him and his partner, who was from Tunisia. She had spent the day making brik, a savoury filo turnover stuffed with tuna, capers and fried eggs, and as I emerged from my room, she was placing a towering plate of them on the table. They were delicious, but I could scarcely do them justice after what I had eaten in the day. I picked at a couple as Claudio asked me questions about my trip before finally escaping to bed at well past midnight.

The next morning he announced that he was not going to give me such a huge breakfast because we were going on a tour of the local neighbourhood, Vuccaria, famous for its fish market, street stalls and restaurants. Among the stalls displaying the day's catch was a man serving *polpo*, octopus, which he bought at harbour every morning and simply boiled in salted water before serving warm with the head split open so the insides could form a creamy coating of the meat. 'The 'ead is the best bit', Claudio mumbled as he licked fishy brain matter from his fingers.

We stopped in for a drink at Claudio's favourite bar, filled with gruff old men, cigarettes drooping from their mouths. Claudio ordered two large, cold bottles of Moretti beer, and while I kept watch over them, he ran around the corner and returned with a plate filled with fried seafood he had bought from another bar. 'The perfect combination', he added, giving me that finger twisted in the cheek movement again. Finally, as we drained the last of our litre bottles of beer, Claudio announced, 'Is time to have some lunch. Follow me.'

I waddled after him, and we ducked into the tiny entrance of a trattoria called Caffè Attico. 'The owner, Giovanni, is a good friend and makes the best food in the city', he assured me, as we were shown to a table outside in a busy alleyway. A couple of bottles of the inky Nero d'Avola were placed in front of us, and Giovanni and Claudio got into a heated discussion, which involved lots of hand-waving and pointing in my direction. Claudio explained, 'He did not think you would like sea urchin. I told him you ate anything.'

A large plate of spaghetti con ricci was placed in front of each of us, the pasta tossed with a sauce made from the fresh sea urchin. It tasted of the sea, and inside I could see Giovanni splitting open more of the spiny creatures, adding them to garlic sizzling in oil.

Claudio apparently knew everyone in the city. As we ate, we were joined by a parade of his acquaintances, all of whom declared that they couldn't possibly stop for a drink, before sitting down and spending the next four hours with us and getting horribly pissed. At one point I was surrounded by seven hard-faced Sicilians, all arguing about food as they tucked into the bowls of home-made semifreddo and cannoli that Giovanni had brought to the table along with bottles of lethal local grappa. It was at this point that Claudio leaned over and pointed to Valentino, the chick with the 'deek'. Valentino was Claudio's upstairs neighbour and a pre-op transexual. She had joined us during the meal, a fact I had missed, despite her appearance, because I was horribly, horribly inebriated.

'She has invited us to supper. Is OK? Because, as I say, she has a deek', he added as though this might matter to me.

'As long as she can cook, I don't care if she has two of them and can tie them in knots', I replied, swaying slightly in my seat.

Giovanni presented us with a bill that I suspect barely covered the cost of the wine we drank, and Claudio and I staggered back to his apartment, arms around each other for support.

'You are good man. You should stay for longer', he told me, fumbling for the key, letting us into the apartment and pointing me towards my bedroom. A few hours later, as I was sleeping it off, he rapped hard on my door. Disturbingly, he looked right as rain and breezily announced, 'Time for supper with cheek with deek'.

Whatever her gender definition, Valentino could certainly cook and had prepared a dish of linguini in a sauce made from veal and thickened with potatoes. It was just what I needed to help soak up the booze, and I raised my glass to propose a toast to Valentino for providing yet another memorable moment on the trip. I somehow knew that I was not going to get any sleep that night as Claudio stood and plopped the corks from another couple of bottles of wine.

At 4 a.m. I realized I only had one hour before my bus to the airport. Claudio insisted on giving me a lift on the back of his scooter, which led to the unlikely sight of a Vespa weaving its way unsteadily through the empty streets of Palermo carrying two men, both the worse for wear, one of whom was carrying a large red rucksack and holding on for dear life. As he deposited me at the bus stop, Claudio kissed me on both cheeks.

'*Ciao*, you come back soon. We have more eating to do.'

With that, he hopped back on his bike and sped off into the night, waving over his shoulder as he weaved unsteadily into the distance. I just said a silent prayer of thanks for the fact I was still alive and for the opportunity to see Sicily through one of its native sons.

40

All Roads Lead to Rome

'*Veni, vidi, vici.*'

Or at least, that's how it should have been when I entered Rome, in triumph. I had been, I had seen and I had eaten. Rome was the last official stop on the trip before I headed off to meet up with TGS for a wine-sodden 'end of the adventure' week back in Spain.

I had been to twenty-nine countries. I had eaten thousands of meals, met hundreds of people and completed a task that had not even entered my mind eighteen months earlier. I should have stormed into Italy's historic capital more unbearable than ever, stayed in a fine hotel sipping on the best wines while unutterably attractive Roman girls gave me shoulder rubs, peeled me grapes and applauded my achievements, all the time whispering in my ear 'You are not a god'.

Cut to picture of shambling forty-something hobbling up five flights of stairs to a tiny room in a grubby hotel, throwing Big Red on the floor and collapsing on the bed in tears. I had developed the tiredness equivalent of a water table, and it only took a small amount of effort to push me over the top into physical meltdown. I had not slept the night before, on my last night in Sicily, and the headache of my grappa-induced hangover had kept me awake on the plane. My foot, which had begun to ache as I reached Palermo, was now beating out constant and painful rhythms that convinced me that it was indeed fractured. I winced as I pulled off my walking shoes and socks and looked at the bright red swollen lump that was now where my foot used to be.

My only previous visit to Rome had been in 1980, a last, reluctant, childhood holiday with my parents at the age of sixteen. They had both been in their pomp – my father a successful surgeon, my mother the local magistrate – and true to form, Gwen Majumdar, who had experienced a secure but modest upbringing, was doing nothing by halves. We stayed in one of the better hotels, ate meals at expensive restaurants, and my father, who remained besotted with my mother from the day they met until the day she died, surprised her with lavish gifts of jewellery. Now, nearly thirty years later, I was far from my pomp and filled with fear.

What was going to happen now I had finished? Did I start looking for another job in publishing? I would certainly need the money. Or was this, as so many people had told me along the way, the beginning of a new chapter? I didn't know, I had not even thought about it much during the trip, but now I would have to. Added to all the other things I was experiencing, my worries began to escape me in floods of salt water.

By the time the waterworks had dried up, I was feeling better, or at least spent. I stripped and had a shower, swallowed a fistful of painkillers to numb the pain in my foot, and took out my guidebook and notes. I may not have been in any shape to conquer Rome, but I was going to have a go.

It is, of course, impossible to do the Eternal City justice when you only have two full days and you can't walk. Not that such impediments could seemingly stop the coachloads of elderly American tourists I encountered at every turn and at every major sight as I hobbled around the town. At the Colosseum I was battered out of the way by a wave of blue-rinsed women who made their way to the front of the queue using their walking frames as a handy weapon, and I saw the same group at the Palatine Hill and in the Forum. It was overhearing the description of the latter as 'a cute bunch of rocks' that made me think I should have some lunch before I said something that would make me a marked man in senior centres all over the USA.

I headed up Via Cavour, dived into a trattoria that I recognized from my internet research and ordered half a litre of house red before my backside hit the leatherette seat cover. Like all other Italians, Romans are obsessive about food and have their own specialities. In particular, they like their pizza, and pizzerias are dotted all over the city, from the corner shop selling it by weight from square blocks with different toppings to the smartest restaurants with wood-fired ovens and the finest ingredients. I have expounded my 'snot on toast' theory about pizza before in this book, so I won't repeat it here, but it is fair to say it is normally something I avoid.

When in Rome, however − even if it does involve eating something resembling mucus. I ordered the Roman favourite, pizza margherita, which, although it actually originated in Naples and is in theory the most simple of all to make, with little more than tomato and mozzarella cheese, is a source of constant discussion among the Romans. While that was being prepared, I fortified myself with another favourite, bucatini all'amatriciana, a dish of tubular, hollow pasta with a sauce made from pork jowl, pancetta and tomatoes. This was much more to my taste, with a slight kick from a hot chilli used in the cooking and the zest from the addition of lemon juice before serving. I was famished and attacked the bowl in a way that won admiring glances from other tables and from the staff, who quickly brought me another bowl of bread when I finished the first one sopping up the sauce.

The pizza arrived. It looked as I imagine a good pizza should: the toppings bubbling and glistening under a sheen of juices and a drizzle of olive oil, the base crispy and cracking under the pressure from my knife. It was a good example of the genre; I just didn't like the genre and this was not going to change my mind. I nibbled at the crust and ate a bit from the centre, but my mind was still going back to the meaty, rich pasta dish. In the end I pushed the plate away, contents half-eaten, indicating that it was fulness rather than disgust that had caused me to fail.

The day, and indeed the trip, had caught up with me, and I decided to head back to my hotel room. I bought a bottle of good red wine and spent the evening drinking, reading and sleeping – all restorative acts that I hoped would at least bring me back to a semblance of normality.

I felt much more energized the next day and, because of my early night, was up and raring to go at 7 a.m. Stopping only for the prerequisite Italian pastry on the way, I found my way to the Vatican City and was the second person in the queue when the doors opened at St Peter's. I was able to stand in awe before Michelangelo's *Pietà* for twenty minutes before another soul appeared. I was not so lucky, however, when I headed out to the Vatican Museum, where already vast queues had begun to form. I was tempted to turn around, but it seemed silly to have gone all the way around the world and not to see one of the truly great pieces of art on my last stop. It was, of course, a hateful experience. Tour groups ruled, with, in these modern times, each tourist attached to a earpiece that made them look like a mismatched assortment of trainees for The Gap.

The solo tourist is the lowest in the pecking order, and I had to fight my way with considerable force until I found myself staring upwards at the ceiling of the Sistine Chapel. It is, despite recent insensitive restorations, which make it look like it has been coloured in with crayons, as remarkable as I had imagined, doubly so because its majesty shines through the pushing and shoving of tourists and guides alike.

The Yorkshire lad in me could not help but look up and think 'A bit of Artex would work a treat there'.

I found my way out of the building and hailed a cab, asking the driver to take me to the Piazza San Salvatore, where I had a likely spot for my last lunch in Rome. I had my mind set on two other Roman specialities and began with one of the most misunderstood of all pasta dishes, spaghetti carbonara, all too often a bowl of limp pasta swamped with cheese and cream, often from a jar. At its best, however, it is a beautiful mix of sautéed onions, crispy Italian bacon, large amounts of pecorino and beaten eggs, which cook in the residual heat of the pasta.

To follow, it was just the time of year to order abbacchio, a dish of beautifully tender, slow-cooked spring lamb, seasoned heavily with lots of garlic, sage and rosemary before being spiced up with the addition of anchovies just before serving. It was a simple yet glorious meal, and I lingered over it for two or more hours while I treated myself to a bottle of Brunello, the smooth, subtle wine from Tuscany, some gelato for dessert and an unfeasibly large grappa to send me on my way, this time more with a slight swaying than a hobble.

I returned to my hotel for another early night. I had to fly to Spain the next morning to meet TGS. I had done a bit of sightseeing and had had at least two excellent meals, but I had scarcely done Rome justice. Mark it up as another place I have to return to one day. I had my excuses, though. General weariness, the sorest foot any human male has ever had to endure without having it amputated, and limited time. Whatever the excuses, it definitely was not a case of '*veni, vidi, vici*', more a case of 'I came, I saw, I conked out'.

41

The End of the Road

For a journey that had involved so many long-distance trips, the final flight was an anti-climax: a short hop from Bilbao, where I had finished a final few days touring La Rioja with TGS to celebrate the end of the journey.

I arrived at my flat shortly before midnight and threw Big Red down on the floor. As it hit the surface, air was squeezed out through a small rip on the side that had appeared in the last two weeks. It sounded like a sigh, which was fair enough for a companion who had done as many miles as I had and in considerably less comfort. Like me, Big Red had endured nearly one hundred flights, almost thirty countries and had seen the inside of countless hotel rooms. It had been my constant companion – often my only companion. Airlines had tried to lose it, and crooks had tried to steal it, but together, in our own very British way, we had muddled through somehow.

I peeled my walking boots off and tossed them to one side. I promised myself, and my foot, still painful and swollen from the stress fracture, that I would not need them again for a little while, if ever. I made myself a large mug of builder's tea and sat down to check my e-mails. There were a handful that said 'well done', but otherwise the end of my journey seemed to have gone as little remarked upon as the day I handed in my notice. Not even a mention on the TV news, which was so desperate for stories that they were talking to a woman who claimed to have seen the face of Jesus in a piece of toast.

Had it been worthwhile? Had I actually achieved anything

after all that time, effort and, of course, money?

Glancing up from my cup of steaming tea, into which I was dunking my second chocolate digestive biscuit, I saw an envelope propped up on the dining-room table. I opened it and a read the note inside. It was from Baba.

'Congratulations on finishing your round-the-world trip. Mum would have been very proud.'

Of course, it had been worthwhile. I might have spent every penny I had in the bank and a little bit more, but it had been worth every last cent. I had made a journey that most people could only dream of but few will ever have the opportunity or inclination to embark upon. I may not have fulfilled my avowed aim to 'Go Everywhere, Eat Everything', but I had given it my best shot. I may not be the first person to have eaten rat in China, elk in Finland, barbecue in Texas, crickets in Manila or cod sperm sushi in Kyoto, but there are not too many people out there who can claim to have done so in a little over a year. One thing is for certain: I am the only Simon Majumdar to have done it, and that was good enough for me.

What about Simon Majumdar? Where does it leave him? Well, apparently it leaves him talking about himself in the third person, which, at the very least, sees a richly deserved slap in his near future if he keeps it up. It leaves me (that's better) broke but incredibly rich in experience. It leaves me with memories that few others will ever have, of standing on the Great Wall of China and riding the rails from Mongolia to Moscow, of the smells in the bodegas of Jerez and the smells of Chinese toilets, of the craziness of India and the rigidity of Japan, of much-loved family members in India and New York and new family members in Manila.

It leaves me with over 12,000 images on my computer, most of the different things I have eaten in all those countries – food that, if I look at the pictures, can still summon up pleasing memories of the tastes and the smells and the circumstances in which it was eaten.

Most of all, it leaves me with hundreds of new people in far-flung corners of this globe that I can call 'friend' and mean it. People like Tomoko in Kyoto and Tana in Santa Cruz. People like Stan and Lisa Cohen in Philly and Bath in Senegal, the Den Dulks in South Africa and Pertti and the Prinsessa in Finland, the strangers who broke bread with me on a train in Morocco and the old friends who welcomed me into their homes all around the world.

A man whose view of the world could at best have been described as jaded before he set out had had his faith in the intrinsic goodness of people restored. That on its own is accomplishment enough, and I suspect it would have been enough to make Gwen Majumdar proud too. I am not sure I need, deserve or want any other accolade apart from knowing that my father is, and my mother would have been, proud of me.

So what now? Perhaps it is time to go back to being a grown-up and get a real job involving a desk, a hole-puncher and a PC, on which I can play solitaire when people think I am working. Perhaps I could look for a different job, something in the food industry, going cap in hand to the many people I now know who do this for a living and asking them if they have room for a balding, forty-something with a dodgy foot.

Or perhaps, just perhaps, I should figure out a way to keep doing exactly what I have been doing for the last year. To keep finding ways to travel around this rapidly changing world of ours in search of the best food and the generosity of spirit that makes it taste so good. The offers and invitations are still flooding in – in fact, even more than when I first set out on the trip. There are still another ninety countries out there whose stamps I would love in my passport, and, of course, there is so much food still to try. Perhaps Big Red and I aren't finished quite yet.

Any ideas?

The Best and the Worst

The Best Twenty Tastes of Eat My Globe

(Of course, if you ask me this tomorrow, you may get a totally different answer). In no particular order:

1) Thiebou djene cooked for me by the sisters of my friend, Bath in Rufisque, Senegal.
2) Tandoori chicken at Bukhara, New Delhi.
3) Yakitori at the bars of Ueno, Tokyo.
4) Sichuan hotpot in Chengdu, China.
5) Boiled new potatoes prepared by the Prinsessa, Finland.
6) Breakfast ribs at the American Royal, Kansas City, Missouri, USA.
7) Seafood kare kare prepared for me by Claude Tayag in Angeles, Philippines.
8) Souvlaki at Lamb on Chapel, Melbourne, Australia.
9) Pho on the streets of Hanoi, Vietnam.
10) Braai prepared by Emil Den Dulk, Stellenbosch, South Africa.
11) Shrimp cocktail, Guadalajara, Mexico
12) Roast chicken with my friend, Tana in Santa Cruz
13) Mee krop, Chote Chitr, Bangkok
14) Mutton kebab rolls, Bade Miyan, Mumbai
15) Mrs King's pork pie, Melton Mowbray, England
16) Jamon Iberico with a glass of Tio Pepe, Jerez, Spain

17) Pani ca meusa, Palermo, Italy
18) Balik ekmek, Istanbul, Turkey
19) Smoked omul and sig on the shores of Lake Baikal,
20) Roti canai, Penang, Malaysia.

The Worst Ten Tastes of Eat My Globe

I ate it so you don't have to.

1) Braised dog in Yangshuo, China
2) Stir fried rat in Yangshuo, China
3) Cod sperm sushi, Kyoto, Japan
4) Mystery meat, Maputo, Mozambique
5) Fermented mare's milk, Mongolia
6) Hákarl, rotten shark meat, Reykjavik, Iceland
7) Deep fried, breaded banana, Castletownbere, Ireland
8) Acaraje fried in dende oil, Salvador, Brazil
9) Dim Sim in Melbourne, Australia
10) Camel Meat, Casablanca, Morocco